Evangelism
for a
Changing
World

Essays in honor of Roy Fish

Harold Shaw Publishers
Wheaton, Illinois

The quote on p. 137 is from "Because He Lives" words by William J. and Gloria Gaither, music by William J. Gaither ©1971 William J. Gaither. All rights reserved. Used by permission.

Unless otherwise noted, all Scripture quotations are taken from *The Holy Bible: New International Version*. Copyright © 1973, 1978, 1984 by International Bible Society. Used by permission of Zondervan Publishing House. All rights reserved. Scripture quotations marked KJV are taken from the King James Version of the Bible.

Scripture quotations marked CEV are taken from the Contemporary English Version of the Bible, © 1991 by American Bible Society.

Scripture quotations marked NASB are taken from the New American Standard Bible, © 1960, 1962, 1963, 1968, 1971, 1972, 1973, 1975, 1977 by The Lockman Foundation. Used by permission.

Scripture quotations marked NKJV are from The New King James Version of the Bible. Copyright © 1979, 1980, 1982, Thomas Nelson Inc., Publishers.

Scripture quotations marked Phillips are taken from *The New Testament in Modern English,* copyright © 1958, 1959, 1960, 1972 by J.B. Phillips.

Scripture quotations marked RSV are from the Revised Standard Version of the Bible, copyright © 1946, 1952, 1971 by the Division of Christian Education of the National Council of the Churches of Christ in the USA, and used by permission.

Scripture verses marked TLB are taken from *The Living Bible* © 1971. Used by permission of Tyndale House Publishers, Inc., Wheaton, IL 60189. All rights reserved.

ISBN 0-87788-240-1

Edited by Timothy K. Beougher and Alvin L. Reid   Cover design by David LaPlaca

---

Library of Congress Cataloging-in-Publication Data

Evangelism for a changing world : essays in honor of Roy J. Fish / edited by Timothy K. Beougher and Alvin L. Reid.
     p. cm.
    Includes bibliographical references.
    ISBN 0-87788-240-1
    1. Evangelistic work. 2. Theology, Practical. 3. Revivals. 4. Missions—Theory. 5. Southern Baptist Convention—Membership. 6. Baptists—Membership. I. Fish, Roy J. II. Beougher, Timothy K. (Timothy Ken) III. Reid, Alvin L.
    BV3795.E894 1995
    269'.2—dc20   95-3410
                                                        CIP

---

02 01 00 99 98

10 9 8 7 6 5 4 3 2

To our wives
Sharon Beougher
Michelle Reid

and our children
Kristi, Jonathan, Kari, and Karisa Beougher
Joshua and Hannah Reid.

We are truly blessed.

Roy J. Fish

Contents

PART 4

Roy J. Fish: Evangelist Extraordinaire

Foreword

It was a dry season for me that year. I was pastoring a small church about eighty miles from Southwestern Baptist Theological Seminary. I commuted every day to class, leaving before daylight and often returning after dark. We had a small son and were expecting another child. At night and on weekends I tried to serve as pastor of the church. I preached each Sunday and on Wednesday nights. Physically, emotionally, and spiritually I was stretched to the max! Class work was demanding, and eighteen semester hours were an unusually heavy overload.

It was during that period of my life that I went to a chapel service one day at the seminary. I wasn't expecting much. A graduate student was to preach, and I had never heard of him. His name was Roy Fish. I entered that chapel discouraged, tired, and exhausted. Roy Fish preached that morning and challenged us to be about the business of winning people to Jesus Christ. He concluded with an illustration I have never forgotten. He told about the illness of their infant son and his brush with death. He described how he felt as his son lay near death in the hospital. He described how he began to ask in his heart, *What would I regret most if my son died?* As he pondered this question, the answer came clear. *I would regret that he died never knowing how much I loved him.*

With that illustration, Roy Fish revealed an insight into the character of God, whose great heart grieves over every lost soul. Surely, Roy said, God grieves because the lost who die without Christ never know how much he loves them. God used that simple illustration and that dynamic message to encourage my heart and plant a burning desire in my soul to see people saved. Perhaps more than any other single message, it shaped my life and launched me into a lifelong ministry to reach those without Christ.

The experience I have had with Roy Fish could be repeated for thousands of others over these years. Few men have ever stood with more integrity and consistency over a lifetime. Whether as a pastor, a seminary professor, a conference speaker, or a friend, Roy Fish has been God's instrument to motivate several generations to accept the challenge of the great commission. How grateful I am for Roy Fish today. I could speak of the phone calls he has made and the letters he has sent to me over the years. At one very crucial time in my ministry, a phone call from Roy helped solidify a decision concerning accepting a pastorate. His sensitivity and counsel has been extended to many. All across this nation and around the world, his students, members of churches he has served, and fellow ministers are the recipients of his love and encouragement.

He is one of the most sought-after speakers in the world. He has graced the platforms of the most significant conferences and conventions of our time. He has guided scores of churches through difficult times as interim pastor, preparing the church to move forward under the leadership of a new pastor. He has often entered troubled churches and brought about healing and new vigor for the task before them.

Mention his name, and strong words enter the mind. *Powerful, insightful, honest, sensitive, compassionate, devoted, committed, godly, consistent, profound yet simple, a communicator, counselor, encourager, scholar, evangelist, soul-winner,* and a myriad of other words leap in the heart. This is a man with no guile, whose life has been mightily used of God to influence thousands and point them to the Savior. Words are inadequate for me to fully express the gratitude of the thousands who have been influenced, encouraged, and challenged by this gifted man of God.

These pages are presented to try in some way to convey the deep gratitude that resides in the hearts of so many for Roy Fish. He has done more to give a positive influence on evangelism in the Southern Baptist Convention than any other person alive today. His friendship and support in my life is cherished. I am deeply indebted to Roy Fish and eternally grateful to God for his life and ministry.

James T. Draper

James T. Draper, Jr., is president of the Southern Baptist Sunday School Board. Draper formerly pastored the First Baptist Church of Euless, Texas. He is the author of several books including Authority: The Critical Issue for Southern Baptists, The Church Christ Approves, *and* Foundations of Biblical Faith.

Acknowledgments

Evangelism for a Changing World has been written in honor of Dr. Roy Fish. In 1995 Fish celebrates his sixty-fifth birthday and begins his thirtieth year of teaching evangelism at Southwestern Baptist Theological Seminary. These nineteen contributors represent students, colleagues, family, and friends who have demonstrated their deep appreciation for Roy Fish by this labor of love. All can testify to the impact he has had on their lives and ministries.

The editors would like to acknowledge all those who have helped make this book a reality. It is impossible to name all the secretarial help utilized by the contributors; we say to them a hearty "thank you." We have been blessed personally with the support of a great team: Carol Fowler and Diane Garvin of Wheaton College; and Becky Greer, Nancy Garst, and Rindi Commons of Houston Baptist University. Also, many of Dr. Fish's former students have encouraged us as we have worked on this project.

The staff at Harold Shaw Publishers, including Vinita Hampton Wright, Joan Guest, and Esther Waldrop, the editors for this project; Stephen Board, the publisher; and Dan Stovall in marketing, have all been exceedingly gracious and helpful. Working with them has been a true joy.

Our wives have been incredibly patient and helpful throughout this process. They have not only provided prayer, insight, and encouragement, they have spent extra time filling in for absent fathers as we worked on the project. To our children, Kristi, Jonathan, Kari, and Karisa Beougher; and Joshua and Hannah Reid, we say thanks for your understanding when Daddy had to be at his office instead of at home. You all are great!

Introduction

Dr. Roy Fish has taught evangelism to more ministry students than probably any other person in the history of Christianity. Thousands of students at Southwestern Baptist Theological Seminary in Fort Worth, Texas (the world's largest Protestant seminary), have sat at his feet to be challenged and inspired.

The book is designed around the recognized strengths of his personal life and teaching ministry. It includes, in the last section, a biographical essay by his son Steve, who highlights Dr. Fish's role as a husband and father who has faithfully practiced what he preached. Steve Gaines then chronicles Fish's professional history, highlighting his ministry experiences and his teaching and writing career.

The essays in this book are divided into four main sections. Dr. Fish has always encouraged his students to be creative and seek new approaches to ministry. Hence, section one has this focus. Section two highlights Fish's emphasis on the evangelistic imperative. The third section acknowledges Fish's interest and emphasis on the significant role of spiritual awakening in evangelism. The final section focuses on Dr. Fish himself. It is our prayer that these writings will not only educate you and inspire you, but also motivate you to share the good news of Jesus Christ with a world of lost and dying people.

We say "thank you, Dr. Fish," for following so diligently the One who promised to make his followers "fishers of men." We commit ourselves afresh, as we challenge you, the reader, to "go and do likewise."

Timothy K. Beougher
Wheaton, Illinois

Alvin L. Reid
Houston, Texas
1995

PART 1
"It's a New Day": Contemporary Approaches to Ministry

In this section the writers give fresh insight on five critical areas of ministry as the church approaches the twenty-first century. Rick Warren highlights the importance of churches being "purpose-driven" to remain faithful to the great commission. Calvin Miller takes a fresh look at maintaining balance in one's life through "praying without ceasing." Bill Pinson discusses the need for solid Christian leadership to meet the challenges of our world. Don McMinn writes about the role of contemporary worship as it relates to evangelism. And Jerry Rankin offers an insightful perspective on the current state of world missions.

1
The Purpose-Driven Church:
A Contemporary Approach to Church Growth

Rick Warren

Rick Warren is the founding pastor of the Saddleback Valley Community Church in Lake Forest, California. Saddleback was honored in 1994 as the fastest growing church in the history of the Southern Baptist Convention. Rick has trained more than twenty thousand pastors and church leaders through his Purpose-Driven Church seminar. He is the author of four books. He holds a D.Min. from Fuller Seminary and an M.Div. from Southwestern Seminary, where he served as Dr. Fish's grader while a student.

"I will build my church."
—Jesus (Matt. 16:18)

"By the grace God has given me,
I laid a foundation as an expert builder."
—Paul (1 Cor. 3:10)

A few years ago I bought some property in the mountains behind Yosemite National Park and built a log cabin. Even with the help of my father and some friends, it took two years to complete, since I couldn't work on it full time. When I began building, it took me an entire summer just to lay the foundation. First I had to clear a pad in the forest by cutting down and uprooting thirty-seven towering pine trees. Then I had to dig over sixty feet of five-foot-deep French drains because the ground was wet from a nearby underground spring. After ten exhausting weeks, all I had to show for my effort was a leveled and squared concrete foundation. I was very discouraged. But my father, who has built over seventy church buildings in his lifetime, said, "Cheer up. When you've finished laying the foundation, the most critical work is behind you."

Foundations determine both the size and the strength of a building. You can never build larger than the foundation can handle. The same is true for churches. A church built on an inadequate or faulty foundation will never reach the height that God intends for it to reach. It will topple over once it outgrows its base.

Churches are started for many different reasons. Sometimes those reasons are inadequate: competition, denominational pride, the need for recognition by a leader, or some other unworthy motivation. Unless the driving force behind a church is biblical, the foundation will be off. The health and growth of the church will never be what God intended. Strong churches are not built on programs or gimmicks, but on the purposes of God.

What Drives Your Church?

If you were to look up the word *drive* in a dictionary, you'd find this definition: "To guide, control, or direct." When you drive a car, it means you guide, control, and direct it down the street. When you drive a nail, you guide, control, and direct it into the wood. When you drive a golf ball, hopefully you drive, control, and direct it down the fairway!

Every church is driven by something. There is a guiding force, a controlling assumption, or a directing conviction behind everything that happens. It may be unspoken. It may have never been voted on by the members. But it is there influencing every aspect of the church's life.

Some churches are driven by tradition. Their favorite phrase is "We've always done it this way." The goal of a tradition-driven church is to simply perpetuate the past. Change is usually seen as negative and stagnation is interpreted as "stability" in a tradition-driven church. Tradition can be such a driving force in a church that even God's will becomes secondary. They brag, "We have a sound church." Yes, sound asleep. Ralph Neighbour says the Seven Last Words of the Church are "We've never done it that way before."

Some churches are driven by personality. Their favorite question is "What does the leader want?" If the pastor has served the church for a long time, he is most likely the driving personality. But if the church has a history of changing pastors every few years, a key layperson is likely to be the driving force. One obvious problem with a personality-driven church is that its agenda is determined more by the background, needs, and insecurities of the leader than by God's will or the needs of the people. Another problem occurs when the driving personality leaves or dies. The church will come to a standstill.

Some churches are driven by finances. The question at the forefront of everyone's mind in a finance-driven church is "How much will it cost?" Nothing else ever seems quite as important. Finances are foremost. The most heated debate in a finance-driven church is always over the budget. While good stewardship and cash flow are essential for a healthy church, finances must never be the controlling issue. The greater issue is "What does God want us to do?" We do not exist to make a profit. The bottom line in the church is not "How much did we save?" but "Who was saved?" I've noticed that many churches are driven by faith in their early years and driven by finances in later years.

Some churches are driven by programs. The Sunday school, the women's program, the choir, and the youth group are examples of programs that are often the driving force in churches. In program-driven churches, all the energy is focused on maintaining and sustaining the programs. The nominating committee is the most crucial group in the church. The goal of this church subtly shifts from developing people to just filling positions. If results from a program diminish, the people blame themselves for not working hard enough. No one ever questions whether the program still works.

Some churches are driven by buildings. Winston Churchill once said, "We shape our buildings, and then they shape us." Too often a congregation is so anxious to have a nice building that they spend more than they can afford. Then funds needed to operate ministries must be diverted to pay the mortgage. The facilities get built, but the actual ministry of the church suffers. Paying for and maintaining the building becomes the biggest budget item. The tail ends up wagging the dog. In other situations, churches build too small because they build too soon. Then the smallness of the building sets the limit for future growth. Staying with a historic but inadequate building takes priority over reaching the community. In essence, the shoe tells the foot how big it can get.

Some churches are driven by events. If you look at the calendar of an event-driven church, you'd get the impression that the goal of the church was simply to keep people busy. Every night of the week, something is going on, one event right after another. As soon as one big event is completed, work begins on the next one. There is a lot of activity, but not necessarily productivity. A church may be active and busy—but for what purpose? Are any lives being changed? Meetings replace ministry as the primary activity of believers, and attendance becomes the sole measurement of faithfulness and maturity.

Some churches are driven by seekers. In an honest attempt to reach unbelievers for Christ and be relevant in today's culture some churches allow the needs of the unbelievers to become the driving force. The primary question asked is "What do the unchurched want?" While we must be sensitive to the needs, hurts, and interests of seekers, we cannot allow them to set the total agenda of the church. That isn't our option. Of course God's purpose for his church includes evangelism—but not to the exclusion of his other purposes. While it is fine for a business to be market-driven (give the customer whatever they want), the church has a higher calling. We must be seeker-sensitive, but the church must not be seeker-driven.

A New Paradigm: Purpose-Driven Churches

I believe what is needed today more than anything else are purpose-driven churches. My goal for this essay is to explain this new paradigm, the purpose-driven church, and offer it as a biblical and effective alternative to the traditional ways that churches have organized and operated. This paradigm is made up of two parts. First, it requires a *new perspective:* I'll help you see how balancing God's five purposes for your church is the key to your church's health and growth. Second, it includes a *simple process:* I'll give you a practical system to help your congregation fulfill God's purposes, regardless of its size. This is not some theory cooked up in an ivory tower. It has been fieldtested for fifteen years, and today it is producing exciting results in thousands of churches.

By focusing equally on all five of the New Testament purposes of the church, your church can develop the healthy balance that makes lasting growth possible. Proverbs 19:21 says, "Many are the plans in a man's heart, but it is the LORD's purpose that prevails." Plans, programs, and personalities don't last. But God's purposes *will* last. Paul said that God will judge whatever we build on this basis: Does it last? "The fire will test the quality of each man's work. If what he has built survives, he will receive his reward" (1 Cor. 3:13-14). He also gives us the key to building something that lasts: Build it on the right foundation. "But each one should be careful how he builds. For no one can lay any foundation other than the one already laid, which is Jesus Christ" (1 Cor. 3:10-11). Strong churches are built on purpose!

The Importance of Being Purpose-Driven

Nothing precedes purpose. Until you know why the church exists, you have no foundation, no motivation, and no direction for your church. If you are starting a new church, your first step, before you do anything else, is to define your purpose. Forget everything else until you've got that clear in your mind. It's far easier to start with the right foundation than to have to tear it down and set it up again after a church has started.

If you serve in an existing church that is plateaued, declining, or simply discouraged, your first task is to redefine your purpose. Recapture a clear vision of what God wants to do in and through your church family. Absolutely nothing will revitalize a discouraged church faster than rediscovering its purpose.

Years ago, in preparing to start Saddleback church, I studied the one hundred largest churches in America. I wrote a personal letter to each of them and found out all I could about the factors that had made each one grow. I also read every book in print at that time on growing churches. I then made a master list of the common denominators of healthy, growing churches. Saddleback was built on those principles.

One of the most important factors I discovered was that growing, healthy churches have a clear-cut identity. They understand their reason for being; they are precise in their purpose. They know exactly what God has called them to do. They know what their business is, and they know what is none of their business!

However, if you ask the typical church member why his or her church exists, you'll get a wide variety of answers. Win Arn once surveyed members of nearly a thousand churches, asking the question "Why does the church exist?" The results? Eighty-nine percent of the church members surveyed said, "The church's purpose is to take care of me and my family's needs." Only 11 percent said, "The purpose of the church is to win the world for Jesus Christ."

Then the pastors of the same churches were asked why the church exists. Amazingly, the results were exactly opposite. Ninety percent of the pastors said the purpose of the church was to win the world, and 10 percent said it was to care for the needs of the members. Is it any wonder why we have conflict, confusion, and stagnation in many churches today? If the pastor and people can't even agree on why the church exists, conflict and disagreement on everything else is inevitable.

Any church that genuinely wants to be healthy and grow needs to develop a purpose statement that summarizes its purposes. Having a clearly defined purpose statement, one that is short enough for everyone to remember, will yield five wonderful benefits for your church.

A clear purpose builds morale

First Corinthians 1:10 says, "Let there be real harmony so that there won't be splits in the church. . . . Be of one mind, united in thought and purpose" (TLB). Notice that Paul says the key to harmony in the church is to be united in purpose. Saddleback is a church with an unusually high morale and sense of harmony. We've been very fortunate to have a warm fellowship in spite of all the enormous changes our church has gone through as it grew. This is because Saddleback members are committed to a common purpose. Our purpose statement is explained in detail to every individual who desires to become a part of our church family, before they join. No one can join Saddleback church without attending the membership class and signing the membership covenant, which includes a commitment to support the purposes of Saddleback.

Common goals reduce conflict in a church. People working together for a great purpose don't have time to argue over trivial issues. When you're helping to row the boat, you don't have time to rock it!

Proverbs 29:18 says, "Where there is no vision, the people perish." Today many churches are barely surviving because they have no vision. They limp along from Sunday to Sunday because they've lost sight of their purpose for continuing. Nothing discourages a church more than not knowing why it exists.

On the other hand, the quickest way to reinvigorate a declining or plateaued church is to reclaim God's vision and purpose for it.

A clear purpose reduces frustration

A purpose statement reduces frustration because it helps us forget about the things that don't really matter. Isaiah 26:3 says that God gives perfect peace to those who keep their purpose firm and trust in him. The fact is, your church doesn't have time to do everything. The good news, though, is that God doesn't expect you to do everything. And there are only a few things really worth doing in the first place. So the secret is to know what really counts, then do what really counts, and don't worry about all the rest.

A clear purpose not only defines what we do; it defines what we don't do: what our business is, and what it isn't. As a pastor I've learned that everybody has a different agenda for the church. People are always saying, "The church ought to do this" or "The church ought to do that." Some of these suggestions may be good activities, but that is not the real issue. The filter must always be: Does this activity fulfill one of the purposes for which God established the church? If it meets that criteria, you must consider it. But if it doesn't, you are obligated to not let it distract you from God's will. Paul told the Philippian church that he wanted to see them "standing firm with one common purpose."

Without a purpose statement it is very easy to be frustrated by all the distractions around us. Many church leaders identify with the way Isaiah felt in Isaiah 49:4—"I have labored to no purpose; I have spent my strength in vain and for nothing."

If a church doesn't clarify its purpose, it will be unstable because it can't make up its mind about what is most important. James 1:8 says that the life of a man of divided loyalty will reveal instability at every turn. An indecisive church is an unstable church. Trying to lead a church without a clearly defined purpose is like trying to drive a car in the fog; you have no clear idea of where you're going, and you're likely to crash.

But in a purpose-driven church, decision making is far easier and less frustrating. When somebody suggests an activity or an event, you simply ask, "Will this fulfill one of our purposes?" If it does, you do it. If it doesn't, you don't do it.

A clear purpose allows concentration

Focused light has tremendous power. Diffused light has no power at all. The power of the sun through a magnifying glass sets a leaf on fire, but alone, sunlight does nothing to a leaf. This same principle is true of the focused life and the focused church. The more focused it becomes, the more impact it has.

As I've said, no church has the time to do everything. A clear purpose allows you to concentrate your effort. Philippians 3:13 says, "I am bringing all my energies to bear on this one thing: forgetting the past and looking forward to what lies ahead." Continually reviewing your purpose keeps your priorities straight and keeps you focused. One of the common temptations I see a lot of churches falling for today is majoring on the minors. We get distracted by good, but less important, agendas, crusades, and purposes. The energy of the church is diffused and dissipated. Power is lost.

In my opinion, most churches try to do too much. This is one of the most overlooked barriers to building a healthy, growing church. We wear people out. Too often, small churches try to get involved in all kinds of activities, events, and programs. Instead of concentrating like Paul ("this one thing"), they dabble in forty different things and aren't good at any of them.

When I started Saddleback church in 1980, all we offered for the first year was a worship service and a limited children's church program. We didn't attempt to be a full-service church. We added other programs only as we had the leadership to manage them. For instance, we didn't have a youth program until we were averaging over five hundred in worship attendance, and we didn't have a singles program until attendance had grown to nearly one thousand.

We determined that we would never begin a new ministry without someone to lead it. We would wait on God's timing, and when we finally had the right leader, we would begin the new ministry. We concentrated on doing a few things very well. Once we got a ministry to an acceptable level of performance, we'd add another one. Once that ministry was going well, we'd add another. But we didn't try to do everything at once.

We must remember that being efficient is not the same as being effective. My friend Peter Drucker says, "Efficiency is doing things right. Effectiveness is doing the right things." God wants churches to be effective.

Churches can be efficient and well organized, but if they're not focused on their purpose, they'll be ineffective. It's like rearranging deck chairs on the Titanic; it may look nice, but that doesn't matter if the ship is still sinking! When we don't focus, energy is wasted on trivial issues. The church that forgets the ultimate becomes the slave to the immediate.

A clear purpose attracts cooperation

People want to join a church that knows where it's going. When a church clearly communicates its destination, people are eager to get on board. That is because people are looking for something that gives meaning, purpose, and direction to life. As the people told Ezra, "Tell us how to proceed . . . and we will fully cooperate." (Ezra 10:4, TLB)

The apostle Paul was always clear in his purpose. As a result, many people wanted to be a part of what he was doing. The Philippian church was especially attracted to his vision and so they gave him ongoing financial support (Phil. 4:15). If you want people to get excited and actively support a church, you must spell out up front exactly where the church is headed.

Have you ever boarded a wrong plane? Once I got on a plane I thought was going to St. Louis but was going to Kansas City. I learned an important lesson: Check the destination before the plane takes off, because bailing out later would be painful! You wouldn't dare get on a bus without knowing where it's going first, so you shouldn't expect people to join your church without knowing its destination either. I tell prospective members that if they don't know where Saddleback is headed, they shouldn't join. That's why we have a required membership class prior to joining. Every member needs to understand your church's purpose.

Proverbs 11:27 says that if your goals are good, you will be respected. Tell people up front where you're going, and it will attract cooperation. Spell out your church's purposes and priorities in a membership class. Clearly explain your strategy and structure. This keeps people from joining under false assumptions.

On the other hand, if you allow people to become members of your church without understanding your purpose, you're asking for trouble. New members, especially those transferring from other churches, often have personal agendas and preconceptions about the church. These issues will eventually cause problems unless you deal with them up front in a forthright way.

People who transfer their membership to your church from another church always carry cultural baggage. They have certain expectations that your church has no intention of fulfilling. This was a lesson I had to learn in the early days of Saddleback. I began the church with a small Bible study in my home before we started public worship services. The group grew to about fifteen people. One of the men in this group had been a member of a large church for twelve years. Every time we started to plan something he'd say, "At my old church they did it like this." This became his recurring refrain. After about eight weeks of this, I finally said, "You know, if you want a church just like your old church, why don't you go back there? It's only thirteen miles up the road." He took my advice and left with his family of five. That was 30 percent of our fellowship at that time—and he was a tither!

I look back on that situation and believe it was one of the crucial decisions that determined the destiny of Saddleback church. If I had listened to that fellow, Saddleback would have ended up just being a copy of that other church. Our future would have turned out very differently. I also learned two important lessons about leadership: First, you cannot let whiners set the agenda for the church. That is an abdication of leadership. I also learned that the best time to get rid of uncooperative members is before they join! Telling people the purposes up front weeds out people who have hidden agendas or should attend another church because of philosophy or personal taste.

Once your church's purposes have been clarified, any goal that fulfills one of those purposes gets automatic approval. For instance, if your church agrees that evangelism is one of God's purposes for the church, the congregation doesn't have to keep voting each year to decide to reach the community for Christ. Define your roles—then set your goals.

A clear purpose assists evaluation

Second Corinthians 13:5 says, "Examine yourselves to see whether you are in the faith; test yourselves." How does a church evaluate itself? Not by comparing itself to other churches, but by asking, "Are we doing what God meant for us to do?" and "How well are we doing it?" These are the two most critical questions for evaluating: "What is our business?" and "How's business?" Your purpose statement must become the standard by which your church's health and growth are evaluated.

There is absolutely no correlation between the size and the strength of a church. A church can be big and strong or it can be big and flabby. A church can be small and strong or it can be small and wimpy. Big is not necessarily better. Small is not necessarily better. Better is better! You measure your church's strength by examining how well you are fulfilling each of God's eternal purposes for it.

Your Church Can Be Purpose-Driven

There are three parts to becoming a purpose-driven church: First you must *define* your purposes. Next, those purposes must be *communicated* to everyone in the church on a regular basis. Finally, you must consistently *apply* those purposes to every phase and function of your church life.

Leading your church to define its purpose

You can lead your church through the process of discovering and defining its purpose by following these four basic steps:

1. Study what the Bible says. The first step is to involve your congregation in a study of the biblical passages on the church. There are four important areas to consider in this churchwide study:

First, examine *Christ's ministry on earth*. Ask, What did Jesus do while he was here? What would he do if he were here today? Whatever he did then, we are to continue today. The elements of Christ's ministry should be present in the church today. What he did while here in a physical body, he wants continued in his spiritual body, the church.

Next, look at each of *the images and names of the church* given in the Bible. The New Testament offers many analogies for the church: a body, a bride, a family, a flock, a community, an army. Each of these images has profound implications for what the church should be and what the church should be doing.

Then study *the examples of the New Testament churches*. Ask, What did the first churches do? There are many different models given in Scripture. The Jerusalem church was very different from the church at Corinth. The Philippian church was very different from that in Thessalonica. Study them all.

Finally, consider *the commands of Christ*. What did Jesus tell us to do?

In Matthew 16:18 Jesus said, "I will build my church." His tone indicated that he has a specific purpose in mind. Our job is not to make up the purposes of the church, but to discover them. Remember it's Christ's church, not ours. He has already established the purposes, and they're non-negotiable. Our duty is to discover and implement them. While the methods may change (and must change!) in every generation, the purposes never change. We may innovate with the style of ministry, but never the substance.

2. Answer two questions. As you review the biblical material on the church, find the answer to two critical questions: What are we to *be* as a church? and What are we to *do* as a church? Focus on both the nature and the tasks of the church.

3. Put your findings in writing. Write down everything you've learned through your study. Don't worry about trying to be brief. Say everything you think needs to be said about the nature and purpose of the church. From this multiple-page document you will eventually distill a single sentence that summarizes what you believe. But don't worry about that right now. It is always easier to edit and condense than to create. Focus only on getting all of the purposes clearly identified. Even when you already know and could simply list the New Testament purposes, it is vital for you and your congregation to review all the Bible has to say about the church and write down your conclusions.

4. Summarize your thoughts in a sentence. Finally, you need to condense what you've discovered into a single paragraph, and then into a single sentence. Begin by grouping similar concepts together under major headings like evangelism, worship, fellowship, spiritual maturity, and ministry. Start with the large and move to the small. Next, try to state all the major themes in a single paragraph. Then begin to edit out unnecessary words and phrases to reduce your purpose paragraph to a single sentence.

Condensing your purpose statement into a single sentence is absolutely important! Why? Because the statement has limited value if people can't remember it!

Somebody once said, "Thoughts disentangle themselves when they pass through the lips and the fingertips." In other words, if you can say it and write it, then you've clearly thought it through. If you can't put it in writing, you haven't really thought it out. Bacon said "Writing makes an exact man."

What makes a great purpose statement?
There are four characteristics of an effective purpose statement:

It is biblical. As said before, we don't get to choose the purposes of the church. Christ established them long ago. But each generation must reaffirm them.

It is specific. Many statements are so vague, they have no impact. Nothing becomes dynamic until it becomes specific. The more specific a statement is, the better. Some churches say, "Our church exists to glorify God." Of course it does! But exactly how do you accomplish that? How do you prove you've done it at the end of each year? How do you improve the way you do it each year?

It is transferable. This means it is short enough to be remembered and passed on by everyone in your church. The shorter it is, the better. I hate to admit this, but people don't remember whole sermons or speeches. They don't even remember paragraphs. What people remember are simple statements, slogans, and phrases.

I don't remember any speech John F. Kennedy gave, but I do remember that he said: "Ask not what your country can do for you, but ask what you can do for your country." Neither do I remember any sermon of Dr. Martin Luther King, Jr., but I remember his phrase "I have a dream!"

For better or worse, every president is remembered by a phrase, not his speeches: Roosevelt's "We have nothing to fear but fear itself"; Truman's "The buck stops here"; Bush's "Read my lips"; Nixon's "I am not a crook!"; and Clinton's "I didn't inhale!"

It is measurable. You must be able to look at your purpose statement and evaluate whether or not your church is doing it. You cannot evaluate the effectiveness of your church unless your purpose is measurable.

How to Make a Purpose Statement

Prior to starting Saddleback church, I took six months to do an extensive, personal Bible study on the church, using the methods described in my book *Dynamic Bible Study Methods* (Victor Books, 1980). Then, during the first months of the new church, I led our young congregation through the same study. Together we studied all the relevant Scriptures about the church. Finally we concluded that although many passages describe what the church is to be and do, two statements by Jesus summarize it all: The great commandment (Matt. 22:37-39) and the great commission (Matt. 28:19-20). I suggested that "A great commitment to the great commandment and the great commission will grow a great church." It became a Saddleback slogan. We decided that these two passages would be the filter for everything we would do as a church. If an activity or program fulfills one of the commands in these verses, we do it. If it doesn't—we don't do it. We are "guided, controlled, and directed" by five purposes we've identified in these two passages:

> *"Love the Lord your God with all your heart and with all your soul and with all your mind. . . . Love your neighbor as yourself." All the Law and the Prophets hang on these two commandments. (Matt. 22:37-40)*

> *Go and make disciples of all nations, baptizing them in the name of the Father and of the Son and of the Holy Spirit, and teaching them to obey everything*

I have commanded you. And surely I am with you always, to the very end of the age. (Matt. 28:19-20)

One day a Pharisee tried to test Jesus by asking him to identify the most important command. Jesus responded by saying, "Here is the entire Old Testament in a nutshell. I'm going to give you the Cliffs Notes summary of God's Word. All the Law and all the Prophets can be condensed to two tasks: Love God with all your heart, and love your neighbor as yourself." Later, in some of Jesus' final words to his disciples, he gave three more instructions: Go make disciples, baptize them, and teach them to obey everything I commanded you to do. These were the tasks the church was to focus on until he returned.

Five purposes from two passages

A purpose-driven church will focus on accomplishing these five New Testament purposes for the church:

Worship: "Love the Lord your God with all your heart." How do we love God with all our heart? By worshiping him! Worship is simply expressing our love to God. It doesn't matter if we're by ourselves or with a small group or with 100,000 people. When we express our love to God, we're worshiping.

The Bible says, "Worship the Lord your God, and serve him only" (Matt. 4:10). Notice that worship comes before service. The first purpose of the church is to worship God! Sometimes we get so busy working for God that we don't have time to express our love for him through worship.

Throughout Scripture we're commanded to celebrate God's presence, to exalt the Lord, to magnify the Lord, and to enjoy doing this. Psalm 34:3 says, "Glorify the LORD with me; let us exalt his name together." We don't worship out of duty. We worship because we want to, because we love God.

Ministry: "Love your neighbor as yourself." Ministry is demonstrating God's love to others by meeting their needs and healing their hurt. Every time you reach out in love to others, you are ministering to them. Jesus said that even a cup of cold water given in his name was considered ministry and would not go unrewarded. The church is to "prepare God's people for works of service" (Eph. 4:12).

Evangelism: "Go and make disciples." We exist to communicate God's Word; we are ambassadors for Christ; our mission is to evangelize the world. As long as there is one person in the world who does not know Christ, the church has a mandate to keep growing. Growth is not optional. It is commanded by Jesus in his great commission. We seek church growth, not for our benefit, but because people need the Lord!

Fellowship: "Baptize them." As Christians we're called not just to believe, but also to belong. We are not meant to live Lone Ranger lives. We are to belong to Christ's family and be members of his body. Baptism is not only a symbol of salvation; it is a symbol of fellowship. It visualizes a person's incorporation into the body of Christ. It says to the world, "He is now one of us!" When new believers are baptized, we welcome them into the fellowship of the family of God. Providing fellowship for God's people is a fourth purpose of the church. We're not alone. We have each other for support. I love the Living Bible version of Ephesians 2:19: "You are members of God's very own family . . . and you belong in God's household with every other Christian."

Discipleship: "Teach them to obey . . . ." Another word for this is edification. It represents the educational purpose of the church. We must not only reach people, we must teach people. We must develop people to spiritual maturity. Paul writes, "building up the Church, the body of Christ, to a position of strength and maturity; until . . . all become full-grown in the Lord" (Eph. 4:12-13, TLB).

If you closely examine the earthly ministry of Jesus, it is apparent that he included all five of these elements in his work. For a summary, see John 17:1-26. The apostle Paul not only practiced these in his ministry; he also explained them (Eph. 4:1-16). But the clearest example of all five purposes is the first church at Jerusalem (Acts 2:1-47). They worshiped, they ministered, they evangelized, they fellowshiped, and they taught each other.

Here's another way of saying it: The church exists to exalt, evangelize, encourage, educate, and equip.

Make it as simple as possible

At Saddleback, we've condensed the purposes into five key words: *magnification* (We celebrate God's presence in worship); *mission* (We communicate God's Word through evangelism); *membership* (We incorporate God's family into our fellowship); *maturity* (We educate God's people through discipleship); and *ministry* (We demonstrate God's love through service).

These five key words, representing our five purposes, have been incorporated into our mission statement, which reads, "We exist to bring people to Christ, enlist them as members, educate them to maturity, and equip them for a meaningful ministry in the church and a life mission in the world, in order to magnify God."

Notice that the five purposes are incorporated into a process. This is absolutely crucial! *To be workable, your purposes must be put into a process.* Instead of focusing on growing a church through programs, focus on growing people by setting up a process, based on God's purposes, that enables people to become what God intends for them to be. If you will do this, the growth of your church will be healthy, balanced, and consistent!

At Saddleback, the process involves four steps: We bring people in, build them up, train them, and send them out. We bring them in as members, we build them up to maturity, we train them for their ministry, and we send them out on their life mission, magnifying the Lord in the process. That's it! This is all we do at Saddleback. Nothing else. This is our entire focus.

To say it in business terms, we are in the disciple-development business. Our business is developing effective lives for God's glory. Once we decided that our product was to be Christlike lives, we set about designing a process to accomplish that goal. If we're not seeing lives changed and God isn't getting the glory for those changed lives, then we're failing. This is what it means to be purpose-driven.

Communicate your purposes clearly

Once you have defined the purposes of your church, you must communicate those purposes to everyone in your congregation. This is the number-one task of leadership. You must continually *clarify* and *communicate* the purposes of your church. If you fail to communicate your purpose statement regularly, it is worthless.

What is the best way to communicate the vision and purpose of your church? Here are essential elements:

Scripture. Teach the biblical truth about the church. Every part of your church's vision needs to be supported by Bible verses that explain and illustrate your reason for doing it.

Symbols. People often need visual representations of concepts to grasp them. A symbol can be a powerful communication tool—whether it is a cross, a swastika, or a national flag. Leaders understand the tremendous power of symbols. At Saddleback, we've designed two symbols, a baseball diamond and a set of five concentric circles, to illustrate our purposes. These will be explained later.

Slogans. Remember, slogans and pithy phrases are remembered long after sermons are forgotten. We've developed and used dozens of slogans at Saddleback to reinforce our church's vision. In fact, I periodically set aside time to think of ways to communicate old ideas in a fresh, succinct way.

Stories. Jesus, the greatest communicator, used simple stories to help people understand and relate to the vision he had to impart. Stories personalize and dramatize the purposes of your church. For example, when speaking about fellowship as a purpose of the church, tell a story of how someone's loneliness was relieved through becoming a part of your church family. Give actual stories of people ministering or evangelizing, and say, "That is the church in action!" At Saddleback we have certain "legends," stories that are told over and over, that powerfully illustrate different purposes of our church.

People tend to do whatever gets rewarded. So make heroes of people in your church who clearly act out the purposes of your church.

Specifics. Give concrete action steps that explain exactly how your church intends to fulfill its purpose. Remember, nothing becomes dynamic until it becomes specific. The more specific your church's vision is, the more it will grab attention and attract commitment.

Because people are distracted with other things, don't assume that communicating your church's vision one time is enough. We all have good forgetters. The fire of vision must be fanned continually. You must state it over and over in as many ways as possible. You must keep it before your people continually.

We use as many different channels as we can think of to keep our purposes before our church family. As I've already mentioned, the purpose and vision of the church are communicated in each monthly membership class. Then once a year, usually in January, I preach an annual "state of the church" message. It is simply a review of our five purposes. I say, "It's that time again, folks!" It's the same message every year. Only the illustrations are updated.

Many pastors do not understand the power of the pulpit. It's the rudder of the church ship. If you are a pastor, use your pulpit on purpose! Where else do you get everyone's undivided attention on a weekly basis? Whenever you speak, always look for the opportunity to say something like "and that's why the church exists." Don't be afraid to repeat yourself. Nobody gets it the first time. You'll need to say it over and over in fresh ways. I call it creative redundancy. It's amazing how many times I've taught or preached on the purpose of the church, and people will say, "I just got it for the first time." You have to say it over and over and over until it finally sinks in enough that they can share it with others.

Other tools we've used to continually communicate our purposes are brochures, banners, articles, newsletters, bulletins, songs, T-shirts, videos, and cassette tapes.

Balance and apply your purposes

It's not enough to define your purpose and communicate your purpose. To be a purpose-driven church, you must integrate your purposes into every area and aspect of your church's life. The key to being purpose driven is balance. Each of the five New Testament purposes must be given adequate emphasis for the church to be healthy.

The greatest hindrance to health and growth in most evangelical churches is imbalance! If you look at the average evangelical church, they already do the five purposes of the church—sort of. But they don't do them all equally as well. One church may be strong in fellowship yet weak in evangelism. Another church may be strong in worship yet weak in discipleship. Still another may be strong in evangelism yet weak in ministry. What causes this? It is the natural tendency of leaders to emphasize what we feel strongly about and neglect whatever we feel less passionate about.

Unless you have thought through a plan—a system and a structure—to intentionally balance the five purposes, your church will tend to overemphasize the purpose that best expresses the gifts and passion of the pastor. This fact can be demonstrated in practically every church. All across America you can find churches that are simply the extension of their pastor's giftedness. Historically, churches have taken five basic shapes, depending on which purpose they emphasize the most.

For instance, if the pastor sees his primary role as an evangelist, then the church becomes a **soul-winning church.** This church is always reaching out to the lost. The main goal is to save souls. In this church, you're likely to hear most often about witnessing, evangelism, salvation, decisions for Christ, baptisms, visitation, altar calls, and crusades. This church is shaped by the leader's gift of evangelism. Everything else takes on a secondary role.

If the pastor's passion and gifts lie in the area of worship, he will instinctively lead the church to become what I call an **experiencing God church.** The focus of this church is on experiencing the presence and power of God in worship. Key terms for this church are *praise, prayer, worship, music, spiritual gifts, spirit, power,* and *revival.* The worship service receives more attention than anything else. You can find both charismatic and noncharismatic varieties of this type of church.

A church that focuses primarily on fellowship is what I call the **family reunion church.** This church is shaped by the pastoral gift. The pastor is highly relational, loves people, and spends most of his time caring for members. He serves more as a chaplain than anything else. Key terms for this church are *love, belonging, fellowship, caring, relationships, potlucks, small groups,* and *fun.* Most churches of this type have less than two hundred members, since that's about all the pastor can care for. I estimate that about 80 percent of American churches fall into this category. A family reunion church may not get much done—but it is almost indestructible. It can survive poor preaching, limited finances, no growth, and even church splits. Relationships are the glue that keep the faithful coming.

The **classroom church** occurs when the pastor sees his primary role as being a teacher. If his primary gift is teaching, he will emphasize preaching and teaching and de-emphasize the other tasks of the church. The pastor serves as the expert instructor. The members come to church with notebooks, take notes, and go home. Key terms for the classroom church are *expository preaching, Bible study, Greek and Hebrew, doctrine, knowledge, truth,* and *discipleship.*

The **social conscience church** is out to change our society. It comes in both a liberal and conservative version. The liberal version tends to focus on the injustice in our society. The conservative version tends to focus on the moral decline in our society. Both feel the church should be a major player in the political process. The pastor sees his role as prophet and reformer. Important terms in this church are *needs, serve, share, minister, take a stand,* and *do something.*

I realize that I have painted these pictures with broad strokes. Some churches are a blend of two of these. The point is that unless there is an intentional plan to balance all five purposes, most churches will embrace one purpose to the neglect of others.

There are some interesting things we can observe about these five categories of churches. First, the members of each of these churches will usually consider their church as the most spiritual. That's because people are attracted to join the type of church that corresponds to their own passion and giftedness. We all want to be part of a church that affirms what we feel is most important. The truth is, all five of these emphases are important. They are the purposes of the church. But they must be balanced!

Much of the conflict that occurs in congregations today is caused when a church calls a pastor whose gifts and passion do not match what the church has been in the past. When a church thinks they are calling a chaplain and they get an evangelist or a reformer, you can expect sparks to fly. That is a recipe for disaster!

Five Major Parachurch Movements

The parceling out of God's five purposes for the church can also be seen in the parachurch movements of the past forty years. From time to time God has raised up a parachurch movement to reemphasize a neglected purpose of the church.

The lay renewal movement, including Faith at Work, Laity lodge, The Church of the Savior, and many other organizations, has been used by God to reemphasize the ministry of all believers.

The discipleship/spiritual formation movement, including the Navigators and books by Richard Foster and others, has underscored the importance of developing believers to full spiritual maturity.

The worship renewal movement, beginning with the Jesus movement in the early 1970s, then the charismatic renewal, the liturgical renewal, and more recently the seeker-service emphasis, has brought us new music, new worship forms, and a greater emphasis on worship.

The church growth movement, which began with Donald McGavran, Peter Wagner, and other seminary professors and now has many practitioners, has refocused the church's attention on evangelism and missions.

The small group/pastoral care movement, including Serendipity, Care givers, the Korean cell model, Stephen's ministry, and other proponents, has stressed the importance of fellowship and caring relationships.

What is wrong with these movements? Nothing! They are all partially right. Each movement has had a valid message for the church. Each has given the body of Christ a wake-up call. Each has emphasized a different purpose of the church. The problem is this: Each one emphasizes only a part of the big picture. Unless you look at the big picture, you'll risk being imbalanced as a church.

For instance, Pastor Smith goes to a seminar A, where he is taught that small groups are the key to church growth. He goes home thinking that's all there is to it until he hears about seminar B, which teaches that evangelism is the key to church growth. Then he gets really confused when seminar C boldly states that doctrinal soundness and discipleship are the key to church growth. You get the point. Each time he receives a true but partial picture of what the church should be doing.

I want to clearly state that there is no single key to church health and church growth! Health occurs when we intentionally balance all five of the New Testament purposes. Then growth is the result of health. This is the essence of being a purpose-driven church.

To help you balance the five purposes, I want to give you two simple diagrams. I developed these in the first year of Saddleback Church (1980), when we had fewer than one hundred people attending. Today (1995), with nearly ten thousand attending, we still build everything we do around these two diagrams. They have served us well, and we've shared them with thousands of other churches. You may have seen a version somewhere.

The concentric circles diagram represents a new way of looking at the levels of commitment and maturity in your church. The baseball diamond represents the process by which you can move people to deeper levels of commitment and maturity.

The Concentric Circles of Commitment

While there may be other ways to measure commitment, in a purpose-driven church we identify people by how many of the five purposes they are committed to. Imagine five concentric circles. Each circle represents a different level of commitment, ranging from very little commitment (like agreeing to attend services occasionally) to very strong commitment (like using my spiritual gifts in ministering to others). If you think of your own church as I describe these five groups, you'll recognize that they exist in your church, too.

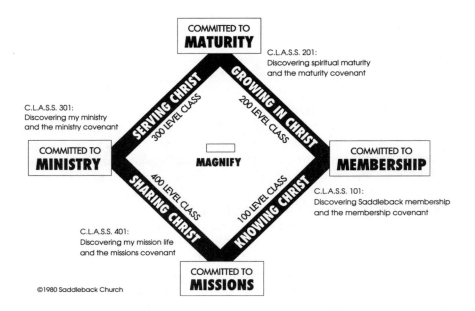

The goal of your church is to move people from the outer circle (low commitment/maturity) to the inner circle (high commitment/maturity). At Saddleback we call this moving people from the community into the core.

The Community. This is your starting point. It is the pool of lost people that live within driving distance of your church. They've made no commitment at all to either Jesus Christ or your church. They are the unchurched who you want to reach. This is where evangelism takes place—in your community. It is the largest circle because it contains the most people.

As Saddleback church has grown, we've narrowed our definition of the community to refer to people we call "unchurched occasional attenders." If you visit a Saddleback service at least four times in a year (and indicate it with a registration card or offering envelope), your name gets put on the "community" database in our computer. These are our hottest evangelistic prospects. As I write this we have over twenty-eight thousand names of occasional attenders of Saddleback. This represents about 10 percent of our area. Our ultimate goal of course is total penetration of our community, giving everyone a chance to hear about Christ.

The Crowd. The next circle in represents the group of people we call the crowd. The crowd includes everyone who shows up on Sundays for services. These people are your regular attenders. The crowd is made up of both believers and nonbelievers. What they have in common is that they attend *worship* every week. That isn't much of a commitment, but at least it's something—and you can build on it. When someone moves from your community into your crowd you've made major progress in his or her life. Currently we have about 10,000 attending in the crowd at Saddleback each weekend.

While an unbeliever cannot truly worship, he or she can watch others worship. And genuine worship is a powerful witness. I have so much confidence in God's Word to change lives that I believe if a person makes a commitment simply to be a regular attender, it is just a matter of time until he will be saved.

Once a person has received Christ, your goal is to move him into the next level of commitment: the congregation.

The congregation is the group of members of your church. They have been baptized and made a commitment to be a part of your church family. They are now more than attenders. They are committed to the *fellowship*. This is a critical commitment. The Christian life is not just a matter of believing; it includes belonging. Once people have made a commitment to Christ, they need to be encouraged to take the next step and commit themselves to Christ's body, the church. At Saddleback, we offer a monthly class (Class 101: Discovering Saddleback Membership) that is required for membership. Only those who have received Christ, been baptized, taken Class 101, and signed the membership covenant are considered a part of the congregation (membership).

At Saddleback we see no use in having nonresident or inactive members on a roll. We remove hundreds of names from membership each year. We are not interested in a large membership, just a legitimate membership of genuinely active and involved people. Currently we have about five thousand active members. Having more members than attenders in a church indicates that membership doesn't mean much. I've been in churches that had one thousand members on their roll, but only one hundred people attend services! What is the value of having that kind of membership? On the other hand, having more attenders than members means the church is being effective in attracting the unchurched and building a pool for evangelism.

The Committed. Do you have people in your church who are godly, growing people—people who are serious about their faith—but for one reason or another are not actively serving in a ministry of your church? We call these people the committed. They pray, they give, and they are dedicated to growing in *discipleship.* They are good people, but they have not yet gotten involved in ministry.

At Saddleback, the people we consider in this group are those who have taken Class 201: Discovering Spiritual Maturity and signed a maturity covenant that says they commit to having a daily quiet time, tithing 10 percent of their income, and being active in a small group. These are three habits we consider essential for spiritual growth. About thirty-five hundred people at Saddleback have signed maturity covenant cards.

The Core. This is the smallest group because it represents the deepest level of commitment. The core of your church are those committed to *ministry* to others. These are people who lead and serve in the various ministries of your church: Sunday school teachers, deacons, musicians, youth sponsors, etc. Without these people your church would come to a standstill. Your core workers form the heart of your church.

At Saddleback we have a very intentional process for helping people find their best ministry niche. This includes taking Class 301: Discovering My Ministry, filling out a S.H.A.P.E. profile, having a personal ministry interview, being commissioned as a lay minister in the church, and attending a core-only monthly training meeting. Currently we have about fifteen hundred people in the core.

I would do anything for these people. They are the secret of Saddleback's strength. If I were to drop dead, Saddleback would continue to grow because it's not built around a single pastor. It has a base of fifteen hundred lay ministers.

What happens when people finally get to the core? We move them back out into the community for ministry!

Jesus' ministry included both feeding the crowd and training the core. Both were appropriate. We need to follow his example of beginning where people are—then slowly, gently leading people to deeper levels of commitment.

As people continued to follow him, he would turn up the heat a notch, redefining more clearly the kingdom of God and asking for a deeper commitment to it. But he did this only when the previous stage was reached.

The first encounter Jesus had with John and Andrew, he didn't say, "Take up your cross and deny yourself!" He simply said, "Come and see!" That's a crowd statement, an enticement for people to come and check it out.

Jesus started where people were, at their level of comfort, but he never left them there. As he spent time with people, they lowered their guard and began to trust him. He kept turning up the heat and raising the level of commitment until he had their total allegiance.

There is a debate today between two views of the church. One group, the "seeker sensitive" camp, says we ought to open up our services to the unchurched—in order to reach the secular pagans in our society. They point out that Jesus said "I didn't come for those who are well. I came for the sick—the unrighteous," and that Paul adapted the style of his presentation on Mars Hill. The other group, the "purist" camp, says, "We must preserve the purity of the church. Being seeker sensitive is caving in to our culture! We cannot water down the cost of discipleship." Recently some in the purist camp have written a number of books and articles filled with biting criticisms of the seeker-sensitive camp.

I believe the strategy of Jesus is the antidote to this conflict: Start where people are—but don't leave them there! That is the idea behind the Circles of Commitment strategy. It recognizes that we must minister to people at all levels of commitment. Each level has unique needs. We must not confuse what we do with the community and the crowd with what we do with the core! They each require a different approach. A crowd is not a church, but a crowd can be turned into a church.

If your church is serious about the great commission and evangelism, you will never have a completely "pure" church because you will always be attracting unbelievers with their questionable lifestyles. You can't clean fish until you first catch them! Evangelism is not clean. It is messy. Even after people become believers, you have to deal with their immaturity and carnality. There will never be a completely "pure" church as long as people are imperfect.

Are there some unrepentant pagans in Saddleback's crowd of ten thousand? Without a doubt! But Jesus said in one parable, "Don't worry about the tares mixed in among the wheat. One day I'll separate them!" Leave it to Jesus.

In Jesus' day, there was another group who used the objection of "purity" to avoid contact with sinners. They were called Pharisees. And Jesus reserved his severest words for them.

Ten Ways to Be Purpose-Driven

At Saddleback church, we have tried to integrate the New Testament purposes into every aspect of our church life. Here are ten ways you can do this too:

1. Strategize on purpose! Use the Circles of Commitment as your strategy. Move people from the community to the crowd, then from the crowd to the congregation, and so on.

Notice that I suggest you grow the church from the outside in, rather than from the inside out. Start with your community, not your core. This is the exact opposite advice of most books on church planting. They say, "Build a committed core, and then start reaching out to the community."

The problem I have found with that approach is that often by the time the church planter has "discipled" his core, they've lost contact with the community and are actually afraid of interacting with the unchurched. A small group that meets in a home for a year or two will become comfortable with that size, and it will be difficult for newcomers to break into that tight fellowship.

When I began Saddleback, I started with the community. I spent eight weeks just going door to door, talking to people and surveying their needs. I then gathered a crowd, using a direct mail piece. For the first year, all I tried to do was build a crowd. At the end of the year we had an average attendance of about two hundred. I then began working on turning that crowd into a congregation, while continuing to work on community and crowd building. The third year I began to turn up the heat and really encourage people to deepen their commitment to the habits that build spiritual maturity. From that group we began to move people into core ministries in a major way. You build a multidimensional ministry by focusing on one need at a time. Build from the outside in.

2. Program on purpose! Design a key program to fulfill each of your purposes, one that meets the unique needs of each circle. For example, at Saddleback the key program for reaching out into our community is our schedule of community-wide events: a harvest party at Halloween, six Christmas Eve services, six Easter services, and other big events that attract the community's involvement.

The key program for the *crowd* is our weekend seeker-services. The key program for the *congregation* is our small group network. The key programs for the *committed* are our midweek worship and Bible studies. The key program for the *core* is our monthly S.A.L.T. (Saddleback Advanced Leadership Training).

3. Assimilate and train on purpose! Saddleback's Christian education focuses on not simply informing Christians, but transforming them into the image of Christ. This happens not by chance but by a Life Development Process that encourages and rewards people to keep growing and learning.

© 1980 Saddleback Church

We use the simple diagram of a baseball diamond to communicate this process to everyone. You get to first base by completing Class 101 and committing to membership in our church. You make it to second base by completing class 201 and committing to the habits necessary for spiritual growth. You make it to third base by completing class 301 and committing to service in a ministry of the church. Finally, you get back to home plate by completing Class 401 and committing to sharing your faith both at home and on mission trips.

As in baseball, you don't get credit for runners left on base. We tell new members that our goal is for them to become "grand slam disciples." Most churches do a fairly good job getting people to first base or maybe even second base. People will get saved and become a regular attender at church, even sometimes moving on to maturity. But a great majority of Christians never use their gifts in a ministry and never win anyone else to Christ.

I believe that a church's health is determined not by its seating capacity but by its sending capacity. You judge the strength of an army not by how many soldiers sit and eat in the cafeteria but by how they perform on the front line.

4. Start small groups on purpose! We don't expect every small group to do the same things. We allow them to specialize: Some are for evangelism, some for fellowship, some meet for ministry, some gather for worship, and some meet for discipleship training.

5. Add staff on purpose! Every person we hire has a job description related to one of the five purposes of our church. We discover which purpose they feel most passionate about and staff accordingly. If I were starting a new church today, I would recruit five volunteers for unpaid staff positions: a music director to help prepare the worship services for the crowd; a membership director to teach Class 101 and oversee the care of members in the congregation; a maturity director to teach Class 201 and oversee the Bible study programs for the committed; a ministry director to teach Class 301 and supervise the lay ministries of the core; and a mission director to teach class 401 and oversee the evangelism and missions programs in the community.

As the church grew, I would move these people to part-time paid staff, and eventually full-time. You can be purpose-driven regardless of the size of your church.

6. Structure on purpose! Rather than organizing by traditional departments, at Saddleback every staff member and every lay ministry is assigned to one of our five purpose-based teams: The missions team evangelizes the community; the music team exalts Christ in the crowd; the membership team encourages the congregation; the maturity team edifies the committed; and the ministry team equips the core.

7. Preach on purpose! In planning your preaching, make sure you balance what your people receive by preparing at least one series related to each of the five purposes: a series that mobilizes people for ministry; a series that helps people grow to maturity (Fruit of the Spirit, etc.); a series on worship

(How to hear God, etc.); an evangelistic series; and a pastoral care series (on fellowship, encouragement, etc.)

8. Budget on purpose! Funds are allocated according to the five purposes.

9. Calendar on purpose! Each purpose team can be assigned two months of the year to give special emphasis to their purpose. For example, January might be ministry month, February might be maturity month, and March might be missions month.

10. Evaluate on purpose! To remain effective, you must build review and revision into your process. At Saddleback we've developed a tool called the "snapshot" that the staff reviews each month. It helps us keep track of how many people are moving through the circles and around the baseball diamond. Remember the two questions: What is our business? and How's business?

No Greater Goal

One of my life verses is Acts 13:36, which says that David served God's purpose in his generation, then he died. What a great tribute! David served *God's purpose* (eternal, unchanging, and timeless) *in his generation* (in a contemporary, relevant, timely way). It is my prayer that people will be able to say that about me when I die—that I served God's purpose in my generation. And it is my prayer that people will be able to say that about you, too. There is no greater use of your life. This is the foundation for effective evangelism.

2
Praying Without Ceasing:
A Contemporary Approach to Spirituality

Calvin Miller

Calvin Miller is writer in residence and professor of communication and ministry studies at Southwestern Baptist Theological Seminary. He is known across evangelicalism for his many writings, including the Singer trilogy. For many years he pastored the Westside Church in Omaha, Nebraska.

The most difficult of all the spiritual disciplines is enduring prayer. In a "hyper-drive" world, finding a praying Christian is rare, and finding a Christian who hungers for an unbroken prayer life is all but impossible. The reason for this lack of people who pray has nothing to do with prayer itself, for everyone wants to pray. It has to do with the focus of prayer. Our prayers lack focus. They are so random they fly at God without ever taking aim at heaven.

Centering is a matter of focusing. To center means to move from the periphery of a circle to its center. Each of us have had the experience of driving a car whose tires are out of balance. They are impossible to steer. The wheels "shimmy." The rubber makes horrible thumping noises. This problem is corrected by taking the car to a technician who "balances" the wheels. How does he perform this marvel? He adds weights to various parts of the rim so that the tire's center is moved synthetically to the center of the axle. The ride then is smooth. Driving becomes enjoyable.

In life we call people who behave erratically in social situations eccentric. By this we mean that their behavior is somewhere on the periphery of our expectancy. Sometimes we say such persons are mentally unbalanced. This parallel to the tire illustration needs no further illumination. Such persons need therapy to try to get the center of their behavior back in the center of our expectancy.

But in the devotional life, to speak of centering means that we are trying to move from the periphery of our preoccupations to the middle of our relationship with God. Centering is the act of being still so that we can know that God is God (Ps. 46:10). Centering is that focus which pulls our wideness of vision into "laser spotlight." It stops all peripheral vision and surrounding noise. It gets us ready to meet God.

But centering is hard work indeed. The mind is a flibbertigibbet. It will not stay put. It flits in and out of the throne room of God. It worries whether the roast will burn. It stews over the bank account even as we try to talk to Jesus. It has a million side-conversations going all the time we are trying to talk to God. It draws us away from our centering on God and dooms our lives to short-attention-span praying. We cannot give God our full attention for long. Our contemptible inner chatter will not permit us an exalted conversation with our King. It is too flighty to allow us the serious work of prayer.

Remember the nursery rhyme of our childhood? We oft recited, "Pussy-cat, Pussycat, where have you been?/ I've been to London to visit the Queen./ Pussycat, Pussycat, what did you there?/ I frightened a little mouse under the chair." One wonders of the tour agents, the money, the arduous travel, the accommodations, the language barrier: All of these are spent to allow the pussycat her moment with her ruler. But alas, she never saw the queen. She was distracted by her flighty attention span. How often our appointment with our Sovereign is distracted in the very throne room of heaven. We fly off to chase our little matters, and God is unseen in our lives. How we need to develop the focused art of centering.

"All who have walked with God have viewed prayer as the main business of their lives," says Richard Foster.[1] These are commonly called *saints*. Yet we are as much threatened by the constancy of their prayers as we are challenged by it. Which of us in becoming concerned about the discipline of prayer are not ashamed to admit we do it neither well nor regularly. Paul's challenge to "pray without ceasing" (1 Thess. 5:17) follows hard upon his challenge to "be joyful always" (1 Thess. 5:16). The connection between these two commands states the fundamental ratio between constant joy and constant prayer. Those who forever pray are those who continually rejoice.

Still, for most of us the idea of praying without ceasing conjures up spiritual nightmares of heavy, unpleasant disciplines. Maybe we can pray without ceasing if we don't get too bored and fall asleep or suffer a wandering mind. Maybe we can do it if we clamp our eyes shut in determination . . . if we grit our teeth in firm intention . . . if we get up two hours early to show God how very serious we are about it all. But usually in five minutes of prayer we can pray for everyone we can think of—the president, Aunt Molly's rheumatism, all of our professed friends, and two or three of our worst enemies. Then we experience that unholy doubling back over all that we have already prayed.

But there is a splendid correlation of deliverance in 1 Thessalonians 5:16 and 17. Can it be that praying without ceasing can be related to the matter of rejoicing? Taken together, do these verses not show the truth that prayer is to be the joy, not the drudgery of the Christian life?

Joy is always found in the appetite of all we are hungry for. Food is never boring to a starving man. It is never drudgery to eat. Malcolm Muggeridge reminds us of that spiritual hunger that ought to exist between Jesus and ourselves:

> . . . this bridge, this reconciliation between the black despair of lying bound and gagged in the tiny dungeon of ego, and soaring upwards into the white radiance of God's universal love—this bridge was the Incarnation, whose truth expresses that of the desperate need it meets. Because of our physical hunger we know there is bread; because of our spiritual hunger we know there is Christ.[2]

Theresa of Avila is reported to have asked God to make her pray four hours every day. "Ah," replied God, "as I do not make the birds to eat, neither will I make you pray; the birds eat because they get hungry. When you are hungry for me you, too, will pray, Theresa."

Prayer as the Focus of Lovers

Indeed, continual praying is possible or not possible depending upon the definition of prayer. If prayer is seen as talking to God, we will have one definition of it. If it is seen as talking and listening to God, we will have yet a second definition of it. And if it is seen as togetherness with God, we shall have yet another definition. In my book *Table of Inwardness,* I long ago opted for this togetherness definition. Prayer is more than talking and listening. It is that state of union with Christ that is fostered by our own spiritual desire. That desire is filled only by our longing for Christ. Those who want to talk to God are *talkers.* Those who want to listen to God are *listeners.* But those who crave his unbroken presence are *pray-ers.* These opening lines of *Table of Inwardness* speak of the life of desire and union.

> In this secluded place I meet a King.
> He comes alone to drink reality
> With me. Sometimes we talk, sometimes we sit
> And sip a life that passes by the crowd
> As inwardness is born—a felted thing
> Of power—a commonality—
> A union where unmended hopes are knit
> Where silence roars as quiet sings aloud.
> O Christ, I love it here! It is our place.
> Speak Lord or not. Touch me or not. Show then
> Your will or bid me wait in patient grace.
> Fill all my hungry need with joy again.
> With simple loaves of bread and chaliced wine
> Heaven, earth and all of God are mine.[3]

This desire is the focus of lovers. Separated lovers are possessed of a common need to be together. This focus is only possible when we have unbroken rapport with God. But our sin is ever in the way. The issue of our sin is one that we have often failed to take seriously. At the midway point of the twentieth century, psychology began to make serious infringements into the biblical understanding of spiritual truth. B. F. Skinner's behaviorism took a "white-rat" view of the morality of human beings. Sin was redefined as behavior, and its spiritual consequence was defined as bad sociological conditioning.

The result of this redefinition has left our current generation "free of guilt" but neurotic and unhealed. In a world where there is no sin, God does not need to be consulted, and Christ's redeeming work is inconsequential. But this vast need for unsought forgiveness has fostered a neurotic world, where no one sits on God's throne but Narcissus. Once humankind no longer needed forgiveness, the race no longer needed God. He still hangs around in our stained-glass religious formality, but he seems frail, old, and anti-feminist to most.

The loss of sin has dulled our once-keen focus on God. When we close our eyes in prayer these days, we see mostly ourselves. We "talk to God," but our own egos, "spongelike," absorb our piety and crown our own souls as central. "God helps those who help themselves," we chirp, all-sufficient in our own self-righteousness. Naturally, we cannot see God. We try divorcing, marrying our ways through piteous cycles of mismanagement. We gear ourselves with a self-lubricating positivism and cry in the dark while we smile and quote optimistic slogans in the hollow daylight.

How we need to cry with the psalmist, "Against Thee, Thee only, I have sinned" (Ps. 51:4, NASB). Then we will find our focus narrowing. Then we will see God and learn the joy of Kierkegaard's prayer:

> Father in Heaven! Hold not our sins up against us but hold us up against our sins, so that the thought of Thee when it wakens in our soul, and each time it wakens, should not remind us of what we have committed but of what Thou didst forgive, not of how we went astray but of how Thou didst save us![4]

Centering is not possible without a consciousness of sin. But let us also remember that just as sin cannot be left out of the relationship recipe, neither can it be central. Just as ignoring sin leaves us with no need of God, focusing on it obscures God. Ignoring our sin sets God at a distance too great to be seen and excessive guilt blocks our vision of God. The hymnist wrote, "My sin, oh the bliss of this glorious thought,/ My sin, not in part, but the whole/ Is nailed to the cross and I bear it no more./ Praise the Lord! Praise the Lord, O my soul!"[5]

Sin must be confessed once, and in that confession nailed to the cross. Once nailed to the cross, the heart is to be free of all thought of it. Then the centering focus becomes possible in a positive walk with Christ. We must yield up all guilt over confessed sin. Notice that 1 Thessalonians 5:16 sets continual rejoicing over against praying without ceasing (v. 17). Is this an arbitrary arrangement of rejoicing and praying? Shouldn't we pray first so that prayer can come naturally ahead of rejoicing? To the contrary, I believe that once we have confessed all sin our attitudes become instantly positive. In confession all that might have prevented our focus is nailed to the cross, and joy then invites our unbroken focus on God. On the contrary, when sin lies unconfessed, rejoicing is replaced by guilt which permits neither joy nor togetherness with God. When rejoicing we find that centering provides unbroken relationship in Christ.

Prayer As Conversation in the Presence of the Enemy

Satan has no power to interrupt our conversations with our Father. Yet we are to be ever mindful of him as we pray. Did not Jesus remind us in the Lord's Prayer that we are always to pray for deliverance from the evil one (Matt. 6:13)? But Paul assured us that with the shield of faith we will always be able to quench all the fiery darts of the evil one (Eph. 6:16). James tells us that if we resist the devil he will flee from us (James 4:7). Yet Peter tells us that resisting the devil is not all that easy. We must be ever on guard, for our adversary, the devil, is like a roaring lion, pacing and dogging our existence (1 Pet. 5:8).

Satan thwarts our centering process in at least two ways. *First, he distracts our hearts from our spiritual duty.* We know we ought to pray always (1 Thess. 5:17), but somehow we never get around to it. Why is this? Because the grand issue of our Christ relationship is always interrupted by the little things. Mary could sit at the feet of Christ, but Martha fidgeted with trivia (Luke 10:38-42). God is called Almighty in the Old Testament (e.g., Gen. 17:1). All his acts are almighty in their significance. He knows no minor issues, offers no little assignments. God, his call, his demands: all are immense. Satan, however, is god of the small and distracting. He is king of the interruptions. His trivia, however, achieves almighty importance. Test the theory if you will. Fall to your knees and see if the phone does not soon ring. Open your Bible; it is inevitably the doorbell. Try to set aside a time to meet God, and your schedule fills up with things that must be done or you will not appear efficient, or caring, or important.

Satan's tyranny with God was the tyranny of rebellion. He challenged the throne of God (Isa. 14:12-15) and took a third of the angels with him (Rev. 12:4, 7). But his tyranny with humans is a tyranny of trifles, a tyranny of the urgent. What must be done ever defeats what should be done. Martin Luther well understood the tyranny of the urgent when he said, "I have so much business I cannot get on without spending three hours daily in prayer."[6] Richard Foster well understands how little tasks interrupt the important work of prayer:

> How often we fashion cloaks of evasion . . . to elude our Eternal Lover. . . .
> For those explorers in the frontiers of faith, prayer was no little habit tacked
> onto the periphery of their lives—it was their lives. . . . For these, and all of
> those who have braved the depths of the interior life, to breathe was to pray.[7]

There is only one way to defeat the tyranny of the urgent. We must be quick
to identify the urgent, assign it to "later," and give the essential our full
focus in the moment. For me, praying is like the "call-waiting" button on
my telephone. If I am talking to the president, I must not let its buzzing
insistence distract me. I must not put aside the important conversation while
I attend to electronic surveyors who want to question me on my favorite
toothpaste. But the buzz is insistent, so I must focus . . . I must center . . . I
must play my focus to the full, as Mary did, while Martha gave herself to
every "call-waiting" that came along.

*But there is a second way that Satan distracts us. He snuggles into our
philosophies.* He is always convincing us that we are not seeing things quite
right. This tactic is far more dangerous than merely distracting us with the
trivial. For in this mode of operating, he actually lives inside our life-defi-
nitions. In such a strategic position, our will to resist him is gone, for his
advice is our counsel. He leads us to believe that prayer is ineffective. He
causes us to remember some agonizing request we prayed for and never
received. He leads us to believe that prayer is only autosuggestion. He
convinces us that action is better than praying. He causes us to say that I
need not talk to God, for "God helps those who help themselves."

To keep from falling into erroneous philosophies of prayer, we must use
the Scriptures in a consistent and periodic way. As we read the Bible, Satan
will be challenged from owning us philosophically. Otherwise, he will
cloud our vision, and our prayer focus will be lost. In the fourth century,
John Chrysostom preached a sermon on the Prodigal Son in which he dealt
with Satan the philosopher as a nestling serpent:

> If we were suddenly aware of a serpent nestling in our bed, we would go to
> great lengths to kill it. But when the devil nestles in our souls, we tell
> ourselves we are in no danger, and thus we lie at ease. Why? Because we do
> not see him and his intent with our mortal eyes.
>
> This is why we must rouse ourselves and be more sober. Fighting an enemy
> we can see makes it easy to be on guard, but one that cannot be seen we will
> not easily escape. Also, know that the devil has no desire for open combat

(for he would surely be defeated), but rather, under the appearance of friendship, intends to insinuate the venom of his malice. . . .

Be on your guard, and arm yourself with weapons of the Spirit. Become acquainted with the devil's plans that you may keep from getting caught in his traps, and instead, expose him. Paul got the better of him because he was "not ignorant of his devices."[8]

Techniques for Quieting the Heart

The incessant chatter of the mind is always the antithesis of Psalm 46:10 (KJV), "Be still, and know that I am God." But for most of us, prayer is not a matter of focus. We go into the throne room and slam down our intercessory demands, while all the time our hearts have played the harlot. We force God to hear us through the swim of all the things we can't quit thinking about. The Almighty swims in the same egoistic thought whirlpool as our refrigerator payment and our afternoon agenda. Our conversation with God is indistinct from all the things that buzz in our brains even while we are in his presence. How do we silence this never-ending inner stream of conversation?

The first rule

The first rule of centering prayer is, Never start praying before you've stopped to look at God. One Christmas Eve, in the panic of last-minute shopping I ran into a perfumery to buy my wife a bottle of cologne. The store was about to close, and I was in a dreadful hurry . . . there was much to be done. I slammed down my credit card and hastily picked up my parcel. I hurried out of the store exactly as I had hurried in. Only as I left the parking lot did it occur to me that I had managed the entire transaction and never seen the salesperson. I think it was a woman, but I am not sure. I wonder if my hurried transaction is not the way that we do business with God. We hurry in and out of God's presence, agitated that we can't give God more time. But it has been well said that worrying in the presence of God does not constitute prayer.

We must be careful lest our pietistic fidgeting is called prayer. We must stop the hurry. We must stop the inner chatter, and only when all is quiet, and angels announce us, should we move into his presence. This is the first work of centering: seeing God, taking our shoes from off our feet, and acknowledging that we are ready to hear the fire from the bush. "I am that I am!" only comes to those who "aren't as they were."

In short, all of this says that we must be empty to attend his filling. How do we empty ourselves of our noisy inwardness? I would like to suggest two ideas. *First, I would like to talk about breathing the name of Jesus till his holy name calls our raucous souls to silence.* In Christian meditation there are essentially two approaches to the subject. There is *apophatic* tradition and the *kataphatic* approach. The *kataphatic* is the affirmative mode of meditating on God. Its strength is that it feeds on positive images and words and symbols. It uses the words of Scripture to make us think of God. In the *kataphatic* approach we read or quote Scripture until there is a firm focus on God that achieves a glorious oneness of prayer relationship with God. Still, it has for its greatest weakness the fact that it often hurries too directly into his presence. It quotes Scripture without taking the necessary time to deal with the state of heart. It is like a little boy who is so excited he breaks away from making mud pies and quickly greets his father as he comes in from work. His father may be flattered by his love, but when the son is more grown up, he will greet his father with clean hands. *Kataphatic* meditation can go to God so directly that it takes little notice of cleaning up the heart.

By contrast, in the *apophatic* emphasis there is an attempt to arrive at meditation by negation. In other words, the person seeks to become focused on God by obliterating all the thoughts or mind-states that distract us from union with Christ. The apophatic meditator spends much time cleaning up the heart to prepare to meet God. But this mind-state so thrives on preparing to meet God that it sometimes misses the conversation. It is, too often, all prologue *to* God and no dialogue *with* God. It is like a beautiful porch with no house behind it. This is the sad course often followed by certain Eastern forms of mantra meditation. Such meditation entails the repetition of a non-content or nonsense word until the mind is freed of all content thinking. This was the same idea used in Transcendental Meditation, as an attempt to stop all the inner chatter, until the silent and quiet consciousness "dived" deeply into ego states of peace and utter quiet. It sounds good, but the real question is, What does the quiet mind dive into? If it only dives into an undefinable peace, it will be a peace that quickly succumbs to defeat, for it is not founded on God. Do not the Scriptures remind us, "Thou wilt keep him in perfect peace, whose mind is stayed on thee" (Isa. 26:3).

I really think that both ideas (kataphatic and apophatic) incorporate the proper approach to prayer. First we need the cleansing emptying process, and then a strong prayer agenda of relationship. I believe, therefore, it is necessary to quiet the heart before God, not by use of a mantra, but by closing the eyes and breathing the name of Jesus, the strongest word of content in the English language. We will find his name able to both cleanse our hearts of busyness and yet quiet and empty our hearts to make room for his coming. How are we to do this? Slowly, I believe. It should be as natural as breathing. In fact, in my life I often do it *as* I breathe. Each time I exhale, I let his name clear my heart of hurriedness. Yet I do not think of the repetition of his name as prayer, but as a time of preparing to pray. Then as his name clears my thinking of inner congestion, I begin to quiet my mind and make it ready to sit in quietness before God. Without some such kind of "centering," I would probably hurry into his presence "full of sound and fury, signifying nothing."

Second, I would like to call the Christ-needy to what I call kenotic meditation. Paul uses the Greek word *kenosis* in Philippians 2:5-7 to speak of how Christ emptied himself of divine prerogatives in becoming human. All ambition was cleared out of Jesus as he "poured himself out" in Incarnation. In a similar way, we can quiet our own hearts by consciously emptying our souls of busy schedules and self-importance as we empty our ego by self-denial (Luke 9:23).

We should not hurry into God's presence so full of self that we find no room in our hearts for him. I said in my book *Table of Inwardness* that a well-bucket will bring up water only to the exact extent of its emptiness when it is lowered into the well. If we send a bucket full of rocks into the well, it will bring up some water, but what really fills it will still be largely rocks. But if a completely empty bucket is sent into the well, it will come back completely full of water. In a similar way, if we send our busy lives directly into God's presence, full of self and schedule, we will return from the throne full of self and schedule. But if we pour the egoistic noise and bulky self-service out of our lives, then we shall come from the throne room filled.

The second rule

The second rule of centering prayer is, While you are in the presence of God, do not let the focus of your praying drift. I have had people tell me they prayed themselves to sleep at night. I cannot imagine doing this. To ramble on in the presence of a great King until we have fallen asleep in his presence is unthinkable. I would suggest instead that we never allow ourselves to forget the nature of him to whom our petition is addressed. For those who want to continue for a long time in prayer, there needs to be a specific agenda that we are going to go through so that our focus is maintained. One of the best tools that we can use is to pray through the Scriptures. Madam Guyon suggests that this approach might use God's own Word to form the words we pray back to him. Not only does this prevent a decay in our devotion, but it allows a focus that permits God to speak to us. Guyon writes:

> But in coming to the Lord by means of 'praying the Scripture,' you do not read quickly; you read very slowly. You do not move from one passage to another, not until you have *sensed* the very heart of what you have read. You may then want to take that portion of Scripture that has touched you and turn it into prayer.
>
> After you have sensed something of the passage and after you know that the essence of that portion has been extracted and all the deeper sense of it is gone, then, very slowly, gently, and in a calm manner begin to read the next portion of the passage.
>
> You will be surprised to find that when your time with the Lord has ended, you will have read very little, probably no more than half a page.
>
> 'Praying the Scripture' is not judged by *how much* you read but by the *way* in which you read.
>
> If you read quickly, it will benefit you little. You will be like a bee that merely skims the surface of a flower. Instead, in this new way of reading with prayer, you must become as the bee who penetrates into the *depths* of the flower. You plunge deeply within to remove its deepest nectar.[9]

The praying of Scripture is probably the most joyous exercise of centering for both the believer and his or her God. It is the author of the piece being thrilled by hearing his children read it back to him. I was doing a poetry reading recently to a group of children. The auditorium where I read was furnished with an exalted stage, from which I seemed to be "reading down" to my audience. As I began one of the poems, I noticed a child on the front row, whose lips were moving with mine as I read. I knew the boy had the passage memorized. It was a most delicious moment for me. I stopped my reading and walked to the edge of the platform and said, "Sir, do you know this poem?" The boy nodded his head in exaggerated, affirmative movements.

"Do you think you could quote this poem in front of all these people?" I asked.

Again the exaggerated movements of the head.

"Come up here, if you will," I begged.

He did. I took my microphone from the stand and gave it to him. He quoted the entire piece to thunderous applause. But the audience could never know the joy I felt in hearing this child read my work back to me. Believe me, my focus and the child's focus were one. Why? He was reading my book back to me. I know the thrill of being an author and having my words given back to me by an adoring child. I tasted only a fraction of the joy that God must feel when we pray his Word back to him in an intensity of centering.

The Pursuit of Union with Christ

Shallowness is never comfortable with depth. It is possible to drown in eight feet of water, yet the depths of the ocean somehow fill us all the more with wonder and dread. It is the depth that provides the mystery and the awe of God. Most Christians are content to splash about in wading pools, intimidated by the deep canyons of the Pacific Ocean. Karl Rahner mused at how shallow people seem content to live without a hunger for God:

> Look at the vast majority of men, Lord—and excuse me if I presume to pass judgement on them—but do they often think of You? Are You the First Beginning and Last End of them, the one without whom their minds and hearts can find no rest? Don't they manage to get along perfectly well without You? Don't they feel quite at home in this world which they know so well, where they can be sure of just what they have to reckon with? Are You anything more for them than the one who sees to it that the world stays on its hinges, so that they won't have to call on You? Tell me, are You the God of *their* life?[10]

But the majestic, engulfing nature of God is the passion of those who want his fathomless love. Many prefer to swim in the ocean for all its risks. And be sure the risks are there. He is so almighty that we cannot understand or measure all he is. We will be awed and sometimes bewildered by his immensity and the overwhelming size of his demands. But we will never be bored, and we will soon know we can never measure him with our simple requirements.

Just how awesome is such awe?

Paul said in 2 Corinthians 4:6 that God has given us the "light of the knowledge of the glory of God in the face of Christ." When we pursue this togetherness with God, we pursue the rapport of splendor. Nothing but God

will slake the thirst of those believers whose thirst is proper. In Psalm 139
God is shown in pursuit of us:

Where can I go from your Spirit?
Where can I flee from your presence?
If I go up to the heavens, you are there;
If I make my bed in the depths, you are there.
If I rise on the wings of the dawn,
if I settle on the far side of the sea,
even there your hand will guide me,
your right hand will hold me fast.
If I say, "Surely the darkness will hide me
and the light become night around me,"
even the darkness will not be dark to you;
the night will shine like the day,
for darkness is as light to you. (Ps. 139:7-12)

But those who know that craving only heaven can fill realize that they too
are in pursuit of God. He alone can fill them with that water that nothing
else can take the place of. William MacNamara wrote:

Nikos Kazantzakis tells the story of a thirsty Moslem who came upon a well
in the desert. He dropped a bucket into the well and pulled it up. It was full
of silver. Emptying the bucket, he dumped it into the well again and pulled
it up full of gold. The Moslem protested: "My Lord God, I know how
powerful you are and what marvels you are capable of. But all I want is a cup
of water." He emptied the bucket of gold, lowered it into the well and
retrieved it. It was full of water. He drank and quenched his thirst.[11]

But it is Frank Laubach who writes of the goal of this pursuit:

I feel simply carried along each hour, doing my part in a plan which is far
beyond myself. This sense of cooperation with God in little things is what
astonishes me. . . . I seem to have to make sure of only one thing now, and
every other thing "takes care of itself," or I prefer to say what is more true,
God takes care of all the rest. My part is to *live in this hour in continuous
inner conversation with God and in perfect responsiveness to His will, to
make this hour gloriously rich.* This seems to be all I need think about.

We can keep two things in mind at once. Indeed we cannot keep one thing in mind more than half a second. Mind is a flowing something. It oscillates. Concentration is merely the continuous return to the same problem from a million angles. . . . So my problem is this: Can I bring God back in my mind-flow every few seconds so that God shall always be in my mind as an after image, shall always be one of the elements in every concept and precept?

I choose to make the rest of my life an experiment in answering this question.[12]

This is the all-consuming pursuit of God's lovers.

Avoiding Sterile Fascination

In the seventies, the deeper-life movement began, when many Christians became so fascinated with God that they had no time for serving him. There is no human merit in worship, however ardent, if the worshipper will not serve. Suppose I asked our son to take out the trash and he replied, "Oh Dad, you are so beautiful and resplendent, I want to just sit here and contemplate your wisdom and power."

"But Son, I might insist my attributes are little if you will not obey me. Take out the trash!"

"When I consider how you are the ground from which I sprung, I am awestruck. When I think of how you conceived me, I consider my own immaturity and praise you all the more."

"Son, *take out the trash.*"

Well, the illustration has gone on long enough to speak of the danger of folding our hands in adoration or lifting them in praise when we ought to be using them to minister. God is never honored by our sterile fascination with him.

I see three distinct dangers in the unrealistic pursuit of God.

The first danger is that the pursuit of holiness breeds its own inner addiction. Since we have already looked at this one, there remains little to say except to express this caveat: Always look for evidences that you are loving the wrong things. Do you love the quietness that you create, and in which you meet God, more than you love God? If so, you are in love with the discipline of quietness more than you are in love with him. If you love the literature of the saints more than you desire to emulate their holiness, you are also captive. If you seem to talk a lot about prayer but pray very little, you have bought only a godly mystique, and not godliness.

The worst thing about all of this is that in appearing to pursue God you will have abandoned more important forms of ministry. We must never keep our hands so folded in prayer that we cannot unfold them to teach and heal and minister. The lesson of Matthew 25 is that we can call Jesus Lord and never minister unto the "least of these" (Matt. 25:45). Remember the Final Judge's condemnation to those on the left:

> *Then he will say to those on his left, "Depart from me, you who are cursed, into the eternal fire prepared for the devil and his angels. For I was hungry and you gave me nothing to eat, I was thirsty and you gave me nothing to drink, I was a stranger and you did not invite me in, I needed clothes and you did not clothe me, I was sick and in prison and you did not look after me." (Matt. 25:41-43)*

I've always wondered if many of these who go off into everlasting fire were not part of a deeper-life group, who busied themselves with the rhetoric of holiness but never took the time to minister.

The second danger is that the pursuit of holiness can breed an other-worldly aloofness. The key fault in such a mystique is that people will not approach the spiritually elite. When someone translates as hyper-godly, most of us become hyper-nervous around them. Saints may be safely read about, but most of us feel a bit uncomfortable in their company. The result is that needy people would rather die in their need than approach a saint whose very lifestyle seems to condemn their own.

The third danger is that the pursuit of holiness can lure us into the "sweet little Jesus" syndrome. I've never much cared for those paintings of Jesus where his halo is over large or his thorn-crowned-bleeding heart is painted on the outside of his toga. This Jesus is the saccharine Christ of gooey pietism. Yet this Christ is where many a lover of God has wound up. There is a valid romance in the gospel, but we want to be sure that our centering disciplines do not at last wind us up in a religious sugar bin. Jesus is the sinless Son of God, but he did not come to be the object of our love.

He came on a rugged, double-fisted agenda to save humankind. He should always be adored within the context of his saving mission. He should always be celebrated within the framework of his calling to our lives.

Centering is the work of focus in our relationship with God. It is desperately important work. In 1970, Richard Lovelace wrote:

> Only a fraction of the present body of professing Christians are solidly appropriating the justifying work of Christ in their lives. Many have so light an apprehension of God's holiness and of the extent and guilt of their sin that consciously they see little need for justification, although below the surface their lives are deeply guilt-ridden and insecure. Many others have a theoretical commitment to this doctrine, but in their day-to-day existence they rely on their sanctification for justification, in the Augustinian manner, drawing their assurance of acceptance with God from their sincerity, their past experience of conversion, their recent religious performance or the relative infrequency of their conscious, willful disobedience.[13]

I believe this deplorable state can only be reversed as Christians begin to see that talking with God is the church's number-one work. It is from this divine conversation that the church secures both her assignment and the power to accomplish it. But even more, this conversation is the only contemporary evidence the church has that she has not gone into business for herself, following some separate agenda from God. Prayer is a relationship of discipline, and that discipline begins in the willful act of centering. Centering is the life-consuming art of approaching God with thought, time, and delightful focus. When the church sees the glory of this calling, Pentecost will visit every day. There will come again a trumpet in our moral wilderness. The old hymn will be the new one:

> Jesus shall reign, where'er the sun
> Does his successive journeys run;
> His kingdom spread from shore to shore,
> Till moons shall wax and wane no more.
>
> To him shall endless pray'r be made,
> And endless praises crown his head;
> His name like sweet perfume shall rise
> With ev'ry morning sacrifice.[14]

Endnotes

1. Richard J. Foster, *Celebration of Discipline* (San Francisco: Harper and Row, 1978), 30.

2. Malcolm Muggeridge, *The Green Stick* (New York: Quill, 1972), 82.

3. Calvin Miller, *The Table of Inwardness* (Downers Grove, Ill.: InterVarsity Press, 1984), 9.

4. Søren Kierkegaard, *The Prayers of Kierkegaard*, ed. by Perry D. LeFevre (Chicago: University of Chicago Press, 1956), 21.

5. Horatio G. Spafford, "It Is Well with My Soul," 1873.

6. Foster, *Celebration of Discipline*, 31.

7. Ibid., 30–31.

8. John Chrysostom, *The Nicene and Post-Nicene Fathers*, ed. by Philip Schaff. Vols. IX, X, XI, XII, XIII, and XIV. (Grand Rapids: Eerdmans, 1989), 37.

9. Madame Guyon, *Experiencing the Depths of Jesus Christ*, ed. by Gene Edwards (Goleta, Calif.: Christian Books, 1975), 7–8.

10. Karl Rahner, *Encounters with Silence*, translated by James M. Demske (Westminster, Md.: Christian Classics, 1984), 5.

11. William MacNamara, *Mystical Passion* (Chicago: Claretian Press, 1977), 58.

12. Frank C. Laubach, *Letters by a Modern Mystic* (Westwood, New Jersey: Fleming H. Revell Co., 1937), 14, 19–20.

13. Richard F. Lovelace, *Dynamics of Spiritual Life* (Downers Grove, Ill.: Inter-Varsity Press, 1970), 101.

14. Isaac Watts, "Jesus Shall Reign Where'er the Sun," 1719.

3
The Visionary Leader:
Contemporary Approaches to Christian Leadership

William M. Pinson, Jr.

William M. Pinson, Jr. is executive director for the Baptist General Convention of Texas. Pinson has served in numerous local church and denominational positions, including president of Golden Gate Baptist Theological Seminary and professor at Southwestern Seminary. He holds a Th.D. from Southwestern and has received four honorary doctorates. He has authored numerous books.

Recently an outstanding Christian business leader sat beside me on a plane and we talked about leadership. With great intensity he declared, "Leadership is not one of the elements required for success of an enterprise. It is the only one." Everyone seems to agree about the importance of leadership. But what is it? And how is it achieved?

When you hear the word *leadership,* what picture comes to mind? A hard-driving charismatic head of a major company? A brilliant, eloquent pastor? A person such as Winston Churchill leading a nation through crisis to victory? A demanding coach who leads a team to the championship?

Certainly all of these are examples of leadership, but they don't come close to illustrating leadership. Leadership is actually for the many, not just the few. No one is a leader in everything, but practically anyone can be a leader in something. Not only presidents and pastors, but also foremen on assembly lines and Sunday school department directors and teachers exercise leadership. If you are responsible for achieving the goals of any organization or group of people, you are in leadership. It is important to be an effective leader. Such leadership is essential for evangelizing our changing world.

Christian leadership has much in common with any sort of leadership, but it is leadership with a plus. There is a dimension to Christian leadership that makes it distinctive. And that distinctive is something any Christian can demonstrate, whether in a church-related or a secular position of leadership. In summary, Christian leaders ought to follow biblical leadership principles, seek God's will and the advancement of God's kingdom in what they do (secular or "sacred"), and demonstrate Christian character. But let's explore in more depth the components of effective Christian leadership in the contemporary world.

What Is Leadership?

Like love, leadership is something we all know exists but find difficult to define. More than eight hundred definitions are known to exist. Thousands of studies have been done searching for an adequate definition and explanation of leadership. However, "no clear and unequivocal understanding exists as to what distinguishes leaders from non-leaders, and perhaps more important, what distinguishes effective leaders from ineffective leaders and effective organizations from ineffective organizations."[1]

Lack of a full understanding of leadership does not mean there is no understanding at all. In fact, much is known. Nevertheless, we need to acknowledge that many different concepts, insights, and theories exist, and approach any discussion of leadership, especially effective Christian leadership, with a heavy dose of humility. I personally think of leadership as the ability to enlist followers and gather and apply resources to carry out a mission and fulfill a vision in keeping with God's will.

In spite of some ambiguity about the meaning of leadership, certain aspects are rather clear. For example, there are some things leadership clearly is not. It is not managing (Management, as is often said, is doing things right—while leadership is doing the right things), or lording it over others, or succeeding at all costs. Leadership does not come from holding a position, regardless of how "high up" in an organization the position is. Leadership is not an office held but a task performed. As such, leadership is not really conferred; it is earned. It is not an inherited quality, although some persons may have characteristics that make it easier for them to be effective leaders.

And some factors are clearly necessary for effective leadership. Leadership requires knowledge, skills, and character, all of which can be learned or developed.[2]

Leadership involves change. Leaders operate within constantly changing circumstances, both within their immediate organization and within society as a whole. One of the chief characteristics of contemporary leadership is that it functions in a world of rapid change. Change has always been part of life, but in today's world the change is extraordinarily rapid. This calls for what some term "white water management," because the leader must take a group or organization through tumultuous, treacherous, ever-changing circumstances. Today's changes are also major ones. Paradigms are changing. The world is in such flux that one observer labeled these as "plastic" times—no longer what was and not yet what will be. We are moving into what some term the Emotile Society.[3]

In the midst of all of this rapid, bewildering contemporary change, the Christian leader strives to bring about change within an organization or group so that it is ever more effective. In fact, Daniel Brown declares, "Accomplishing legitimate, meaningful change may well be the real test of leadership."[4] Carrying out change is difficult enough in itself, but the contemporary leader is called on to bring about change while the world itself is rapidly changing. What a challenge! It is no wonder Christian leaders seldom if ever complain of boredom.

Leadership, therefore, involves a process. It does not so much focus on a project to be completed or a product to be produced as on a process to be carried out over a period of time. Currently the process is thought of more in biological than mechanical terms. To be sure, projects and products may be part of the process, but the major focus is on bringing about change in a system so that the group or organization is equipped to function effectively in the future. And that certainly means with quality. Because quality can be continuously improved and because circumstances constantly change, the leader's job is never done. Leadership is truly a never-ending story. And that story involves both what a leader does and who a leader is. Let's take a look at what effective leaders do and then at what qualities characterize the effective contemporary Christian leader.

What Do Effective Christian Leaders Do?

A careful study of effective leaders in the Bible, throughout history, and in the contemporary world reveals some actions that effective Christian leaders have in common. These are not a surefire formula for success, but they do indicate how a person faithful to God's Word can accomplish more than would otherwise be possible. The actions are not necessarily in any order of importance; nor are they sequential steps. Some need to be carried on simultaneously with others, and some will occur throughout the leadership experience.

Prayer is essential for effective Christian leaders in both church-related and so-called secular occupations. These leaders follow the Bible's instruction to "pray without ceasing" (1 Thess. 5:17, KJV). They realize their need of God's guidance and power. Profoundly aware of their own limitations, they seek the One who is omniscient, omnipotent, and omnipresent.

Prayer for God's guidance is vital. Surely we ought to beware of developing plans and then asking God to bless them. Rather, from the beginning God's will should be sought. After all, "It is God which worketh in you both to will and to do of his good pleasure" (Phil. 2:13, KJV). God's answer may take many forms. Sometimes it is a clear-cut vision or call, such as the call Paul received as a missionary to go to Macedonia. More often it is an increased sensitivity to circumstances or awareness of opportunities. It may come from the counsel of godly persons, or God may answer with an heightened intuition, a gentle nudge in a direction, or a "holy hunch." Of course, we must avoid interpreting our own wishes for that of God's answer to prayer. Admittedly it is sometimes difficult to distinguish between the two. But that difficulty should never stand in the way of a Christian leader seeking God's guidance.

Prayer for God's power is also necessary. Puny human efforts will fall short of the great challenges faced by Christian leaders in the contemporary world. Jesus declares that all power is his and that we can go forth to do his will confident of his presence and power (Matt. 28:18-20).

Commitment is essential for the Christian leader—commitment to God's will and Word, commitment to the task at hand, and commitment to fellow believers. Commitment takes many forms. It is willingness to pay the price necessary to accomplish the assigned mission, even to suffer and perhaps to die. Although most leadership roles do not call for martyrdom, they do demand enduring criticism and sometimes verbal abuse. The hardship, frustration, and difficulty of leadership may cause a leader to abandon the process unless there is deep commitment to the Master and his mission.

Commitment is recognized as essential for even secular leaders. Without it a person is not likely to stay at the task long enough to bring about the change required in the system to make a difference. When a leader abandons ship and another replaces him or her, precious time is lost, momentum is slowed, and disaster may ensue. How much better to have a leader committed to staying the course. When a person accepts a leadership position, it is important to realize that more than position, prestige, and perks, the role will likely demand hard work, sacrifice, and frustration.

Mission, purpose, the reason for the existence of the organization or group—the effective leader will make certain that these are clearly understood and well stated. It is essential for a leader to know the purpose or mission. Peter Drucker declares, "The first job of the leader is to think through and define the mission of the institution."[5]

A mission statement needs to be clear, brief, simple, and true to the real purpose of the organization. It answers the question "Why do we exist?" Too often mission statements are vague, long, and off target, filled with lofty phrases that are operational, focusing on what people are expected to do in the organization to carry out the mission. Finally, the mission ought to be specific. If an organization tries to do everything, it will fail. That means saying no to many good causes. A sound mission statement ought to tie an organization to that which utilizes its competence and the commitment of its personnel to respond to actual opportunities.

A leader is responsible not only for guiding an organization to clearly define its mission but also for keeping it focused on the mission. Peter Drucker says of effective leaders, "They know what their mission is, and they make no apologies for sticking to that."[6]

Vision is absolutely essential for an effective leader—a vision of what the organization ought to become in order to best carry out its mission. Burt Nanus declares, "There is no more powerful engine driving an organization toward excellence and long-range success than an attractive, worthwhile, and achievable vision of the future, widely shared."[7] Mission and vision are sometimes thought of as the same thing, but they are distinctly different.[8] Mission describes why an organization exists; vision describes what an organization ought to become. Mission focuses on the present, on reality; vision focuses on the future, on possibility. As Bennis and Nanus remind us: "With a vision, the leader provides the all-important bridge from the present to the future of the organization."[9]

Where does such a vision come from? Sometimes a leader more or less receives the vision. Through prayer, examination of the organization and its possibilities for the future, and reflective thought, the vision takes shape, and then the leader comes down from the mountain and delivers the vision to his followers—that is a popular concept. However, research into leadership reveals that more often vision comes from a process of interaction among several people. Persons with a common purpose pray, talk, discuss, and dream together about what ought to be—about what can be—and a vision takes shape. As such it is a shared vision, and those involved in the development of it feel ownership and are able in turn to share the vision with others in the organization. For Christians the Holy Spirit plays a big part in this process. This was the case with the early Christians in Antioch when the vision grasped them of sharing the gospel with the pagan world through sending out missionaries (See Acts 13). To be of any real value, the vision must be put into action.[10]

The leader must clearly and movingly communicate the mission and the vision. In whatever way a mission statement and a vision are developed, they must be communicated in order to bring about change. James Belasco insists, "Vision must exist at all levels of the organization."[11] Seeing that this happens is a major responsibility and opportunity of the leader. Thus a leader must be a communicator. That does not necessarily mean being a great orator or writer, but it does mean developing or possessing the skills necessary to help others in the organization not only understand the mission and vision but want to help carry them out. Information and inspiration are both important.

A part of this communication is the leader's own obvious commitment to the mission and vision. Words alone are not enough. The leader must walk the talk, incarnate the vision, and demonstrate belief that the vision is attainable. Along with effective public speaking and clear writing must go authentic behavior if the leader is to adequately communicate the mission and vision. This is not a once-and-for-all kind of task but a continuing process. New people come into the organization without a knowledge of the mission and vision. Continuing members forget, or their enthusiasm wanes. Therefore the leader must constantly hold up the mission and share the vision.

The leader also is primarily responsible for enlisting and developing a team to carry out the mission and fulfill the vision. No one can accomplish these alone. A group functioning as a team is absolutely essential. The leader should enlist the best persons possible for the tasks to be done, even if some of them clearly excel the leader in certain qualities or perhaps even over all. The ideal is for persons to be enlisted who fill in for the weaknesses of the leader as well as complement the strengths.

Once they are enlisted, persons need to know and embrace the mission and vision of the organization. They need to be developed and equipped for the roles they are to play. Equally important, they need to be inspired and motivated, encouraged and rewarded, empowered and affirmed. Effective leaders strive to get everyone in the organization to feel a part of the overall operation and to be responsible for success. They don't nag; they inspire. They affirm team members, treating them with respect and courtesy. They create an atmosphere of community where people enjoy working together.

Christian leaders should develop a strategic plan for utilizing human and other resources to carry out the mission and to accomplish the vision. Strategic thinking calls for determining what is necessary in terms of goals, organization, action, and resources to fulfill the vision. This is not so much the development of projects or action plans as it is the development of an overall process. The process calls for a continuing cycle: Research, plan, resource the plan, carry out the plan, monitor the results, and alter the plan to make it more effective.[12]

At the heart of strategic planning, or positioning as some prefer to call it, is understanding both the system of the organization and the system within which the organization functions. An organization, whether it is a church, school, Sunday school class, or business, does not exist or operate in isolation but in relation to internal and external factors. Often when failure is blamed on persons, a malfunctioning system is really the cause. The leader is best positioned both to understand and to change the system so that it functions better and better. In fact, a leader's major role may well be to effect change in the system so that it functions more and more effectively, resulting in the quality necessary to accomplish the vision of the group or organization. If all of that sounds complicated and difficult, that is because it is. Change is seldom easy. Change of systems never is. Knowledge, skill, experience, commitment, and more are called for to be successful—that is the leader's job.

Work is also essential for success. Hard work, rigorous thinking, and long hours are the lot for most leaders, especially for those of complex organizations. True, many leaders enjoy the work they do and the pace they keep, but that does not alter the conditions of the leader's life. "Work smarter, not harder," "Delegate, don't disintegrate," and all kinds of cute sayings don't take away the fact that leaders must work hard if the organization is to achieve its vision.

In the midst of all these demands, it is crucial for the leader to maintain focus on priorities, on what is truly important. In every organization distractions exist. The urgent clamors for attention, and to respond is to leave the important unattended. Crises, personnel disputes, and petty grievances can eat up all of a leader's time. Few things in leadership are more difficult than staying focused on the priorities necessary to achieve the vision of the organization, but perhaps nothing is more important. Only through discipline, reflection, and review of the priorities will the leader be able to maintain attention to them.

Finally, **persistence** in carrying out all of the above is vitally important. In the midst of distractions, faced with criticism, plagued by opposition, pummeled by difficulties, and discouraged by setbacks, the leader must stay at the task, remain focused on the vision, and carry out the mission. In the secular world the premier example of the persistent leader is Abraham Lincoln.[13] In the religious world a marvelous model of persistence is the missionary Paul. In all the world the most exemplary model is the Lord Jesus.[14]

What Are the Qualities of Effective Leaders?

Effective leaders are not all alike. In fact, they differ greatly in many ways. Some are extroverts and others are shy. Some are big, booming personalities, while others are quiet and unassuming. Some act largely on intuition, and others demand plenty of facts and time to study them.

They also differ in leadership styles. Some are very directive, even dictatorial, while others follow a participatory approach. The fact is that no one style of leadership seems best for all circumstances.[15] For example, the kind of leadership called for in fighting a war may not be the best kind for governing in peace; Ulysses S. Grant is a case in point, being a brilliant general but a poor president of the United States. A pastor or leader who functions well in a growing suburban community may not fare so well in a transition neighborhood.

Clearly, there is no set of qualities that guarantees effective leadership. Yet there are certain characteristics that are common among leaders. Generally these fall into three categories: knowledge, skills, and character.[16] Effective leaders possess certain knowledge, exercise particular skills, and incarnate various character traits. Each of these is important, no one more so than the others. Thus the order in which these are set forth here is not in itself significant.

An effective leader must possess certain **knowledge**—knowledge about himself or herself, knowledge of the organization and the systems in which it operates, knowledge of the persons who are co-laborers in the task, knowledge of the process of leadership itself, and certainly a knowledge of God.

Self-knowledge is extremely important and often difficult to acquire. To "know thyself" is no easy accomplishment. Various personality tests, consultation with experts, discussions with good honest friends, and healthy introspection all help. Through these means a person can identify how he or she perceives reality, processes information, relates to other persons, and draws energy for the tasks at hand. A person can identify qualities that are strengths and weaknesses for the leadership role in which he or she is involved. Knowing these, the leader can work on strengthening weaknesses and utilizing existing strengths. The leader can also come to know to what degree he or she is goal oriented or person oriented and how this affects decision making and leadership style.

Knowledge of God and of self can also lead to a healthy sense of self-worth, important in a leader. When we confess that we are sinners, we realize our utter dependence on God's grace and in a sense our unworthiness. But there is more to know—much more. We are created in the image of God. God loves us so much that he sent his beloved Son to die for our sins. As redeemed sinners we are the children of God. With this knowledge we become aware of how much we are worth in the sight of God. This ought not lead to any sort of cockiness, but to genuine humility and a sense of healthy self-worth. With that knowledge also comes a confidence, a confidence not so much in our own ability but in God's grace and care. Regardless of how much we fail in our leadership efforts, we are confident of God's love and of our ultimate victory with him.

Knowledge of the organization in which leadership is provided is also important. This calls for knowing the structure, the products, the persons involved, the customers, the history, the problems, the internal and external relations—in other words, just about everything. Many leaders find it helpful to walk around observing the daily operations. Others call together persons from various parts of the organization for discussion. Seldom does a leader acquire the knowledge needed by sitting in an office, reading reports or memos.

Knowledge of leadership itself is needed. Leadership is an art, not an exact science. No one can ever know all there is to know. Concepts of leadership constantly change. The effective leader is a lifetime learner, always looking for ways to improve—reading, attending conferences, listening to tapes, visiting with effective leaders.

Certain **skills** are also vital for effective leadership. Few if any leaders excel in all important skills but leaders who excel will constantly strive to improve skills, such as decision making, communicating, handling conflict constructively, disciplining one's self, timing, and relating well to other persons, including one's own family.

The ability to make good decisions is a key to leadership effectiveness. Making right decisions is even more important, but the right decision is often determined by factors beyond the leader's control or knowledge. The leader should concentrate on processes that result in good decisions and realize these may not always turn out to be right. No one can be right all of the time. To be afraid of making a wrong decision will paralyze a leader. A leader must concentrate on decisions that lead to accomplishing the mission of the organization and not on avoiding those that lead to failure, just as a good skier focuses on finishing the course rather than on not falling.

The skill of communication, both oral and written, is vitally important to a leader and can be developed by just about anyone. Mission, vision, decisions, and specific courses of action need to be communicated effectively or they are practically worthless. Communication should be accurate and clear. In most cases it needs also to be inspirational and motivational. If communication is garbled or fuzzy, people will not know what is expected of them. If the communication lacks motivation, people may not want to do what is expected of them. In either case the success of the organization in achieving its vision is hampered.

An effective leader must know how to handle conflict constructively. Conflict is an inevitable part of any human organization or activity. The Bible is filled with examples of conflict that arose even among people dedicated to carrying out God's will. The great missionary Paul spent much of his time dealing with conflict in the early churches.[17] The presence of conflict is a sign, not of failed leadership, but of human nature at work in the midst of cooperative efforts to achieve a vision, to carry out a mission. In dealing with conflict the leader ought to care for the health of the whole organization and commit to being the leader of the whole, not any one faction. This likely means suffering criticism and abuse from both (or all) sides in the conflict because the leader will not join with them. The leader ought to strive to be a peacemaker even while he realizes that reconciliation is God's work—people cannot be forced to be reconciled with one another. Often reconciliation comes through prayer and through calling diverse factions to concentrate on a common cause, mission, or vision.

The effective Christian leader must also master the skills of self-discipline. If a leader displays little or no self-discipline, he can expect little discipline from followers. As much as possible the leader ought to be in control of his emotions. Self-pity and temper tantrums are not marks of good Christian leadership. Remaining calm under pressure or in the midst of a crisis is important. Vital is discipline regarding prayer, Bible study, worship, witness, and meditation. Discipline in regard to diet, exercise, rest, and schedule is also important.

An exemplary leader will develop the skill of timing. Some people seem to have a natural sense of timing, such as that possessed by many great athletes. However, anyone with practice can improve timing—when to act and when to remain inactive, when to speak and when to remain silent, when to reprimand and when to praise. The difference between a good decision and a right decision is often a matter of timing, a skill that comes with experience and wisdom.

Leaders must master the skill of delegation.[18] No one can do everything, and enlisting the aid of others is essential. Good delegation involves clear explanation of what is expected, the time framework involved, and what will be the measure of success. It helps if the person being delegated to buys into the task. Good leaders thwart "upward delegation," the effort of someone to pass back to the one who made the assignment all of the decisions involved in carrying it out, often to avoid blame if things don't go well.

The effective leader relates well to other persons, including his or her own family.[19] Some leaders are by nature people-centered, while others are job- or goal-centered. However, anyone can develop the attitudes and skills necessary to relate to other persons in a positive, constructive way: Be aware of others. Put yourself in their place, attempting to see things from their point of view. Be concerned about the welfare of others. Seek input from others. Praise people for their efforts and accomplishments, not taking them for granted. Arrange time to be with people, listening to them and showing genuine interest in them. Be thoughtful and courteous. In summary, follow the biblical guidelines for human relations.

In addition to knowledge and skills, character is vital for effective leaders, and especially so for Christian leaders.[20] The downfall of all too many leaders has not been lack of knowledge or leadership skills but flawed character. Some character traits relate almost exclusively to Christians; others can be developed by anyone. Both kinds are important.

Some distinctive character traits come from a relation to Jesus Christ as Savior and Lord. For example, the Christian is to follow a will-of-God ethic, in which the passion of life is to trust God and be faithful to his will, especially as expressed in God's Word, the Bible. For the Christian, "all leadership is under Lordship."[21]

Similarly, the Christian leader is to live a Cross kind of life, following Jesus' command to deny self, take up one's cross, and follow him (Matt. 16:24-26). Among other things this kind of life means voluntary sacrifice for the good of others, in the will of God, out of love. Indeed, Christian love is a key ingredient in the life of the Christian leader—love for self, for God, and for others (Matt. 22:36-40).

All of this means that a servant spirit will characterize the Christian leader. His or her desire is not to be boss, to order others around, or to be adulated, but rather to serve others. This means that the leader does not view the organization as existing for his or her benefit, but rather the other way around. After all, that was the spirit of the leader Jesus Christ (Phil. 2:7) and central in his teachings (Mark 10:42-45; John 13:16).

The Christian leader will also embody purity of thought and action. Lust, greed, selfishness, hate, jealousy, covetousness, and desire for revenge have no place in the attitude of the Christian leader. Adultery, dishonesty, lying, cruelty, and stealing have no place in the actions of the Christian leader.

Other qualities ought to characterize Christians and non-Christians alike. Trustworthiness is certainly among these, which comes as a result of a person's demonstrating responsibility and integrity. Max De Pree defines integrity as "a fine sense of one's obligations."[22] A key to trustworthiness is being truthful. Travis Berry declares that "leaders must be transparently truthful."[23] People trust persons who clearly know what they are doing, who carry out their responsibilities carefully and thoroughly, and who, when they make mistakes or fail, accept the responsibility for these, don't blame others, acknowledge that they are not perfect, and move on to the next task. Such action engenders confidence.

Courage is another key quality in a leader, as distinguished from fool-hardiness or rashness. The courageous person is neither afraid to fail or succeed. He or she is a risk taker, but takes risk with reasonableness and with a focus on success. Such a person is an innovator, exhibiting courage by being willing to try new ways of doing things.

A drive for excellence is another mark of the effective leader. Good leaders are not lazy. They take no pride in ignorance. They are not satisfied with mediocrity. They are action- and results-oriented. They make things happen. As such they may appear hard taskmasters, but good leaders know that a job well done brings a sense of pride and even joy to those who are part of the task.

Flexibility is often found in effective leaders. They are willing to examine new paradigms, to be open to new ideas, to try new ways of achieving the mission of the organization. Leaders must beware of embracing every fad that comes along, but they must equally avoid being stuck in a routine that worked well at one time but has become outdated.

Optimism, hope, and a generally positive attitude stand out among effective leaders. They are also realistic and face facts, but they see opportunity where others see only obstacles. Such people are not easily diverted from a compelling vision just because fulfillment is difficult. In fact, they are often motivated by what seems almost impossible and usually have a capacity for visualizing success.

A kind of wholeness is evident in effective leaders. They are not totally consumed by their responsibility or job but provide time and attention for family, church, and community. They practice balance in life, with a time for work and a time for play. Somehow this wholeness seems to help them accomplish more in a shorter period of time than those who are wed to their work for unusually long hours each day.

Stamina and patience are noted in the character of outstanding leaders. They stay at a task in spite of setbacks. Failures and mistakes are seen as learning opportunities. Neither ridicule nor criticism thwart their deep commitment to fulfilling the mission and vision of the organization. They simply refuse to give up.

Conclusion

Effective Christian leaders are desperately needed in these challenging days. While some seem born with leadership qualities, practically anyone can become an effective leader in some sphere of activity. Leadership is something that can be learned or developed. You learn how to be a leader by practicing leadership under supervision or by observing effective leaders and following their example. As with any other art or skill, some will be better at leadership than others, but all can develop some ability and with time and practice improve on it. Given the tremendous needs of our time in churches and Christian organizations, as well as in the so-called secular world, surely every follower of the Lord Jesus Christ will strive to become an effective leader.

Endnotes

1. Warren Bennis and Burt Nanus, *Leaders* (New York: Harper and Row, 1985), 4. In a 1994 speech, Warren Bennis declared that there are over eight hundred definitions of leadership in recognized literature. Rather than add another he said, "You'll know it when you see it." Frederick Roach, *The Leadership Center,* 31 January 1994, 1.

2. Many programs for leadership development exist, some from a secular point of view and some from a Christian. One that combines the two is The Leadership Center, Baylor Health Care System, 3500 Gaston Avenue, Dallas, Texas 75246.

3. Arnold Brown and Edith Weiner of Weiner, Edrich, Brown, Inc. (200 East 33rd Street, New York, New York 10016) utilize this term extensively in describing the setting for modern leadership, one in which relationships are constantly changing, causing persons to desire a semblance of certainty afforded at least in part by spelling out agreements in explicit detail. An abundant number of books, videos, and articles exist describing the current rapid changes in our world.

4. Daniel Brown, *Leadership Workbook* (Pasadena: Charles E. Fuller Institute, n.d.), 20. See Thomas North Gilmore, *Making Leadership Changes* (San Francisco: Oxford, 1989) for an excellent practical work on leadership in the midst of change.

5. Peter Drucker, *Managing the Non Profit Organization* (New York: Harper-Collins, 1990), 3.

6. Peter Drucker, "Managing to Minister," *Leadership III/89,* Spring Quarter 1989, 17.

7. Burt Nanus, *Visionary Leadership* (San Francisco: Jossey-Bass, 1982), 3.

8. See George Barna, "Don't Confuse Vision and the Mission," *The Power of Vision* (Ventura: Regal, 1992), 37–44.

9. Bennis and Nanus, *Leaders,* 90.

10. For a very practical approach, see Benjamin B. Tregoe, John W. Zimmerman, Ronald A. Smith, Peter M. Tobia, *Vision in Action* (New York: Simon and Schuster, 1989).

11. James Belasco, *Teaching the Elephant to Dance* (New York: Penguin Books, 1990), 98.

12. See George Steiner, *Strategic Planning* (New York: The Free Press, 1979) for an extensive presentation. It should be noted that not everyone agrees with the importance of long range or strategic planning; see Henry Mintzberg, *The Rise and Fall of Strategic Planning* (New York: The Free Press, 1994).

13. For an intriguing survey of Lincoln's leadership see Donald T. Phillips, *Lincoln on Leadership* (New York: Warner Books, 1992).

14. See Leighton Ford, *Transforming Leadership: Jesus' Way of Creating Vision, Shaping Values, and Empowering Change* (Downers Grove, Ill.: InterVarsity Press, 1991).

15. Robert Dale, in his excellent book on biblical models of leadership, identifies three basic leadership approaches: organic, charismatic, and consensus; he prefers organic leadership. He also describes four styles found in leaders: catalyst, com-

mander, encourager, hermit. Robert Dale, *Good News from Great Leaders* (Washington, D.C.: The Alban Institution, 1992), 42.

16. See William M. Pinson, Jr., *Ready to Minister* (Nashville: Broadman, 1984) for an elaboration of this concept.

17. For a case study of Paul's dealing with conflict, see Dale, *Good News from Great Leaders,* 95–100.

18. Jethro helped his famous son-in-law, Moses, understand the importance of delegation. See Exodus 18:13-27.

19. Of sixty CEOs of highly successful companies interviewed, "almost all were married to their first spouse. And not only that: they were also indefatigably enthusiastic about marriage as an institution." Bennis and Nanus, *Leaders,* 25.

20. A major emphasis on character, values, and principles appears in recent works on leadership. Perhaps the best known advocates are Peter Drucker and Stephen Covey.

21. Dale, *Good News from Great Leaders,* 5.

22. Max De Pree, *Leadership Is An Art* (New York: Dell, 1989) 85.

23. Travis Berry, "The Ethics of Leadership," *The Baptist Standard,* June 1, 1994, 4.

4
The Power of Praise:
Contemporary Worship and Evangelism

Don McMinn

Don McMinn serves on the staff of The Center for Marriage and Family Intimacy and is director of The Worship Connection. He formerly was minister of music at the First Southern Baptist Church of Del City, Oklahoma. McMinn earned his Ph.D. from North Texas State University. He has written several books on the subject of worship, including The Practice of Praise.

Worship is the missing jewel in modern Evangelicalism.
We're organized, we work, we have our agencies.
We have almost everything, but there's one thing that the churches,
even the gospel churches, do not have: that is the ability to worship.
We are not cultivating the art of worship.
It's the shining gem that is lost to the modern church,
and I believe that we ought to search for this until we find it.
—A. W. Tozer[1]

God is not seeking worship. He *is* seeking worshipers. And in his searching, he looks beyond all personal pretense and examines the heart, for worship is an issue of the heart. God sees all types of hearts—hardened, pure, indifferent, cold, fervent, apathetic, wicked, sincere, tender, clean . . . but he responds favorably to those who have a heart "after his own heart" (1 Sam. 13:14). Perhaps this is why King David, the sweet psalmist of Israel, enjoyed such deep intimacy with God: God saw in David a heart of worship.

What Is Worship?

Some subjects are so broad they defy definition. St. Augustine once lamented, "What, then, is time? If no one asked of me, I know: if I wish to explain to him who asks, I know not." If Augustine thought *time* was hard to explain, what shall we do with the topic of *worship?* Perhaps a place to begin is to learn the meaning of the word *worship* in the English, Greek, and Hebrew languages.

The English word *worship* comes from the Anglo-Saxon word *weorthscipe,* which denotes one who is worthy of honor and reverence. In this sense, when we are worshipping God we are declaring to him his worth; we are confessing that he is worthy. In Revelation 4, the twenty-four elders worship the Lord by confessing that he is worthy to receive glory, honor, and power.

The Hebrew word for worship is *shaha.* It means to "bow low" or to "prostrate oneself." Worship involves our bowing low before the Lord, not only physically, but in our hearts. When a Hebrew came into God's presence, he would bow low; his posture demonstrated his reverential fear of God.

The Greek word for worship is *proskuneo,* which literally means to "kiss the hand of one who is revered" or to "do obeisance to another." If a member of the early church were to have an audience with Jesus, and he wanted to worship his Lord, he would get close enough to kiss his hand. Notice that the New Testament concept of worship involves closeness and intimacy. The God who was unapproachable under the old covenant may be approached with boldness in the new covenant, and without the slightest fear of being shunned (Heb. 4:14-16).

Worship is the expression of a love relationship. Worship presupposes a *relationship,* which correctly implies that those who do not have a personal relationship with God cannot and will not worship him. Worship also requires open, public *expression;* concealed love is to be questioned. It's like the husband who winked at his wife—in the dark. He knew what he had done, but nobody else did. And worship occurs in a *love* relationship, not an association prompted by commerce, politics, or convenience.

The scope of worship can be wide or narrow. In one sense, everything we do that gives glory to God is worship. Paul said, "Whether you eat or drink or whatever you do, do it all for the glory of God" (1 Cor. 10:31). So every act that is in his perfect will and performed with a pure heart could be considered worship: washing the dishes, mowing the lawn, even the mundane functions of life can be an offering to him.

But worship also involves times of intense intimacy, moments when we are alone with God and we exchange thoughts of love and commitment. These moments may occur during private devotions or during corporate services.

So the scope of worship can be wide or narrow, but in the course of life it must be both. Worship must be a lifestyle that regularly manifests itself in "acts" of worship. We must worship God by faithfully performing daily, mundane acts, but we must also devote time to intimate, focused communion. We must not settle for just "living for Jesus" without the times of direct expressions of adoration and praise. It takes both.

Worship First

The New Testament church has a threefold purpose: to exalt God, to edify the saints, and to evangelize the lost. Just as a stool must have three legs to stand on its own, every church should be strong in all three areas if it is to be both balanced and effective. While all three are necessary, perhaps there is a preferred order of priority. Oswald Chambers once commented, "Worshipping God is the great essential of fitness. If you have not been worshiping . . . when you get into your work you will not only be useless yourself, but a tremendous hindrance to those who are associated with you."

Having considered the meaning of the word *worship* and defined worship as *the expression of a love relationship,* it would seem unnecessary to argue that worship is a necessary function of the church and perhaps even a prerequisite for effectiveness in evangelism and edification. One who has genuinely worshiped the King will be better equipped and more motivated to serve in the kingdom.

In the evangelical missionary world, there is perhaps no name more revered than that of Hudson Taylor. This remarkable man is considered by many to be the father of modern faith missions. What was it that made Hudson Taylor the man he became and was, right to the end?

His son and daughter-in-law, who traveled constantly with him in his later years, testify that very often they would be traveling over a hard cobblestone road for many hours in a springless cart. Arriving at a Chinese inn late at night, they would endeavor to obtain a little corner in a room for their father, for usually in those inns there was just one large room where everybody slept. He was now an aged man; but, without fail, every morning just before dawn there would be the scratching of a match and the lighting of a candle, and Hudson Taylor would worship God. This was the key to his life. It was said that even before the sun rose on China, Hudson Taylor was worshiping God.[2]

Worship in Today's Church

God is restoring the ministry of praise and worship in his body. Churches all across America are discovering the same joy that the Israelites experienced when the ark of the covenant was placed on Mount Zion. They offered free and uninhibited praise day and night. And just as the Israelites responded in praise to the presence of God in the ark, God's people are lifting up shouts of praise as God tabernacles among us today. Traditions are crumbling (Isa. 29:13), the fear of man is losing its grip (John 12:42-43), and God's people are confessing as sin their being ashamed of Jesus (Mark 8:38). They are learning to confess aloud the excellencies of him who brought us out of darkness and into his marvelous light (1 Pet. 2:9). We are seeing the bride make herself ready! We are learning that it is a good thing to give praise unto the Lord (Ps. 92:1), that there is nothing wrong with it (Ps. 33:1), and that it's even scriptural (it's in the Bible)!

In the past twenty years, several styles of worship have surfaced, incorporating new and varied forms. This is not unusual, for throughout Christian history, forms of worship, particularly musical forms, have changed with the passing of time. During the Reformation, Martin Luther gave both the Bible and the hymnbook back to the people after centuries of lifeless ritual. He introduced hymns with more familiar tunes and in the language of the people. The Pietists of the late seventeenth and early eighteenth centuries began writing subjective hymns, reflecting their emphasis on "religion of the heart." At the same time, English dissenters such as Isaac Watts, who some call the "father of English hymnody," began writing hymns that gained popularity in Congregational, Baptist, and Presbyterian worship.

The hymns of Charles Wesley, who wrote over six thousand, were crucial to the theology of early Methodism. During the Evangelical Awakening in eighteenth-century England, John Wesley preached in a practical, application-oriented manner, to which Charles wed hymns utilizing secular tunes. This was not unlike the practice of the German Reformation. As Donald P. Hustad commented, "Worthy lyrics sanctify the secular melody."[3] The worship during the camp meetings of the Second Great Awakening were characterized by simple, emotional hymns, many with evangelistic appeals at their heart.

In today's religious culture, those churches that have not embraced any of the new styles are described as having a "formal, traditional" approach to worship, while the other group is described in terms of being "informal, spontaneous, and free." In fact, it is too simplistic to refer to only two categories, for a broader spectrum exists.[4] However, for the purposes of this chapter, the broad categories of "praise and worship" and "traditional and formal" will be used.

What are some observable characteristics of a "praise and worship" type service? We might consider eight elements:

1. The service is God-focused. Though Christ is hopefully the reason for which we gather, he is not always the primary focus of our attention. We often talk about the kingdom of God, the programs of God, our service to God, but sometimes we neglect talking about, or to—God. In a praise and worship service, adequate time will be given to allow our spirit to focus on him.

2. There is an emphasis on congregational involvement. Fundamentally, praise and worship is something you do, not something you watch others do. A satisfying praise service (one that is satisfying to God and to us) will be congregationally oriented; it will allow ample time for God's people to express themselves to him.

3. There is flexibility in the order of service. Many churches have used the same order of worship for years. If the Spirit of God is still freshly anointing it, fine; but if we consider our form of worship sacred and refuse to change, we will reach a stalemate. There must be a pliableness in our approach to planning worship and a flexibility in the actual execution of the service.

4. There are long periods of uninterrupted worship. If the service is "chopped up" into multiple sections, which include actions foreign to worship (announcements, etc.), worship will be elusive. The continuity of the worship time must be protected.

5. New songs are constantly being integrated into the worship repertoire. Psalm 33:3 instructs us to "Sing to him a new song." Of course, there's nothing wrong with the old songs, but there is great value in singing new songs. Some churches sing the same thirty to fifty songs year after year, which may lead to mindless singing. A constant flow of new songs will keep the music fresh and contemporary and will even breathe new life into the old songs.

6. Music is seen as a means to an end, not an end unto itself. The goal of Christian music is not to exalt a person or music, but to exalt God. Therefore, in a worship service, care should be given to what music is selected and even to the arrangement of the music.

7. The service has a definite direction—it is moving into the presence of God. There is a difference between a song service and a worship service. A song service can be nothing more or less than a collection of favorite songs, which may or may not be related thematically. The goal of a song service is simply to get people to sing. The goal of a worship service is to have a spiritual encounter with God.

8. Sometimes there is the use of body language. The psalmist has declared that "we were formed for the praise of his glory." Our entire being—body, soul, and spirit—has been fashioned as an instrument of praise. Physical acts such as kneeling, applauding the Lord, and lifting of hands can enhance the worship experience if done from a pure heart.

Sometimes a distinction is made by asking, "Is your church into praise and worship?" Such a question is poorly constructed because it infers that all that has gone on before was not praise and worship, and that is not necessarily the case. But there is a difference between the old and the new, and regardless of the merits of either, most churches are having to address the issue: How much, if any, of these new forms are we going to incorporate into our services?

It should be noted that some churches continue to use the traditional format and find it to be fulfilling. Particularly older congregations and those in more rural areas tend to see traditional hymns and services as adequate. This is not surprising, because praise and worship is an issue of the heart. When the heart is right, any form that is intrinsically appropriate can be used to satisfy the soul's longing for God. The bottom line, after all, is not style but substance: Does the experience take us to the heavenlies in true worship of Almighty God? However, many churches are discovering that new forms provide a fresh experience in worship. Having been anesthetized by doing the same thing for years, these churches find that the new forms provide an alternative to what for some have become traditions learned by rote. This is especially true in urban areas, and even more so among younger, baby boomer-dominated congregations. Younger adults tend to be less attached to past traditions and not only accept change, but expect it. Thus, more personal, relevant songs such as praise choruses and Scripture songs appeal to younger congregations.

The new forms of worship are not necessarily better than the old forms, just different. In varying degrees, most churches, particularly those effective in evangelism, are experiencing a metamorphosis in their approach to worship, and that's healthy. The new is challenging the old. In any given situation, if the old prevails it will be stronger and newly appreciated; if the new is blended with the old, the new composition will be attractive and balanced; if the new is exclusively endorsed, it will be fresh and appropriate.

Worship and Evangelism

Evangelism must be a high priority of the New Testament church. It was certainly important to Jesus, as seen in his practice and his teaching, and most importantly because the salvation of hopeless humanity is the very reason he came. The church would cease to exist if we did not evangelize. Evangelism is the one activity of the church that will not continue in heaven. If the gospel is to be shared, it must be proclaimed during this life. An evidence of one who is wholly given to the Lord is a burden for the lost. We often think that the ministry of evangelism and the ministry of praise and worship are mutually exclusive because one focuses on the lost and the other on God. But in truth they are complementary, and one can be used to magnify the effectiveness of the other.[5] In addition, true devotion and worship of God involves obedience, including obedience to the great commission.

Christ is magnificent! His deeds, his ways, his mannerisms, the words he speaks, the way he looks, his response to any given situation; he is excellent and attractive in every way! Therefore, in New Testament evangelism, we don't need to *sell* people on Jesus; we just need to *show* people Jesus. He doesn't need a defense lawyer; he needs a dynamic witness who will uphold his glorious personage. Oscar Thompson was right when he said most people don't reject Jesus; they reject a caricature of him.[6] Christ himself is the focal point of salvation. In him we see our need for salvation (as we observe his holiness), and in him we see the provision for salvation (his sacrifice at Calvary). Though the fear of hell, or a tragic event, may convince us of our need for Christ, it is ultimately the love of Christ and the efficacy of his shed blood to which we are drawn.

This is why praise is such a powerful tool for evangelism. In praise we are lifting up Jesus. We are magnifying his character and ability to meet our needs, and we are testifying of his past faithfulness. In recent centuries music employed in worship has increasingly become central to the evangelistic ministry of the church. Ira D. Sankey (1837–1899) was the first "music evangelist" who teamed worship with an evangelistic meeting during his years of campaign ministry alongside D. L. Moody. Sankey led congregational worship and sang solos. Sankey was followed by scores of others, including Charles Alexander, who traveled with R. A. Torrey and J. Wilbur Chapman and "brought the 'gospel choir' to its nadir";[7] Homer Rodeheaver, who teamed with Billy Sunday; and more recently, Cliff Barrows of the Billy Graham team.

More recent days have seen contemporary Christian music become a significant evangelistic tool, with artists who sing evangelistic numbers followed by gospel invitations in their concerts, the rise of contemporary Christian radio stations, and the use of such music in churches.

Biblical texts give insight into the relationship between worship and evangelism. Psalm 136 is a praise history of the children of Israel. Every other phrase is a refrain of praise: "His love endures forever." When hearing such a song, the heathen stand in awe of a God so great. Psalm 126 declares the praise of God's people who have been set free from the Babylonian captivity. After decades of exile, the people of Israel returned to Jerusalem, singing songs of praise: "Our mouths were filled with laughter, our tongues with songs of joy." Notice then the rest of verse 2: "Then it was said among the nations, 'The LORD has done great things for them.' " The people around Jerusalem took delight in the praise of God's children.

A similar scenario is recorded on more than one occasion in the Acts. Unbelieving multitudes actually praised God as they observed the early church. The typical response was that many came to Christ. In Acts 2:47 we read the early church was "praising God and enjoying the favor of all the people. And the Lord added to their number daily those who were being saved" (see also Acts 4:21; 5:11-14).

I have been in services where Jesus was so exalted and his presence so real that the lost could do nothing else but come to him. They were drawn to the Savior as they witnessed the admiration and devotion with which his children approached him. Simply stated, as Christ was lifted up in their midst, they could see no one but him. The lost person needs to see Jesus as Isaiah did, "high and lifted up." The stone-hearted Saul of Tarsus was converted when he saw and heard the magnificent Christ. We don't need to beg or plead with the unconverted; we simply need to present them with a clear picture of who Jesus is. Inasmuch as Christ inhabits our praise (Ps. 22:3), when we praise him, the lost are in the "arena of praise," and they will be convicted of their need for him. I have been involved in personal witnessing experiences in which the person with whom I shared for some reason just could not make a decision for Christ. Right in the middle of the sharing time I would lead in a time of praise, and usually sufficient freedom would be granted for the person to respond to Christ.

A church flowing in the fullness of the Holy Spirit will naturally want to enter into praise and do so in a grand manner for "Great is the LORD, and most worthy of praise." (Ps. 48:1). Some may think that this great praise will offend the lost person. Quite the opposite is true. Those without Christ need to see and hear the church unashamedly and zealously confess its love for the Lord. Dynamic praise will do nothing but convince lost people of the reality of the God we serve.

Worship and Evangelism in the Early Church

A brief perusal of the early church will reveal many instances in which praise and evangelism went hand in hand.

In Acts 2, the disciples of Christ were obediently waiting for the promised Holy Spirit. When the Spirit came and filled the apostles, they began "declaring the wonders of God" in other languages. As a result of the outpouring of the Spirit, the declaration of the wonders of God, and Peter's sermon, three thousand souls were saved and baptized in one day. This models an effective order of worship: outpouring of God's Spirit, praise, and anointed preaching.

In Acts 13, the appointment of the first missionaries and their ordination came in the midst of a praise gathering. The church at Antioch was "worshiping the Lord and fasting" (v. 2) when the Holy Spirit instructed that Barnabas and Saul be set aside to do the work of missionary evangelists. So the beginning of the most significant evangelistic expansion in the New Testament was birthed in worship! This is a reminder that the Holy Spirit is not the resource of the church, but the church is the resource of the Holy Spirit. Out of true worship the church was positioned to obediently be about fulfilling the great commission.

Though praise may not always precede salvation, it inevitably follows it. In the same chapter in Acts, when the word of salvation was preached to the Gentiles, many believed, and they "were glad and honored the word of the Lord" (v. 48). I have a friend who has discovered an effective part in the immediate follow-up of those he leads to Christ. Immediately following their confession of faith in Christ, he has them pray a simple, personal prayer of praise and thanksgiving to God for their salvation. What a way to begin the Christian life, by practicing the praise of God!

The one who worships God has a tender heart and is open to divine revelation. In Acts 16 we read of a woman named Lydia who was a "worshiper of God." As she listened to Paul preach the good news of salvation through Jesus, the Lord "opened her heart to respond to Paul's message" (v. 14). Lydia was saved, along with her household. A similar story is seen in Luke 7, where the immoral woman came and worshiped at the feet of Jesus. Through her worship, she opened up her heart to Jesus and she left the house a changed person. On the other hand, the Lord's host, Simon the Pharisee, did not honor the Lord in worship (he didn't even offer the Lord a traditional foot-washing). He remained cold-hearted—and lost.

The salvation of the Philippian jailer and his household was preceded by a praise service led by Paul and Silas as they were "praying and singing hymns of praise to God" while in prison (Acts 16:25). Though the jailer did not hear the singing (he was asleep), he became a benefactor of the spiritual transformation that followed the time of praise led by Paul and Silas.

Worship's Effect on Man's Flesh

A dramatic event from King David's life also illustrates the powerful effect that praise can have on those who would normally be resistant to the Spirit of God. In 1 Samuel 19, David is on the run, fleeing from Saul, who is trying to murder him. David and Samuel the prophet go to Naioth in Ramah, and along with other prophets, they begin to prophesy.

Before we continue the story, we need to understand the meaning of "they were prophesying." Other Old Testament Scriptures help clarify the meaning:

After that you will go to Gibeah of God, where there is a Philistine outpost. As you approach the town, you will meet a procession of prophets coming down from the high place **with lyres, tambourines, flutes, and harps being played before them, and they will be prophesying.** *(1 Sam. 10:5, emphasis added)*

David, together with the commanders of the army, set apart some of the sons of Asaph, Heman and Jeduthun for the ministry of **prophesying, accompanied by harps, lyres and cymbals** *. . . under the supervision of their father Jeduthun,* **who prophesied, using the harp in thanking and praising the** **LORD.** *(1 Chron. 25:1, 3, emphasis added)*

Prophesying involved a time of praise, accompanied by musical instruments. So when David, Samuel, and the prophets began to prophesy, it was not just a time of foretelling the future; it was a praise service! They were declaring aloud the praise of Jehovah, and probably doing so with musical instruments.

Now on with the story. Saul discovered that David was at Naioth, so he sent messengers (probably members of his elite group of bodyguards) to take David. But when the messengers came into the "arena of praise" established by the prophesying, they were so overcome by what was happening that their evil plan was thwarted and they also began to prophesy.

It must be noted that these men were under direct orders from Saul to capture David. To disobey would mean certain death. But despite this sure sentence of death, which would motivate them to obey, they disobeyed Saul because they were overcome by a greater power—the Spirit of God.

When word got back to Saul he sent another group of messengers, perhaps with this admonishment: "Your comrades who disobeyed—are history. And you will be likewise if you don't return with David." And yet when they entered the company of the prophets, their evil motives were overcome and they too began to participate in the praise service.

Saul sent a third group of messengers, and the same thing happened to them. Finally Saul decided that a personal appearance was necessary, so he went to Naioth himself. In addition to being demon-possessed and having murderous intentions in his heart, Saul had to have been angry and upset—kings were not accustomed to being humiliated by disobedient servants.

And yet when Saul entered the spiritual environment of constant praise, he too was overcome. Saul "stripped off his robes and also prophesied in Samuel's presence. He lay that way all that day and night" (1 Sam. 19:24).

In like manner, when there is a great expression of constant praise to God in his church, it will prevail over any other spirit or attitude that may be present. Those who are without Christ will be confronted with the reality of a living Savior.

Worship's Catalyst

Not only is praise a tremendous tool of evangelism, but the fruits of evangelism provide the impetus for a great praise service. Luke 15:10 says that there is joy in the presence of the angels of God over one sinner who repents. The corridors of heaven are filled with angelic praise when a mortal soul receives salvation. Holy angels cannot fully understand or appreciate the depths of salvation (because they have not experienced the cleansing power of the blood of Jesus); nevertheless, they rejoice because they see the great joy the Father has when one is born again, the joy Jesus has because his shed blood has provided atonement for yet another, and the Holy Spirit's joy that his ministry of conviction has once again brought someone to Christ.

Evangelistic churches usually have a high level of praise because there is a constant stream of new life! A church that rejoices greatly in seeing people come to Christ is in unity with the Father, whose joy is made full in such occasions. The joy of the Lord springing forth from the testimony of new believers is fuel for the furnace of praise.

It is doubtful that we even possess the power necessary to evangelize until we have worshiped God. Evangelism should spring forth from and overflow in our lives. This filling to capacity comes from worship. Without a fresh touch from the Lord, evangelism is an obligation rather than an opportunity, and we may function out of duty instead of joy.

There seems to be a pattern established with the Bible in regard to worship and evangelism. The pattern is to worship first and then share the gospel. The famous commission found in Matthew 28:19-20, "Therefore go . . ." is preceded by the experience of Matthew 28:17, "When they saw him, they worshiped him." The fact that the disciples saw Jesus and worshiped him gave them the needed impetus to go into the world. Note the testimony of the prophet Jonah. Jonah received a commission from the Lord, "Go to the great city of Nineveh" but failed miserably: "Jonah ran away from the LORD and headed for Tarshish." However, prior to the next call of God, Jonah had a worship experience. Right in the stomach of that great fish, Jonah met God and proclaimed, "But I, with a song of thanksgiving, will sacrifice to you. What I have vowed I will make good. Salvation comes from the LORD" (Jon. 2:9). Chapter 3 records the postworship encounter: "Then the word of the LORD came to Jonah a second time: 'Go to the great city of Nineveh. . . .' Jonah . . . went to Nineveh. . . . The Ninevites believed God" (vv. 1-5). What a striking illustration of what an encounter with God will do for our evangelistic zeal!

Salvation and praise are always seen together because they originate and culminate in the love of God for a lost world. Have you bragged of Jesus today to a lost friend? Has that lost neighbor seen your heart full of praise though your circumstances may be trying? Have you praised him today for saving you? We can testify, along with the song writer:

I will praise him, I will praise him.
Praise the Lamb for sinners slain.
Give him glory, all ye people,
For his blood has washed away my stain.
—Harris

Endnotes

1. A. W. Tozer, *Worship—The Missing Jewel of the Evangelical Church* (Harrisburg: Christian Publishers, 1961), 1.

2. Joseph Carroll, *How to Worship Jesus Christ* (Nashville: Riverside Press, 1985), 15–16.

3. Donald Hustad, *Jubilate! Church Music in the Evangelical Tradition* (Carol Stream, Ill.: Hope Publishers, 1981), 127.

4. For a more detailed consideration of various forms of worship in the Southern Baptist Convention, see Paul Basden, "Something Old, Something New: Worship Styles for Baptists in the Nineties," in *Ties That Bind: Life Together in the Baptist Vision* (Macon, Ga.: Smyth and Helwys, 1994), 171–190.

5. See James Emery White, *Opening the Front Door: Worship and Church Growth* (Nashville: Convention Press, 1992).

6. Oscar Thompson, *Concentric Circles of Concern* (Nashville: Broadman, 1981), 17.

7. Hustad, *Jubilate!*, 134.

Portions of this chapter were excerpted from the author's previously published books on worship and are used by permission:
Practice of Praise (Nashville, Tenn.: Word Music, 1992)
Entering His Presence (South Plainfield, N.J.: Bridge Publishers, 1986)
A Heart Aflame (Irving, Tex.: NCM Press, 1993)

5
Finishing the Task:
Contemporary Approaches to World Missions

Jerry Rankin

Jerry Rankin is president of the Southern Baptist Foreign Mission Board. He was a longtime missionary in Indonesia and other parts of Southeast Asia. He earned an M.Div. from Southwestern Seminary and received an honorary degree from Mississippi College.

The final exhortation of Jesus to his followers was to make disciples of all nations (Matt. 28:18-20). He came to earth to provide redemption for a lost world. He revealed the love of the heavenly Father and taught kingdom principles. He set an example of compassionate ministry and focused witness. But his ultimate objective was that the Good News of salvation would reach the uttermost parts of the earth.

This purpose began in the heart of God before the foundation of the earth. It began to be revealed to the Old Testament patriarchs and prophets as they spoke of a messianic kingdom (2 Sam. 7:16; Eph. 3:4-5; 1 Pet. 1:10-11). It became a reality when Jesus came and died and rose again that repentance and forgiveness of sin might be preached in the whole world (Luke 24:47). It is a purpose that has been committed to every generation of believers who come under the lordship of Christ and in obedience strive to preach the gospel to all creation (Mark 16:15). It is a purpose that has been empowered by the Holy Spirit, through whom we become his witnesses (Acts 1:8). God has never been diverted from his purpose; nor has that power been withdrawn.

The fervor with which first-century Christians began to disperse and proclaim the gospel to the nations lost its momentum in successive generations as the church became institutionalized and New Testament doctrines diluted. Although "Christianity" spread through the expansion of the Roman Catholic church and the perfunctory missionary efforts that accompanied subsequent European colonialism, it was in the latter years of the eighteenth century that the global mission of the church was reignited.

When William Carey sailed for India after challenging Baptists in Kettering, England, to form a missionary society and accept responsibility for evangelizing the pagan world,[1] the modern missionary movement began. This momentum accelerated with the colonial expansion of the nineteenth century and exploded upon the whole world by the mid-twentieth century. Two world wars assisted in bringing a global world view to American evangelical churches, many of which had been limited by denominational provincialism. Advances in communication and travel following World War II further stimulated an awareness of a spiritually needy and hurting world and resulted in unprecedented advances in mission efforts.

The 1950s and 1960s saw a great influx of missionary personnel becoming available in response to God's call to share the gospel cross-culturally. Churches responded with financial support and a sharpened focus on the global task. What earlier had been somewhat of a holding pattern on a limited number of fields such as China, Brazil, and Nigeria now went forth to touch the global community of nations. As doors to a missionary presence closed in China and the communist world, this apparent deterrent became one impetus among others to deploy witnesses of the gospel in every country possible.

As we move toward the twenty-first century, the providence of God seems to be moving us toward the actual fulfillment of his purpose of world redemption. Few nations remain closed to some type of missionary witness. Previously unevangelized people groups are being penetrated by the cooperative, concerted efforts of mission agencies working together. Rates of church growth overseas are surpassing the most optimistic projections. The prophecy of Jesus in Matthew 24:14 that "this gospel of the kingdom will be preached in the whole world as a testimony to all nations, and then the end will come" is beginning to be seen as a possibility within the current generation.

Contemporary approaches to missions are being drawn into a paradigm of God's providence and power. Although the essential element of his power and blessings upon our cross-cultural evangelistic efforts have always been acknowledged, strategies and methods have at times been formulated as if finding the right programs or implementing the correct combination of principles would result in success.

Developments in the last few years have impressed missiologists with a renewed sense of a divine *"kairos,"* in which God is moving to extend his kingdom in ways that defy human explanations. While missionary expulsion from China, the premier mission field of the early twentieth century, was seen as a setback for many mission programs, it actually helped provide the impetus for a larger global vision and expansion as personnel were redeployed. Who would have ever anticipated the tremendous spontaneous growth of the church in China in an indigenous movement of the Spirit in subsequent years?

While Christians were bemoaning the closed doors of the communist world, and some were devising efforts to contravene the iron curtain, no one was anticipating the collapse of the communist governments. It was not simply economic tensions nor the influence of Western capitalism that caused the Berlin wall to crumble; nor was it the result of mission strategies that have allowed the countries of Eastern Europe to be impacted openly with a gospel witness.

There is a divine dynamic at work in our world, fulfilling a kingdom purpose of God. As God's people we have been given the privilege of being actors in a plan of world redemption that began before the foundation of the world. Contemporary approaches to missions must humbly acknowledge that God has determined that all the peoples of the earth will one day have an opportunity to hear and respond to the gospel. John envisioned the culmination of the missions era when Christ would come again, and he saw "a great multitude that no one could count, from every nation, tribe, people and language, standing before the throne" (Rev. 7:9). Every nation and people will be represented in the kingdom due to response to the gospel. God has called us as his people to be the actors, empowered by his Spirit, to carry the gospel to the ends of the earth.

The primary challenge we face is not to invent up-to-date methodologies for global evangelization, but to be sensitive to where God is at work, discern the opportunities to join him in his mission, and be submissive to his leadership. It is foolish to presume that the task of reaching our world for Christ is our mission, or that we can devise a strategy to fulfill that mission. It is God's mission, and God has a strategy to fulfill his kingdom purpose. Those who are privileged to be a part of that strategy are not those who take pride in their own accomplishments or the success of their mission organization and endeavors, but those who will exalt Jesus Christ and give him the glory. Yet God has led in the application of unique contemporary approaches in current mission efforts.

Technology and Communication

Modern technology and advances in the "information age" are being utilized to enhance the effectiveness of mission methods. Research and computerized networking have provided an understanding of the missions task as never before. Rather than presumptions being made on the needs and status of Christian outreach, statistics and demographics can be analyzed.[2] The world is being seen, not as a pattern of artificial geopolitical nations, but as a more realistic matrix of people groups identified by their ethnicity and other significant criteria. Research into sociological characteristics and cultural mores is being applied so the gospel can take root and permeate a people group with minimal conflict with traditions and relationships.

Advances in travel and communication have allowed the mobilization of personnel and resources at an accelerated pace. Missionaries are being deployed more rapidly where God is at work. There is greater mobility for shifting personnel to places of greatest need, rather than their being locked into an isolated assignment regardless of what is happening. Volunteers, who previously represented an occasional, peripheral element of mission strategies, are now able to join those on the field in a cross-cultural witness in massive numbers.

Streamlined decision making by mission administrators, global networking and consultation, and immediate transfer of resources are made possible by the prolific application of computer modems, facsimile machines, and satellite communication. This has created a dimension of interactive planning that has diversified strategies. No longer do processes have to flow through a time-consuming, bureaucratic organizational structure from the field to the home office and back to the field, but decisions can be made instantaneously and field personnel empowered to implement appropriate responses to emerging opportunities.

Unreached People Groups

One of the most notable contemporary approaches to the missions task is a focus on people groups. Few countries represent a monolithic cultural identity. Most are composed of multiple language and ethnic groups, some of which transcend recognized national boundaries. They represent diversity not only in terms of language and traditions, but also in terms of response to the gospel.

In the past, missionaries simply entered a country, sought to plant churches within the borders of a geographic entity, and seldom distinguished why certain groups and types of people became Christians while others did not. Churches were planted throughout countries such as Indonesia and India, but vast ethnic groups remained untouched. Recent statistics reported 18 million Christians in India, but these were primarily among the Malayalam, Tamils, and Telugu in the south and the tribal population in the northeast. Most of the remaining ethnic groups, castes, and tribes remained untouched by the gospel.

Indonesia, the largest Muslim country in the world, has been one of the most responsive, yet the gospel has bypassed large people groups such as the Sudanese, Minangkabau, Achenese, Madurese, and others. Add to these those living in remote areas geographically or isolated culturally in the Muslim or Hindu world, often with restricted religious freedom due to Marxist governments, and researchers have identified more than two thousand ethnic-linguistic groups that had no access to the gospel.[3]

These groups have been identified as "hidden peoples" because they were usually overlooked in mission strategies, or people were largely unaware of their existence. There has been a recent focus on the Central Asian republics of Kazakhstan, Kyrgyzstan, Uzbekistan, Azerbaijan, Turkmenistan, and Tajikistan, an area some have identified as the "black hole of missions" because it has escaped notice until recently. All of our mission maps ended at the Middle East or India and Pakistan in Asia. It was as if the veil of the Soviet Union obscured these 50 million people.

Recently the unreached people groups have been referred to as the "10/40 window," because 80 percent of peoples with no indigenous church are in a rectangular box between 10 degrees and 40 degrees latitude north, stretching across North Africa, the Middle East, Central Asia, and into India and China.[4] The most prominent contemporary approach to missions has been an emphasis on completing the great commission by focusing on these unreached people groups. Entire mission organizations have been formed in the last few years with the sole purpose of implementing innovative strategies for introducing Christ where he has not been known.

Because most of these people groups were in countries closed to missionary presence, personnel have been deployed as "nonresidential missionaries" with the task of developing innovative strategies to impact the target group. Networking among multiple organizations has emerged through these unprecedented cooperative efforts. Scriptures have been translated and distributed, and radio broadcasts have been sponsored.

In addition to these outside approaches, channels have been found through which Christians can gain access to a restricted area by meeting an acknowledged need of the people. Development and health-care workers have offered services, teachers and businessmen have responded to requests by third-world governments, and athletic teams and cultural exchanges have established friendships. Through these various channels, missionaries in unique assignments, or tentmakers working for multinational companies or under direct contract, have been able to incarnate the gospel and expose people to the Christian faith for the first time. With increased mobility and international travel, there have been opportunities to present a witness to expatriate segments of people groups in other countries, such as Kurds living in Germany or Iranians living in London.

Expanded Media Channels

While film evangelism and radio broadcasts have been in the missionaries' toolboxes for many years, the proliferation of technology in developing countries has greatly expanded the potential for utilization of media. Scripture in the heart language of the people continues to be the foundation upon which other strategies of electronic and print media are based. Increased awareness and access of the people-group focus has resulted in accelerated progress in Scripture translation. The complete Bible has been translated into 337 languages. At least one book of the Bible was available in 2,062 additional languages where translation was in process in 1994. As Scriptures are translated, evangelistic tracts are also produced, closely followed by discipleship and study aids that are essential to an emerging group of new believers.

In gauging the accessibility of a people or culture to the gospel, two channels of media have been traditionally identified as key factors—Scripture translations and Christian radio broadcasts in the language of the people. That has now been joined by a third medium that is proving to be one of the most effective modern developments in global evangelization—the *Jesus* film. This two-hour film, produced by Campus Crusade for Christ, uses the actual text of the Gospel of Luke.[5] It has been distributed and is being utilized in 306 languages by many missionaries and organizations. An additional 163 language versions are in production. The mushrooming growth of television (even in most third-world countries), VCRs, satellite transmissions, and cable networks, allows an impressive graphic portrayal of salvation and the hope that it may be seen by millions.

Chronological Storying

Even with technological advances in the developing world that enable the gospel to be spread through electronic channels of mass media, a large portion of the world remains uneducated and illiterate. With birthrates highest in undeveloped countries, increasing numbers continue to be deprived of education and economic benefits that accrue in more developed nations. Many have no access to the media nor would they be able to read the Scriptures and evangelism materials if they were available.

The New Tribes Mission organization introduced a method for communicating the gospel among illiterate populations which has gained widespread application throughout the world. In the oral traditions of these societies, a sequence of well-designed stories are told to acquaint the people with theological truths concerning God, human sinfulness, and the salvation that has been uniquely provided in Christ. Through a systematic presentation of biblical highlights, a group is led to faith in Christ. By the time a commitment to Christ is made, people who had no background for understanding the Christian faith are well-grounded in basic truths. Often the group is eager to know how they can be properly related to God well before they come to the story of Jesus!

While initially intended for illiterate tribals, the storying method has proved to be effective in a variety of settings, even among educated people in urban areas who have no knowledge of the true and living God. Also, because the method of presentation is so simple and indigenous, the stories are told and retold by the listeners with an expanding ripple effect. Recently in one African country eighty-six villagers were baptized and a church started as the result of several months of "storying." The stories were being told in forty other locations.

Accelerated Harvest

Contemporary approaches to missions have had to take into consideration the accelerated harvest where there has been freedom to propagate the gospel. Researchers say that the continent of Africa could become 50 percent Christian if the present rate of evangelism and church growth continues. Some have suggested that there are countries in Latin America where 25 percent of the population is now Protestant! A generation deprived of the gospel in Eastern European countries is responding readily as they hear the Good News from missionaries and thousands of short-term volunteers.

Just as God will hold us accountable for those who do not have an opportunity to hear the gospel, so will he hold us accountable for failure to reap the harvest where his Spirit is moving to create response. Creative methods, modern technology, and newly emerging opportunities must not tempt us to overlook the basic ingredient of fulfilling our global mission—a multiplying, reproducing network of local indigenous churches. When the gospel is proclaimed, it is the very nature of the message, indwelt by God's Spirit, to draw people to saving faith in Jesus Christ. When people are born again, the Holy Spirit draws them together into a fellowship of believers, baptized in public testimony of their faith. It is that local group of baptized believers—a church—that becomes a nucleus of witness and ministry that grows and multiplies throughout a community.

The Southern Baptist Foreign Mission Board has been committed to evangelism that results in churches, in recognition that the objective of the missions task in proclaiming the gospel is that groups of people of God become the body of Christ in another culture or area. In the last six years, this organization has seen baptisms surpass a quarter of a million and the number of Baptist churches affiliated with their mission efforts double.

No missions method or innovative approach can be successful if it omits this basic objective of church planting. No country or people group has been evangelized until local congregations proclaiming Jesus Christ are accessible to the population. Scripture distribution, preaching crusades, radio broadcasts, and film evangelism can touch the masses, but there will not be lasting fruit unless those responding are discipled and congregationalized.

In spite of new tools and resources, missions and church planters are finding that the ageless principles of church growth continue to be the most effective approach, because in the kingdom task of missions, biblical and spiritual principles must be maintained. The gospel bridges barriers and unites differences, but the gospel flows naturally in common sociological entities. The most prolific growth is among homogeneous groups where people can readily receive the message with credibility from their own kind of people. They relate and function effectively, even spiritually, in the context of their own natural community.

The church is most likely to grow and multiply if it is indigenous, fitting naturally within its cultural environment in forms of worship and patterns of relationships. There is a tendency to gain quicker results by infusions of financial aid and personal assistance, but too much dependence on outside resources will inhibit the spontaneous expansion that God desires.

Responding to Human Needs

The modern missionary movement gained momentum following World War II, when the Western church encountered a devastated and hurting world. Few societies and economies were unaffected by the global conflagration. People, left disillusioned and insecure by the collapse of governments and cultural traditions, were responsive to the spiritual hope found in the message of Christ. Compassionate Christian ministries were often the channel for receptivity, with hospitals and schools often being the norm of missionary methodologies.

Even with the rapid development being seen in third-world countries today, rising populations, changing economies, and natural disasters are causing the quality of life to deteriorate and are leaving many destitute. Wars and ethnic conflicts are inflicting suffering and displacing massive populations. In the 1990s there are an average of forty-three wars going on at any given time, compared to only twenty-two in the 1980s. At any given time this results in more than 16 million refugees, driven from their homes in Afghanistan, Indochina, Somalia, Liberia, Rwanda, and multiple other countries.

Deforestation has decimated once fertile agricultural land. Cycles of drought and flooding have frustrated hope for rehabilitation in places such as Bangladesh, India, and West Africa. Into such situations a missionary presence, providing agricultural and development assistance, can bring hope to the hopeless and win a hearing for the message of eternal life. Medical aid following earthquakes and typhoons can often express the incarnational love of Jesus more effectively than any other contemporary approach. These needs will continue to escalate rather than diminish, providing unique opportunities for cross-cultural witness.

Partnership and Cooperation

As the second millennium draws to a close, evangelical believers are being drawn together in common mission efforts in ways that are unprecedented.[6] In the past denominational mission agencies worked rather independently and exclusively, perhaps in opposition to popular ecumenical tendencies among mainline churches. Parachurch agencies were held under suspicion or even shunned as an interference and threat to support.

However, mission agencies have recognized that no one will be unilaterally successful in global evangelization. God has raised up many organizations, each with a unique perspective on the task of missions. As each one brings its special gifts and ministries in submissive cooperation with others, the result is a synergistic effect. Those organizations with a commitment to bringing the peoples of the world to saving faith in Jesus Christ have been identified as "great commission" Christians, an identity that has facilitated working together in unified strategies.

Many evangelical mission agencies have united in a project called CoMission to provide thousands of teachers in the schools of the former Soviet Union, seizing a unique opportunity to bring biblical teaching into this former communist society. Through Cooperative Services International, the Southern Baptist Foreign Mission Board has put strategy coordinators into place among unreached people groups with an assignment to network with a multitude of organizations and mobilize a diversity of resources.

The imminence of A.D. 2000 has brought numerous mission groups into official and ad hoc configurations for the sake of coordination of research and information, partnership in cross-cultural programs, and encouragement of a rising tide of third-world missions that will soon outnumber Western agencies.

Prayer Strategies

Doubtless one of the most remarkable contemporary developments is the rediscovery of a basic biblical precept that the power and miraculous movement of God is unleashed by intercessory prayer. Just as the outpouring of the Holy Spirit on the day of Pentecost was preceded by several days of prayer and fasting, a vast network of intercessors are being mobilized to focus on a lost world. Barriers are crumbling, miraculous breakthroughs are occurring, and the strongholds of Satan are being opened to the light of the gospel because of a deliberate strategy of prayer.

Organizing a prayer network with massive intercession on behalf of an unevangelized people group or closed nation has become a foundational approach. Years before countries like Albania and the Russian republics opened to freedom of religion, people were praying for these countries and unreached people groups. Beginning in 1987, Baptist churches in West Virginia focused united prayer efforts on Mongolia, a communist country closed to outsiders. In 1990 volunteers were able to gain access to the country and found only a handful of Christians. Now there are missionaries in Mongolia and hundreds of baptized believers. Prayers were being offered for the Kurds when most people in the West had never heard of them, and then the Gulf War thrust them into the awareness of the whole world. Countries have opened and people groups have been impacted with the gospel because of prayer strategies that have broken down the strongholds of Satan.

The first task of a strategy coordinator in seeking to impact an unreached people group with the gospel is to enlist a network of prayer supporters. It is not cleverly devised platforms of ministry, fluent communication skills, or modern tools of technology that overcome the opposition of the powers of darkness, but the prayers of God's people.

Regardless of the location or culture—whether a people group is responsive or resistant to the gospel—God is moving to call a people to himself. He has commissioned the church to make Christ known to the ends of the earth. Where that task is being successfully carried out, there seem to be three characteristics invariably present: a passion to share Christ and win the lost, a devotion to prayer, and a bold faith that expects God to manifest his power in response to relevant human needs.

Communication and travel are reducing our world to an inter-related global community. Modern technology is providing tools applicable to the missions task. Burgeoning populations, political upheaval, and social disruptions are creating unique needs and unprecedented opportunities for proclaiming the gospel. Countries are being evangelized, and unreached people groups are gaining access to the gospel at a pace unimaginable a few years ago. The methodologies and approaches are unlimited, but the task will remain unfinished if it is ever presumed that man's programs or organizational strategies are the key to an evangelized world.

God will be faithful to fulfill the great commission through those who follow in humble obedience, submissive to the lordship of Christ and empowered by his Holy Spirit. Creative and innovative approaches are opening doors and being used with great success, but these are simply manifestations of the revealed wisdom of God providing channels for the power of the gospel to produce its eternal fruit.

Endnotes

1. William Carey, *An Enquiry into the Obligations of Christians to Use Means for the Conversion of the Heathens* (Leicester, U.K.: Anne Ireland, 1792).

2. See, for example, David Barrett, ed., *The World Christian Encyclopedia: A Comparative Survey of Churches and Religions in the Modern World A.D. 1900–2000* (Nairobi: Oxford Univ. Press, 1982). The *International Bulletin of Missionary Research* updates this information in its January issue each year.

3. "A Church for Every People": *The List of Unreached and Adoptable Peoples* (Colorado Springs: Adopt-A-People Clearinghouse, 1993).

4. Luis Bush, ed., *A.D. 2000 and Beyond Handbook,* 3rd edition (A.D. 2000 Project: Colorado Springs, 1993), 2-3.

5. Further information may be obtained by contacting The Jesus Film Project, P.O. Box 72007, San Clemente, California 92674, 1(800)432-1997.

6. James H. Kraakevik and Dotsey Welliver, eds., *Partners in the Gospel: The Strategic Role of Partnership in World Evangelization* (Wheaton, Ill.: Billy Graham Center, 1992).

PART 2
"By All Means Save Some": The Evangelistic Imperative

Ultimately evangelism involves the telling of the good news of the gospel to lost persons. In this section the writers examine different approaches for communicating the timeless gospel. John Avant begins by highlighting the crucial importance of a strong biblical and theological foundation for evangelism. Darrell Robinson examines the importance of personal witnessing in the life of the believer. O. S. Hawkins addresses the role of proclamation in sharing the gospel message. Kelly Green takes a fresh look at the often-used method of mass evangelism. Jack Stanton calls attention to the personal life of the witness. Billie Hanks, Jr. shows how the key to effective follow-up is friendship.

6
The Biblical Foundation for Evangelism

John Avant

John Avant is pastor of the Coggin Avenue Baptist Church in Brownwood, Texas. Prior to this he pastored the Northrich Baptist Church in Richardson, the Sand Flatt Baptist Church in Cleburne, and the Hay Valley Baptist Church in Gatesville, all in Texas. He earned a Ph.D. in evangelism at Southwestern Baptist Theological Seminary, where Fish was his dissertation supervisor. Avant also earned an M.Div. at Southwestern and graduated summa cum laude from Baylor University. Avant currently serves on the Home Mission Board of the Southern Baptist Convention and on the Board of Overseers for Criswell College.

The challenge of fulfilling the great commission involves not only evangelism for a changing world, but also the changing world of evangelism. Never in the history of the church has there been such a diversity of methods to share the gospel message. Just a few decades ago, who could have dreamed of seeker services and satellite communications, contemporary Christian music and computer technology, power evangelism and power teams? Change is everywhere in the world of evangelism, and there does not appear to be anything on the horizon but continued diversity.

In the midst of methodological changes, we must be alert to the danger of theological changes that could compromise the message we proclaim. Today evangelicals openly debate the eternal nature of hell and the necessity of accepting Christ for salvation, issues once questioned only by the nonevangelical world. Many denominations have virtually abandoned evangelism altogether. Historically, evangelicals have maintained the stability and continuity of their message by affirming the infallibility or inerrancy of Scripture.[1] The Word of God has been the unchanging foundation for what we proclaim and how we proclaim it. Never has that foundation been needed more than now.

The purpose of this chapter is to examine briefly the relationship between the authority of Scripture and evangelism in the United Methodist Church and the Southern Baptist Convention, the two largest Protestant denominations in America.[2]

The United Methodist Church

Bishop Richard Wilke of Arkansas offers a frank diagnosis of the state of the United Methodist Church in his book *And Are We Yet Alive?* He says:

> Our sickness is more serious than we at first suspected. We are in trouble, you and I, and our United Methodist Church. We thought we were just drifting, like a sailboat on a dreamy day. Instead, we are wasting away like a leukemia victim when the blood transfusions no longer work.
>
> Once we were a Wesleyan revival, full of enthusiasm, fired by the Spirit, running the race set before us like a sprinter trying to win the prize. . . . Circuit riders raced over hill and valley. New churches were established in every hamlet. Our missionaries encircled the globe. Now we are tired, listless, fueled only by the nostalgia of former days, walking with a droop, eyes on the ground, discouraged, putting one foot ahead of the other like a tired old man who remembers, but who can no longer perform.[3]

The United Methodist Church has certainly changed both in doctrine and evangelistic practice since the days of its founder John Wesley. Methodism began on the solid theological foundation of the total reliability of Scripture. Wesley repeatedly insisted that the Bible is infallible. He wrote, "Nay if there be any mistakes in the Bible there may as well be a thousand. If there be one falsehood in that book it did not come from the God of truth."[4]

Virtually every early Methodist theologian followed suit. Adam Clarke said, "Men may err, but the Scriptures cannot; for it is the Word of God himself, who can neither mistake, deceive, or be deceived."[5] By the end of the nineteenth century, however, a definite shift in Methodist theology was under way. Robert Chiles says, "The last fifteen years of the nineteenth century saw the theological leadership of American Methodism change hands almost completely. The shift signaled the end of one theological era and the beginning of another."[6]

The Wesleyan doctrine of Scripture began to be questioned. By the early decades of the twentieth century, most Methodist theologians not only departed from the theology of Wesley, they openly criticized it. Highly respected scholar Albert Knudson said that the doctrine of biblical infallibility held by Wesley and others had "lost practically all value."[7]

At the same time, Methodist evangelistic fires began to wane. By 1938, W. E. Sangster wrote, "In the eighteenth and nineteenth centuries it was generally understood that a Methodist church was a place where one went to get one's soul saved. . . . If only we could win that reputation again."[8]

American Methodism had recorded one of the most astounding growth records in the history of Christianity, exploding from a membership of 14,988 in 1784 to 7,729,791 in 1939![9] Robert Coleman notes, "Above all, undergirding the Wesleyan way of life and constraining their outreach was a simple faith in the gospel of salvation."[10] But as theology changed, both the rate of growth and the commitment to evangelism began to suffer. Wesley had once given his followers a prophetic warning. He said:

> I am not afraid that the people called Methodists should ever cease to exist in Europe or America. But I am afraid lest they should only exist as a dead sect, having the form of religion without the power. And this undoubtedly will be the case, unless they hold fast both the doctrine, spirit, and discipline with which they first set out.[11]

By the end of World War II, American Methodism was in danger of fulfilling Wesley's prophecy. The theological changes in American Methodism in the last fifty years have left the denomination with a serious identity crisis. Albert Outler writes:

> We can scarcely identify ourselves to ourselves. . . . Our doctrinal norms are ill-defined and anomalous. . . . The simplest proof of this is the frequent mention of "our doctrines" with no definition of what the phrase refers to. It is as if, once upon a time, an earlier generation understood it all and then forgot to tell their children—who never asked.[12]

In the years after World War II, almost every prominent Methodist theologian had rejected the infallibility of Scripture.[13] By 1965 an important survey revealed that only a small percentage of Methodist clergy held orthodox views of Scripture. In fact, only 49 percent believed that Jesus physically rose from the dead.[14] More conservative Methodists were beginning to express concern.

However, in 1972, Methodists took an even more radical step when they declared "theological pluralism" to be the official position of the denomination.[15] It now appeared that one could believe almost anything and remain in good standing in the United Methodist Church. Though pluralism was dropped from the doctrinal statement in 1988, it does not appear that there has been any substantial change in doctrine. John Ed Mathison, pastor of Frazier Memorial United Methodist Church in Montgomery, Alabama, one of the fastest growing United Methodist churches in the country, says, "Our leadership and structures will not allow a quick return to Wesleyan theology."[16]

One of the reasons that a move toward a more conservative theology is unlikely is the continuing acceptance of pluralism in United Methodist seminaries. According to James Ward, associate dean for academic affairs at Perkins School of Theology in Dallas, none of the thirteen seminaries could be considered evangelical.[17] James Heidinger says, "All our seminaries are dominated by liberal theology."[18] Ed Robb says,

> The liberals control the seminaries. This has resulted in a rejection of supernatural Christianity. Probably 80 percent of seminary professors would reject the validity of such miracles as the virgin birth.[19]

The writer's own experience as a student at Perkins School of Theology in 1990 certainly validated what many have said about the theology of Methodist seminaries. The writer was the only one in his seminar, including the professor, who believed that Jesus physically rose from the dead.

The United Methodist Church is not without a conservative wing. The Good News movement was formed in 1967, and continues to this day to be a strong force for biblical theology within Methodism. They have thus far been unable, however, to stem the tide of liberal theology. The founder of the movement, Charles Keysor, has left the denomination. Theological confusion has created evangelistic confusion among Methodists. The incredible growth and evangelistic fervor of the United Methodist Church is now a distant memory. The denomination has declined in membership every year since 1964, and its rate of growth began declining nearly twenty years before that.[20] By 1988, the membership had dropped below 9 million, which was a decline of about 200,000 in two years.[21] The membership hemorrhage has continued every year since then, bringing the total loss of members since 1964 to almost 3 million. The decline in the church school has been even more drastic. From 1964 to 1984, United Methodists lost half their church school attendance, going from 4.2 million to 2.1 million people, and attendance is now less than 1.8 million.[22] Warren Hartman, who compiles statistics for the denomination, says that the principal cause of the membership decline is the sharp reduction in the number of confessions of faith.[23] In recent years, half of all Methodist churches have received no one by profession of faith.

While it is clear that the Methodist doctrine of Scripture has become more liberal while evangelism and church growth have declined, can it be shown that the one caused the other? It may not be possible to "prove" such a causal relationship, but the evidence certainly suggests it strongly. Many prominent United Methodists have come to this conclusion. Bishop Earl Hunt says:

> It is my conviction that many maladies characteristic of our denomination in the 1980s are traceable to the plain, simple, and extremely unfortunate fact that, gradually across recent years, we have compromised our earlier understanding of the Bible as God's Word.[24]

Joe Harding, the assistant general secretary for evangelism at the Board of Discipleship of the United Methodist Church, says, "Theology has had a profound effect on the decline of the church. It comes down ultimately to the loss of a Wesleyan view of the authority of Scripture."[25] Even Douglas Johnson and Alan Waltz, two Methodist writers who support theological pluralism, agree that pluralism damaged the growth of the denomination.[26]

Of greater importance than what any of these people say, however, is the empirical evidence that liberalism concerning the Word of God has been a major factor in United Methodist decline. Almost without exception, the growing churches of United Methodism are led by conservative, evangelical pastors. Also, Hartman, perhaps the most significant statistician in Methodist history, has concluded that in both smaller and larger United Methodist churches, demographic factors in growing and declining churches are not different enough to be considered a major factor in the numerical decline.[27] For instance, the two regions of the denomination that have experienced the sharpest decline in recent years are the western region and the industrial northeastern region. These two areas are very different demographically and socially. What they share in common is the fact that they are the two most liberal regions of Methodism.[28]

One of the strongest pieces of evidence is that Hartman's research reveals that those who are the most liberal in United Methodism are the least likely to be interested in evangelism, and those who are the most dissatisfied with the liberal theology of the church are the most likely to be evangelistic.[29] This seems to provide a direct, empirical link between liberal theology, including a rejection of the infallibility of Scripture, and the evangelistic failure and decline of the United Methodist Church. How the world needs the evangelistic fires of the Wesleyan revival again! Many in United Methodism are today attempting to rekindle those fires through applying Wesleyan strategies of evangelism again. If Wesley's strategies are to be recovered by United Methodists, then so must his theology, including his firm belief in the inerrancy and authority of Scripture—the biblical foundation for evangelism.

The Southern Baptist Convention

One would find it difficult, if not impossible, to find any crack in the biblical foundation of early Southern Baptists. L. Russ Bush and Tom Nettles summarize well the early Baptist view of the Bible:

> Historically, Baptists have built their theology from a solid foundation. Holy Scripture was taken to be God's infallible revelation in words. What God said, Baptists believed. . . . Scripture has been the cornerstone, the common ground, the point of unity.[30]

While sweeping theological changes were taking place in many Protestant denominations during the early decades of the twentieth century, Southern Baptists did not move away from their orthodox view of Scripture. This refusal to drift with the theological tide of the day spared Southern Baptists the internal division of the fundamentalist-modernist controversy. As Nancy Ammerman says, "There were not enough modernists around in the Convention to generate a good fight."[31] George Marsden agrees, saying that "the conservatives were so overwhelmingly dominant . . . that there was no possibility of protracted controversy."[32]

Southern Baptists were so unified doctrinally during the early years of this century because with virtually no exceptions their leaders held to a very high view of Scripture. Long before the formation of the Southern Baptist

Convention, the founder of the first modern Baptist church, John Smyth, wrote, "The Holy Scriptures viz. the Originalls Hebrew and Greek are given by Divine Inspiration and in their first donation were without error most perfect and therefore canonical."[33]

Virtually every Southern Baptist scholar through the early decades of this century would follow in his theological steps. John Dagg, an early Southern Baptist theologian, writing to defend the Scriptures against skeptics, says, "Positively, it is divine truth; negatively, it is not human error."[34] James Boyce, the first president of Southern Baptist Theological Seminary, wrote, "It must be secured from all possibility of error, so that its teachings may be relied on with equal, if not greater confidence than those of reason."[35] Basil Manly, professor at Southern, and the first president of the Sunday School Board, believed that "in every part of Scripture there is both infallible truth and divine authority,"[36] and that God keeps his Word "free from error."[37] John Broadus of Southern Seminary was also clearly an inerrantist. He said that "the inspired writers were preserved by the Holy Spirit from error," even in the areas of history or science.[38] Some have claimed that the great scholar A. T. Robertson departed from a belief in the inerrancy of Scripture,[39] yet he made his position clear in the following excerpt from a sermon:

> It has been objected by some that there are discrepancies and inconsistencies in the Word of God. . . . The whole question is whether there were any errors in the original manuscript. . . . It is in accord with God's dealings in his world when he gave a revelation to make it free from errors. I believe he first made it inerrant as he made nature so. . . . Hence, I boldly maintain that the analogy of nature is in favor of the inerrancy of God's original Scriptures.[40]

Others have claimed that E. Y. Mullins was not an inerrantist. Though he held to what he called the "plenary dynamic theory," he still believed that "men were able to declare truth unmixed with error."[41] Mullins was greatly admired by fundamentalists such as J. Gresham Machen, and Mullins himself actually contributed to *The Fundamentals*.[42]

There is certainly no doubt where the founder of Southwestern Baptist Theological Seminary stood. B. H. Carroll believed that "inspiration was an inspiration of the records, which made those records inerrable, not only in idea, but in word."[43]

Not only was Carroll an inerrantist, but he viewed it as a grave danger that anyone might depart from that view. He said:

> It has always been a matter of profound surprise to me that anybody should ever question the verbal inspiration of the Bible. The whole thing had to be written in words. . . . When you hear the silly talk that the Bible "contains" the word of God and is not the word of God, you hear a fool's talk. I don't care if he is a Doctor of Divinity, a President of a University covered with medals from universities of Europe and the United States, it is fool talk. There can be no inspiration of the book without the words of the book.[44]

The list is almost without end. J. M. Frost, the founder of the Sunday School Board, said that the Board would "insist upon the absolute inerrancy and sole authority of the Word of God."[45] Jeremiah Jeter, the first president of the Foreign Mission Board, believed that there was no "possibility of error" in the Bible.[46] John Sampey, former president of Southern Seminary and three-term president of the Southern Baptist Convention, believed that one was only a conservative if one held to the inerrancy of Scripture. He said, "Conservatives hold that the writers were preserved from all error by the inbreathed Spirit guiding them."[47]

Finally, J. B. Cranfill, editor of the Texas *Baptist Standard,* financial secretary for Baylor University, and superintendent of mission work in Texas, wrote that "the Bible is either true or it is false. There is no halfway ground."[48] The writer could discuss many more individuals, but certainly those discussed here are sufficient to demonstrate an amazing theological unity among Baptist leaders concerning the Bible before World War II. Southern Baptist seminaries certainly reflected the theological conservatism of Baptist leadership. Glenn Hinson says that until 1945, "Southern Baptist colleges and seminaries insulated students from the impact of the liberal tradition."[49] James Hefley says:

> Though the term [inerrancy] was infrequently used, it was assumed that missionaries, teachers, and other denominational employees believed the Bible to be without error. If one should believe otherwise, he was expected to resign.[50]

The truth of Hefley's statement is supported by the resignation of Crawford Toy from Southern Seminary in 1879. Toy was asked to resign because he taught the documentary hypothesis and believed there were errors in the Bible. President Boyce said, "No professor should be allowed to enter upon such duties as are there undertaken, with the understanding that he is at liberty to modify the truth, which he has been placed there to inculcate."[51]

There can be no doubt that among the leadership of Southern Baptists before World War II, and in their schools and institutions, the Bible was almost universally presented as the inerrant Word of God.

The commitment to evangelism by early Southern Baptists is as clear as their theology. The Convention was formed for the purpose of evangelizing the world. Roy Fish says, "From the time of its organization, the Convention has placed major emphasis on reaching people for a commitment to Jesus."[52] Baptists reaped great evangelistic harvests during the late nineteenth century and even during the early twentieth century, when other denominations were beginning to abandon evangelism. Historian Robert Baker says:

> At a time when liberal winds were blowing, causing many denominations to magnify the social aspects of the gospel, sometimes even in opposition to the initial need for individual regeneration, Southern Baptists were placing great emphasis upon evangelism and mass revival meetings.[53]

The denomination's Home Mission Board kept evangelism before the Convention as the top priority, and the seminaries trained their leaders in how to do it. L. R. Scarborough, president of Southwestern Baptist Theological Seminary, said in 1939, "It is found that so long as the heart of an institution burns hot with the fires of soul-winning, it is not likely to drift in its theology."[54] Scarborough required that all professors be actively involved in evangelism, and kept records of the number they led to Christ. From 1920–1924, for instance, the professors and students at Southwestern conducted 4,166 revivals and saw 55,861 professions of faith and 35,422 baptisms.[55] This was with a faculty of ten and a student body of less than four hundred!

As a result of their evangelistic fervor, Southern Baptists exploded in growth. The Convention almost doubled from its inception in 1845 to 1860. From that time until World War II, the Convention recorded continual growth, always exceeding that of the population. From 365,000 members in 1845, Southern Baptists grew to 5,367,129 by World War II and were clearly one of the strongest religious forces in America.[56]

When a denomination's theology changes, that change almost always begins in the seminaries that train its leaders. That has certainly been true in the Southern Baptist Convention. Ammerman says that a "New SBC" emerged after World War II, and the seminaries began to change.[57] The change took the form of a growing rejection of the inerrancy of Scripture, and a growing acceptance of historical criticism. C. R. Daley, long-time editor of Kentucky's *Western Recorder,* who admits to being happy about the changes, says:

> When I came to [Southern] Seminary [in the 1940s], I can remember only one professor who stood up strongly for the Mosaic authorship of the Pentateuch. . . . The seminaries have been moving in that direction. If you want the Mosaic authorship of the Pentateuch, the historicity of the first eleven chapters of Genesis, and Job and Jonah as historical figures, go to Mid-America [seminary].[58]

Conservatives grew increasingly concerned as it became clear that Southern was moving to the left theologically. By 1977, controversy began to swirl around the book *Jesus Christ* by Southern professor Glenn Hinson, who said that the Gospels contained the mind of the early church more than the mind of Jesus, and "when sifted, it leaves little that one can confidently attribute to Jesus himself."[59] A 1976 thesis by a Southern student showed that the longer one studied at Southern, the less orthodox he became, even to the point of doubting the existence of God.[60] As late as 1986, Wayne Ward said that "he knew of no faculty member at Southern who was an inerrantist."[61] This of course, represents a complete change from the positions of the founders and early faculty of the school.

At Midwestern Baptist Theological Seminary in 1961, controversy raged over professor Ralph Elliott's book *The Message of Genesis,* which among other things questioned the historicity of Adam and Eve and argued that Abraham only thought God told him to sacrifice his son. Elliott was dismissed, but it was now clear that his teaching was not isolated. Daley said:

> Elliott is not a glaring example of heresy among a host of safely orthodox teachers in our seminaries. If he is a heretic, then he is one of many. . . . Professors in all our seminaries know that Elliott is in the same stream of thinking with most of them, and is more in the center of the stream than some of them.[62]

At Southeastern Baptist Theological Seminary, formed in 1951, it appears that few if any of the early faculty were inerrantists. Morris Ashcraft, who resigned as faculty dean in 1987, says:

Since 1950 I have also taught in Midwestern Seminary and Southeastern Seminary. I have never studied with, nor served as a colleague with, a professor who identified himself or herself as an inerrantist with reference to the Scripture.[63]

President Randall Lolley agreed that there were no inerrantists on the staff.[64] Alan Neely, who was professor of missions at Southeastern until 1988, lists the infallibility of the Bible, the virgin birth of Christ, the substitutionary atonement, the bodily resurrection of Christ, and the premillenial second coming as the doctrines of fundamentalism. He says that he never knew a seminary professor before the 1980s who affirmed all these doctrines.[65]

It is important to note that not all Southern Baptist seminaries have been identical in theology. In fact, studies done by both Ammerman and James Guth show that Southwestern, New Orleans, and Golden Gate seminaries had seen far less theological change. Ammerman writes:

> There were also clear differences among graduates of the six Southern Baptist seminaries. Three of those seminaries had reputations as "liberal" and three were reported to be more "conservative." To see if those reputations had any substance, we compared their graduates. As expected, those who went to Southern, to Southeastern, or to Midwestern were nearly three times as likely to be moderate in theology as were graduates of the other three schools.[66]

Whether one believes that the theological changes in Southern Baptist seminaries are dangerous or not, there can be little doubt that they have taken place. Certainly, recent changes in leadership at several seminaries appear to be moving the pendulum back toward the historic Southern Baptist position on Scripture, but it is too early to judge what effect this will have. Both Ammerman and Guth conclude that not only did the theology of the seminaries change, but through the mid-1980s, these changes were affecting the belief systems of Southern Baptist pastors and thus their churches.[67]

It might seem on the surface that Southern Baptist growth has been totally unaffected by changes in the denomination, since membership has tripled to over 15 million since World War II. However, since the mid-fifties, Southern Baptists have seen a general decline of their growth rate. The rapid growth of the forties and early fifties has disappeared. Moreover, Sunday school growth has clearly plateaued. The rate of growth began to sharply decline about thirty-five years ago, and in many individual years since then, the actual enrollment numbers have declined.[68] With a few temporary deviations, baptisms have also been on a plateau for almost forty-five years. Though baptisms rapidly increased in the first half of this century, the trend has remained level at about 386,000 since 1950.[69]

It is also disturbing to note that since membership has continued to grow and baptisms are stagnant, Southern Baptists as a whole have become less effective in reaching people for Christ. It takes more than twice the number of Baptists today to win one person to Christ as it did in the forties. A Gallup poll taken in 1980 suggests that evangelism has become less important to Southern Baptists than perhaps ever before. The poll found that only 44 percent of laity and 78 percent of pastors in the Southern Baptist Convention believed that "to help win the world for Jesus Christ is the top priority for a Christian."[70]

Regardless of disagreements on other convention issues, most Southern Baptists agree that evangelism is weaker than in past years. Larry McSwain says that "evangelism generally is not faring well."[71] Lewis Drummond says that evangelism in the Southern Baptist Convention "is at one of the lowest depths it's ever been."[72]

It is more difficult to determine a possible correlation between theology and evangelism and growth in the Southern Baptist Convention than in the United Methodist Church because Baptists are still growing, though slowly. Is it possible that Southern Baptists are still growing because the majority still hold to a high view of Scripture, but that growth has slowed and evangelism has suffered because there has been a move away from inerrancy? The evidence suggests that this is the case.

The evidence presented by local Southern Baptist churches appears clear and convincing. The churches that baptize the largest number of people are almost without exception led by pastors who hold to the inerrancy of Scripture.[73] Zimmerman found that differences in how evangelism was perceived, how it was practiced personally, and how it was stressed in the local church, were all dependent upon theology. The most dramatic difference in practice between those she calls moderates and those she calls fundamentalists was that moderates were far less likely to emphasize and practice evangelism.[74] Zimmerman also identified some states as predominantly conservative and some as moderate. The writer studied the statistics of these states, and without exception the conservative states have better records in membership growth, decadal growth rates, Sunday school growth, and baptisms.[75] Also, virtually every available study provides support for the writer's thesis, even studies conducted by those who personally hold to more liberal theology.[76] In every denomination, history has shown that as J. I. Packer says, "Any position other than inerrancy is incapable of sustaining and informing the Christian mission."[77] Finally, it is of great significance that the timing of the theological change at the seminaries and the beginning of a decline in the rate of growth in membership, Sunday school, and baptisms correlate almost exactly. It is unlikely that all three of these trends would begin just after the theological shift purely by coincidence.

When taken as a whole, the evidence overwhelmingly supports the position that a move away from the doctrine of the inerrancy of Scripture has been harmful to Southern Baptist growth and evangelism.

Conclusion

Apart from all of the other evidence, is it not a possibility that God simply chooses to bless those individuals, churches, and denominations who believe and honor his words? I believe that this is the case. It is an awesome and sobering thought to realize that the eternity of millions is at stake this very day. I believe that in a changing world, and in a day of changing evangelism, it is time for all believers to say with the psalmist, "Your Word is truth," and upon that solid foundation, evangelize a needy world.

Endnotes

1. The author will use the terms *infallible* and *inerrant* as synonyms.
2. For further study, see the author's dissertation, "The Relationship of Changing Views of the Inspiration and Authority of the Scripture to Evangelism and Church Growth: A Study of the United Methodist Church and the Southern Baptist Convention in the United States since World War II" (Ph.D. dissertation, Southwestern Baptist Theological Seminary, 1990).
3. Richard Wilke, *Are We Yet Alive?* (Nashville: Abingdon, 1986), 9. See also Robert E. Coleman, *Nothing to Do But Save Souls: John Wesley's Charge to His Preachers* (Grand Rapids: Francis Asbury Press, 1990).
4. John Wesley, *Journal of the Rev. John Wesley,* ed. Nehemiah Curnock, 8 vols. (London: Epworth Press, 1909), 6:117.

5. Adam Clarke, *Miscellaneous Works,* 13 vols. (London: T. Tegg, 1839–45), 12:132. See also Thomas Langford, *Practical Divinity: Theology in the Wesleyan Tradition* (Nashville: Abingdon, 1983), for further study of Methodist theologians.

6. Robert E. Chiles, *Theological Transition in American Methodism: 1790–1935* (New York: Abingdon, 1965), 65.

7. Albert C. Knudson, "Henry Clay Sheldon—Theologian," *Methodist Review* 108 (March 1925): 187.

8. W. E. Sangster, *Methodism Can Be Born Again* (New York: The Methodist Book Concern, 1938), 38. Though Sangster was a British Methodist, he discusses American Methodism in this book.

9. Frederick A. Norwood, *The Story of American Methodism* (Nashville: Abingdon, 1974), 410.

10. Robert E. Coleman, *Nothing to Do But Save Souls,* 20.

11. Quoted in Luke Tyerman, *The Life and Times of the Rev. John Wesley,* 3 vols. (New York: Harper & Bros., 1872), 3:519.

12. Quoted in Dennis E. Kinlaw, "American Methodism at 200: The Unclaimed Heritage," *Christianity Today* 28 (Nov. 9, 1984): 28.

13. Jeffrey K. Hadden, *The Gathering Storm in the Churches* (Garden City, N.Y.: Doubleday, 1969), 57.

14. Ed Robb, "The Predicament of Methodism," *Christianity Today* 8 (Oct. 25, 1963): 9.

15. *The Book of Discipline of the United Methodist Church* (Nashville: UMC Pub. House, 1968), 7.

16. John Ed Mathison, interview by phone, August 26, 1994.

17. James Ward, interview by phone, Jan. 22, 1990.

18. James Heidinger, "The United Methodist Church," in *Evangelical Renewal in the Mainline Churches,* Ronald H. Nash, ed. (Wheaton, Ill.: Crossway, 1987), 27.

19. Ed Robb, interview by phone, Jan. 16, 1990.

20. Douglas Johnson and Alan Waltz, *Facts and Possibilities: An Agenda for The United Methodist Church* (Nashville: Abingdon, 1987), 27.

21. Helen Parmley, "United Methodist Membership Declines," *The Dallas Morning News,* 6 January 1990, 39 (A).

22. James Holsinger and Evelyn Laycock, *Awaken the Giant* (Nashville: Abingdon, 1989), 18.

23. Warren Hartman, "Factors Related to Church Growth and Decline," *Discipleship Trends* 5 (Feb. 1987): 3.

24. Earl G. Hunt, *A Bishop Speaks His Mind: A Candid View of United Methodism* (Nashville: Abingdon, 1987), 89.

25. Joe Harding, interview by telephone, Feb. 15, 1990. Cf. Jerry Walls, "The Fruit of Theological Liberalism," *Challenge to Evangelism Today* 22 (Summer 1989): 5; and Ed Robb, "Should Evangelicals Leave the United Methodist Church," *Challenge to Evangelism Today* 19 (Winter 1986-87): 2.

26. Johnson and Waltz, *Facts and Possibilities,* 31.

27. Warren Hartman, "Size and Regional Differences," *Discipleship Trends* 6 (April 1987): 2.

28. Robert Wilson and William Willimon, *The Seven Churches of Methodism* (Durham, N.C.: Duke Divinity School, 1985), 17.

29. Warren Hartman, *A Study of the Church School in The United Methodist Church* (Nashville: Discipleship Resources, 1976), 36.

30. L. Russ Bush and Tom J. Nettles, *Baptists and the Bible* (Chicago: Moody Press, 1980), 18. This book is the most complete historical study available of the Baptist doctrine of Scripture.

31. Nancy Ammerman, *Baptist Battles: Social Change and Religious Conflict in the Southern Baptist Convention* (New Brunswick: Rutgers Univ. Press, 1990), 69. This is an extremely important book because Ammerman is a sociologist who writes from a more "moderate" perspective than the writer, and yet her research supports the writer's position.

32. George Marsden, *Fundamentalism and American Culture* (New York: Oxford Univ. Press, 1980), 165.

33. John Smyth, *The Works of John Smyth,* ed., W. T. Whitley, 2 vols. (Cambridge: University Press, 1915), 1:279.

34. John L. Dagg, *The Evidences of Christianity* (Macon, Ga.: J. W. Burke & Co., 1869), 224.

35. James P. Boyce, *Abstract of Systematic Theology* (Phil.: American Baptist Pub. Society), 48.

36. Basil Manly, Jr., *The Bible Doctrine of Inspiration* (New York: A. C. Armstrong & Son, 1888), 59.

37. Ibid., 29–30.

38. Quoted in James T. Draper, Jr., *Authority: The Critical Issue for Southern Baptists* (Old Tappan, N.J.: Fleming H. Revell, 1984), 62.

39. See James Robison, *The Unfettered Word* (Waco, Tex.: Word, 1987), 95, where he says that Robertson "avoided not only liberalism on the left, but also the fundamentalist view of biblical inerrancy on the right."

40. A. T. Robertson, "The Relative Authority of Scripture and Reason," an unpublished sermon, n.d. In an interview with the writer, L. Russ Bush said that there are other unpublished sources where Robertson takes a similar position.

41. Edgar Young Mullins, *The Christian Religion and Its Doctrinal Expression* (Valley Forge, Pa.: Judson Press, 1917), 143–44. This book explains further his theory of inspiration.

42. See J. Gresham Machen, "The Relation of Religion to Science and Philosophy," *The Princeton Theological Review* 24 (January 1926): 38–66.

43. Benjamin Harvey Carroll, *Inspiration of the Bible*, ed. J. B. Cranfill (New York: Revell, 1930), 113.

44. Ibid., 48.

45. J. M. Frost, *Our Church Life* (Nashville: Sunday School Board of the Southern Baptist Convention, 1899), 37.

46. Jeremiah B. Jeter, "The Inspiration of Scripture," in *Baptist Doctrines*, ed. Charles A. Jenkins (St. Louis: Chancy R. Barnes, 1881), 49.

47. John R. Sampey, *Syllabus for Old Testament Study* (Nashville: Sunday School Board of the Southern Baptist Convention, 1923), 59.

48. Quoted in James Hefley, *Truth in Crisis,* vol. 4 (Hannibal, Mo.: Hannibal Books, 1989), 226.

49. Glenn E. Hinson, "Southern Baptists and the Liberal Tradition in Biblical Interpretation, 1845–1945," *Baptist History and Heritage* 19 (July 1984): 17.

50. Hefley, *Truth in Crisis,* vol. 3, 35.

51. James P. Boyce, *Three Changes in Theological Institutions* (Greenville, S.C.: C. J. Elford's Book & Job Press, 1856), 35. Toy went on to teach at Harvard and became a Unitarian.

52. Roy J. Fish, "Evangelism in Southern Baptist History," *Baptist History and Heritage* 22 (Jan. 1987): 2-3. I would like to add a personal word of appreciation here to the man who taught me so much about evangelism and continues to have a profound impact on my life.

53. Robert Baker, *The Southern Baptist Convention and Its People: 1607–1972* (Nashville: Broadman, 1974), 336.

54. L. R. Scarborough, *A Modern School of the Prophets* (Nashville: Broadman, 1939), 162.

55. Ibid., 139.

56. Baker, *The Southern Baptist Convention,* 330.

57. Nancy Ammerman, "The New South and the New Baptists," *The Christian Century* 103 (May 14, 1986): 487.

58. C. R. Daley, "Lecture on Denominational Ethics," delivered to a Southern Seminary class in 1984.

59. Glenn E. Hinson, *Jesus Christ* (n.p.: McGrath Pub. Co., 1977), 78. See the writer's dissertation, 189-91 for a more detailed examination of Hinson's book.

60. Noel Wesley Hollyfield, "A Sociological Analysis of the Degrees of 'Christian Orthodoxy' among Selected Students in the Southern Baptist Theological Seminary," (Th.M. thesis, Southern Baptist Theological Seminary, 1976), 31. See Appendix F in the writer's dissertation for a full summary of Hollyfield's findings.

61. Quoted in Hefley, *Truth in Crisis,* vol. 2, 35.

62. C. R. Daley, "Daley Observations," *Western Recorder* 136 (Sept. 27, 1962): 39.

63. Morris Ashcraft, "Revelation and Biblical Authority in Eclipse," *Faith and Mission* 4 (Spring 1987): 16.

64. Quoted in Hefley, *Truth in Crisis,* vol 4, 80.

65. Alan Neely, "Southern Baptists' Quiet Conflict," *Christianity and Crisis* 50 (March 5, 1990): 64.

66. Ammerman, *Baptist Battles,* 223.

67. Ibid., and James Guth, "The Education of the Christian Right: The Case of the Southern Baptist Clergy," *Quarterly Review* 4 (Summer 1984). Guth did a survey of a random sample of 460 Southern Baptist pastors.

68. See 249–50 and Appendix J of the writer's dissertation.

69. James Lowry, "Selected SBC Trends," *Quarterly Review* 49 (April–June 1989): 53.

70. *George Gallup Polls America on Religion* (Wheaton, Ill.: Christianity Today Books, 1981), 139.

71. Larry McSwain, interview by phone, May 15, 1990.

72. Lewis Drummond, interview by phone, July 2, 1990.

73. Quoted in C. B. Hogue, *I Want My Church to Grow* (Nashville: Broadman, 1977), 39.

74. Ammerman, *Baptist Battles,* 173.

75. See the author's dissertation for statistics and graphs.

76. See Dean M. Kelley, *Why Conservative Churches Are Growing,* Rose ed. (Macon, Ga.: Mercer Univ. Press, 1986) and Dean Hoge and David Roozen, "Research on Factors Influencing Church Commitment," in Hoge and Roozen, eds. *Understanding Church Growth and Decline, 1950–1978* (New York: Pilgrim Press, 1979).

77. J. I. Packer, *Beyond the Battle for the Bible* (Westchester, Ill.: Cornerstone Books, 1980), 250.

7
The Priority of Personal Evangelism

Darrell W. Robinson

Darrell W. Robinson is vice president of the Evangelism Section, Home Mission Board, Southern Baptist Convention. Robinson pastored Dauphin Way Baptist Church in Mobile, Alabama; First Baptist Church of Pasadena, Texas; and other churches. Robinson is author of Total Church Life, People Sharing Jesus, *and* Doctrine of Salvation.

The priority of personal evangelism was modeled by Jesus. He took time to deal personally with the lost in all kinds of situations. He did not delegate the work of winning individuals to his disciples while reserving for himself the task of preaching to the multitudes.

Jesus, the Model of Personal Evangelism

The story of the Gospels is to a great extent the story of Jesus' dealing with individuals.[1] He gave the great message of John 3 to one lone lost man, Nicodemus, in the middle of the night. He gave of himself to go through Samaria to reach the Samaritan woman at Jacob's well in John 4. He forgave the woman taken in adultery in John 8 and dealt with the man born blind in John 9. He reached Matthew the publican, Zacchaeus, and Bartimaeus. Finally, while dying on the cross Jesus, ignoring his own agony, reached out to save the penitent thief.

If we follow Jesus, we will be his witnesses. While Jesus was walking by the Sea of Galilee, he met Peter and Andrew, who were casting their nets into the sea. "Jesus said to them, 'Come with me! I will teach you how to bring in people instead of fish.' Right away they left the boat and their father and went with Jesus" (Matt. 4:19-22, CEV).

Personal evangelism was the pattern of life of those who experienced salvation. Andrew shared with his brother Simon Peter. Philip found Nathaniel and told him about Jesus. After Pentecost the Christians witnessed daily. When they were threatened and forbidden by the authorities to speak about Jesus, they prayed, were filled anew with the Holy Spirit, and spoke the word of God with boldness (Acts 4:31). When the disciples, except the apostles, were driven from Jerusalem and scattered after the stoning of Stephen, they "went from place to place, telling the good news" (Acts 8:4, CEV). The gospel spread like wildfire in the first century as believers shared Christ with people wherever they went.

Jesus gave his strategy for reaching a lost world in his last words to his followers (see Acts 1:8). Roy Fish has well said that the strategy has not changed. It still involves each local church acting in *total penetration* of its community with the gospel through the *total participation* of its members in sharing Christ.[2] As it happened in Jerusalem, the circle of gospel witness of the church will be an ever-expanding one. As a church saturates its area of ministry and influence, the gospel will spread through the outlying areas and to the ends of the earth.

The main thing Jesus said to do to reach people is the one thing the average church today is doing less of than anything else, i.e., each person who experiences his salvation is to share Jesus with others. Many churches are trying all kinds of gimmick approaches, spectacular events, indirect methods, marketing techniques, and innovative and creative approaches to attract people to their meetings and gain members. However, personal evangelism is still the basic biblical method for reaching the lost. It is foundational for all other forms of evangelism, including the following:

Mass evangelism becomes effective as individual Christians share Christ with their families and acquaintances and bring them to the revival meeting or evangelistic event. Billy Graham, whose crusades have been mightily used of God, has said that most of the people reached in his crusades were reached one-on-one. Personal and mass evangelism are complementary as sowing the seed and harvesting are complementary.

Ministry evangelism is essential to effective evangelism. But it is necessary for ministering Christians to share the gospel and ask those to whom they are ministering to receive Christ and follow him. If Christians minister without doing the work of personal evangelism, relatively few of those to whom we minister may be saved.

A Christian involved in apartment ministries, tutoring children, and other caring ministries became discouraged. The ministry was not growing. People were not being saved. As the ministry was studied it was found that those who were ministering were not witnessing and attempting to lead the lost to Christ. They were giving the names of people to whom they were ministering to the trained soul-winners of the church, expecting them to do the witnessing. Of course, the ideal person to share Christ is the one who has built a witnessing relationship through caring ministry. Ministering without witnessing is little different from the work of a secular agency.

Pulpit and educational evangelism can certainly be effective evangelistic methods. However, for many lost people to be reached, personal evangelism must undergird the preaching and teaching of the gospel. Otherwise, few lost people will attend to hear the gospel.

Living a consistent, committed Christian life is essential to effective personal evangelism. Wrong living will discredit any attempt to share Christ. Surely we must live the life or our words of witness will be powerless. However, some Christians have come to believe that their life *is* their witness. They feel that if they live an upright life and go to church, this constitutes their witness. Nothing could be farther from the truth. People need the gospel of Christ. *The gospel,* not the lives we live, is "the power of God for the salvation of everyone who believes" (Rom. 1:16). Consequently, the lives you and I live plus the words we speak equals our witness.

Other methods are also effective, but personal evangelism must remain our priority. Witnessing is telling what you know about Jesus to others. *Effective personal witnessing is sharing Jesus Christ in the power of the Holy Spirit and leaving the results to God.*

The Priority of Personal Evangelism

It is clear in the New Testament that personal evangelism is a priority of our Lord for every believer. In each of the Gospels and the book of Acts Jesus emphasized that evangelizing the lost is the assignment of every Christian.

Some would argue that they do not have the gift of the evangelist, therefore, they cannot witness.[3] The reality is that witnessing is the assignment of our Lord for every Christian. When we know Jesus, it is a privilege to share him with others. Witnessing is a joyfully obedient response to the command of our gracious Lord. A few of the passages that point to the priority of personal evangelism are Matthew 28:18-20, Mark 16:15, Luke 24:46-49, John 20:21-23, and Acts 1:8.

Priority of leadership and laity

Both committed leadership and dynamically involved lay people are critical to the implementation of the evangelistic strategy of our Lord. Pastors, evangelists, and vocational church leaders can never reach the world with the gospel. They could not in the first century and they cannot today. As C. E. Matthews has well said, witnessing is every Christian's job![4] But pastors and church leaders must take the lead in witnessing! If they do not, the people will not! People do what leaders lead them to do. *Everything rises and falls on leadership.*

Pastors and church leaders must be personally obedient to the commission of Christ or their spiritual lives will become empty and powerless. A preacher has no right to stand in the pulpit for public proclamation if he does not share Christ consistently with lost people and seek through the Holy Spirit's power to lead them to Christ. The people of a church must have the role model of the pastor and leaders in winning the lost to Christ.

Priority of equipping the laity

Lay people must be motivated and equipped to share Christ and win the lost to him. The pastor and church leaders are responsible and accountable to God for the work of encouraging, enlisting, equipping, and engaging the laity in reaching the lost (see Eph. 4:12ff.). Herein lies the hope of reaching our world for Christ. Multitudes can be reached if someone will take the initiative to become a bridge to reach outside the four walls of the church building to get involved with them and share Christ with them at the point of their need.

As a pastor, it was my goal to encourage and equip every member of the church I pastored to be able to clearly share the gospel and lead a person to Christ. Eventually every Christian who cares about the lost and consistently seeks to witness will have the opportunity to lead someone to our Lord. An illustration of this reality is the case of a lovely but shy young lady named Shelley. Shelley was one of our members who was equipped through a People Sharing Jesus seminar. She developed confidence through the work of the Holy Spirit and through the People Sharing Jesus witness equipping strategy. She found great joy in leading an acquaintance to Christ.

Soon Shelley was called on to be on a jury panel to try an older man who was formerly a significant leader of the Ku Klux Klan. He was charged with being an accomplice to a murder. Under the pressure of the interrogation, the old fellow collapsed in the court room. It was ruled a mistrial. He was set free, but God broke Shelley's heart for him. She was deeply impressed to find him and witness to him.

Our associate pastor assisted her in finding him. Shelley shared with the old gentleman, but he would not accept Christ. He did promise to sit with Shelley in church on Sunday. The Holy Spirit works on both ends at the same time. God had given me a sermon on "God's Unfailing Grace." Shelley and the old fellow were seated on the second row. When the invitation was given, he tottered down the aisle on his cane. He said, "Pastor, I want to receive Jesus. I have never felt such love in my life. I only regret that my wife did not live to know this love."

The former Ku Klux Klan leader prayed, expressing repentance and faith as he received Christ. Then he said, "Many times I have driven down this street and passed this church and wanted to go in. I would say to myself, *You need to go in there.* Then I would say, *No, you could never go in there. You are not as good as those people.*"

Thank God for a precious, shy young lady named Shelley who became a bridge to reach with the love of Jesus a man whose life had been lived in hostility and turmoil. Multitudes of people will never be reached for Christ unless someone cares enough to pay the price to become that kind of bridge to reach them where they are. The equipping and involving of every Christian in witness is the means by which this can happen. When the pastor and people of a church are obedient to Christ in witness, the church will be revived, Christians will experience growth and victory, and lost people will be saved.

Christians involved in the redemptive mission of Jesus will experience the most exciting and highest achievement a person can experience. Sharing Jesus with the lost will keep the spiritual lives of Christians vital and refreshed. It will drive the Christian to prayer for God's help, to Bible study for knowledge of his Word, and to consistent living and dependence on the Holy Spirit. Witnessing is one of the keys to experiencing the growing and victorious life.

Maintaining the priority of personal evangelism

The priority of personal evangelism is difficult to maintain by a church or an individual Christian. If it is to be maintained, it requires vigilance. Several factors make constant attention to witnessing necessary.

First, **Satan violently attacks personal evangelism.** He knows that his domain of darkness will be penetrated with the light of the gospel of Christ if every Christian is faithful to share Christ in his or her marketplace. He knows that masses of lost people will be saved as Christians witness. But he can be overcome (Rev. 12:11).

In Acts 4 Satan attacked the church through the religious and political officials of Jerusalem. They arrested Peter and John. They forbade them to speak anymore in the name of Jesus. They threatened to put them in prison or put them to death. Satan and the world without God has continued through the centuries to attempt to intimidate the church and Christians into silence about Jesus.

Today, not only the world outside the church, but many within the church attempt to intimidate Christians into silence about Jesus. Pollsters have surveyed some non-Christians, asking them what it would take to reach them. Of course the response was that they prefer not to be personally confronted with the gospel by a Christian. This is not at all unusual; nor would it be unanticipated. Lost people do not know what it will take to reach them. They are spiritually blind and do not understand the things of God. They need the Word of God and the conviction of the Holy Spirit in their hearts. Christians must intentionally seek to share Christ. Christians do not go to the lost because they have been sent for by the lost, but because they have been sent by their Lord!

Second, **churches and Christians tend to move away from rather than toward evangelism.**[5] It happened to the great church at Ephesus. They left their first love and soon departed from the first work of reaching the lost for Christ. Jesus admonished them to repent and do again the first work.

Third, **backslidden Christians are not comfortable with witnessing and soul winning.** They will be negative and critical of it. Personal evangelism requires the leadership, fullness, and power of the Holy Spirit. Carnal, self-centered people should not be permitted to determine the mission and priority of the church. They should be objects of prayer, concern, and instruction.

Fourth, **personal evangelism is hard work.** It is an intensely spiritual work. It is easy to drift to other involvements in the service of Christ and the church and minimize involvement in personal witnessing. It is less threatening to participate in a prayer group, sing in the choir, teach a class, go to a Bible study, and a thousand other things than to go to a lost person and seek to lead him or her to Christ. Priority time must be planned in the church's schedule and calendar and in the individual Christian's schedule if personal evangelism is to be done. It takes time to reach people—time to get acquainted, build relationships, share the gospel, and time to lead them to Christ.

The Principles Undergirding Personal Evangelism

Personal evangelism is based on foundational spiritual and biblical principles that guide and motivate Christians in witnessing. Winning people to Christ is a human impossibility. Human ingenuity, concern, knowledge, and persuasion are helpless in converting the lost. The Holy Spirit draws lost people to Christ and then performs the miracle of spiritual transformation. But he uses the instrumentality of those who have experienced salvation themselves to share their personal witness, present the gospel of Christ, and guide the lost through the conversion experience. To be effective in personal evangelism, a Christian must be grounded in the following truths:

First, every person needs Christ. Every person without Jesus is lost. The entire human race is under the dominion and rule of sin, separated from God, and without hope apart from Christ (Rom. 3:9, 23). Like a covering of clouds that separates the earth from the warmth of the sun on a cold and dreary day, an impenetrable barrier of sin separates the entire human race from the person and presence of God. Incurably religious humanity attempts to justify itself and make its own way to God. The results are much human effort toward good works, the development of religious movements and philosophies that attempt to break through the sin barrier and reach God.

As a witness for Christ, you can be assured that you will never meet a person who does not need Jesus. You cannot witness to the wrong person. In following Jesus, Christians should seek to share him with each person they meet. There are only two types of people in our world: the saved and the lost (see John 3:18). If you witness to a saved person, you can rejoice together—you have found a brother or sister in Christ. God will use you to be an encouragement. If you witness to a lost person, he or she needs your witness. God will use your witness either to sow the seed of the gospel, nurture the development of faith, or reap the harvest by leading the person to Christ.

The lost need the witness of a Christian and the illuminating work of the Holy Spirit. They are spiritually blind and cannot understand the things of God (see 2 Cor. 4:4). The mind of the lost person must be enlightened through the work of the Holy Spirit and the gospel of Christ.

The lost are without hope as they are (see Eph. 2:12). They do not know Jesus and his forgiveness. They have no peace. They live in perpetual turmoil like the incessantly churning waves of the sea (see Isa. 57:20-21).

The lost feel the depths of their inadequacy and lack of esteem. They need God but resist him. They try to make their own way to God. But what humanity could never do, God did as he intervened in human history to come in the person of Jesus Christ to penetrate the sin barrier and make the way for lost people to come to God through him (see John 14:6).

Second, God loves every person and has provided for the salvation of each one. You can be confident that you will never meet a person that God does not love (see John 3:16). God loves every person regardless of his or her race, nationality, culture, age, or lifestyle. God wants to reveal his love to each person through his people. God wants to love lost people through you. Through his kindness God leads lost people to repentance (Rom. 2:4).

Third, God desires to save and seeks to save every person. God gave his Son for everyone who will believe on him (see 1 John 2:2). May God break our hearts for the lost. As surely as Christ died for us, he died for them. How can we who have experienced Jesus and his salvation contain the message of his desire to save and not share it with those who need Christ?

To be consistent in personal witness, we need a heart like that of God. God calls on us to pray (1 Tim. 2:1-4).

Fourth, God has chosen to give the message of salvation through those who have experienced what they share. Every Christian is on a mission for Christ. Jesus revealed his heart and purpose to reach the lost in Luke 19:10 (CEV), "The Son of Man came to look for and to save people who are lost." If our heart beats as does the heart of the Master, it beats for souls. What a privilege that redeemed sinners can join with the Creator of the universe on the greatest mission in all eternity.

Christians are on a team of three that God uses to reach the lost for Christ. He uses the Word of God, the work of the Holy Spirit, and the witness of the believer. It gives great confidence to the child of God to realize that he or she is a part of God's work in reaching the lost.

First, *God uses his Word* to bring the lost to himself (Rom. 1:16; 10:17). The Word of God pierces deep into the heart and mind of a lost person to reveal Christ. The gospel is like a seed being planted. It has a germ of life that will burst forth and eventually bear fruit.

It is tragic but true that some have all but lost confidence in the gospel. The power is not human ingenuity, effort, psychology, or methodology. God may utilize any or all of these in bringing people to Christ, but we must never lose sight of the fact that the power is in the gospel.

Second, *God uses the work of the Holy Spirit* to bring the lost to himself. The Word of God is the sword of the Holy Spirit (Eph. 6:17). The Holy Spirit uses the Word to draw the lost to Christ and to convict and convert (John 16:8).

Third, *God uses the witness of the believer* to share the Word of salvation with the lost. As the Holy Spirit draws and convicts the person, the believer may have the opportunity to be used of the Spirit to guide the person through the conversion experience.

This truth is illustrated by the conversion of the Ethiopian in Acts 8. Philip was led by the Spirit away from a great evangelistic harvest in Samaria to the desert of Gaza. His path crossed the path of an Ethiopian caravan on its way back from Jerusalem to Ethiopia. The treasurer of the queen was reading from the book of Isaiah when Philip encountered him. Philip asked, "Do you understand what you are reading?"

The Ethiopian answered, "How can I, unless someone explains it to me?" Philip began there and guided him to Jesus.

Many, like the Ethiopian, need a witness for Christ to take them by the hand and guide them through the conversion experience and ask them to personally commit their lives to him. Many are waiting for someone to ask them to receive Christ.

Preparation for Personal Evangelism

While witnessing is every Christian's job, so great is the task of personal evangelism that meaningful preparation should be made for it. The Holy Spirit can use whatever we yield to him. Winning people to Christ is the Holy Spirit's work, but he uses the yielded, prepared witness as an instrument to reach the lost.

Spiritual preparation is essential. It should not have to be said, but it is too important to assume—a witness for Christ must be saved. Salvation comes before soul winning. We must be born-again children of God to be soul-winners. We cannot share what we do not have. Of course, a lost person can memorize the plan of salvation and present it to another. But he or she could not truly share Jesus without knowing him. There can be no real service to Christ if one does not belong to him.

Spiritual preparation includes one having assurance of his or her own salvation. How could one have the boldness to witness effectively while uncertain about his or her own salvation? This could well be one reason some American church members never lead someone to Christ.

Divine empowerment of the Holy Spirit is a primary part of the spiritual preparation for soul-winning. Witnessing is a spiritual work. It must be done in the power of the Holy Spirit. The instrument God uses effectively must be cleansed from known sin. Prayer, confession of sin and cleansing from sin, and receiving the fullness of the Holy Spirit are essential for power to witness.

The Holy Spirit's power is given for witness (Acts 1:8). As Christians yield to the Holy Spirit and obey him in witness, Holy Spirit power flows. When members of a church obediently share Christ, the lost are reached, people are saved, and revival fills the church. However, when members live in disobedience to the assignment of Jesus to witness, few people will be saved and spiritual coldness and decline will characterize the church.

Love for Jesus and love for people are essential for witnessing. When we love Jesus and we love people, we will do our utmost to bring the two together. A discouraged pastor was ready to resign from his church. One night God moved in the church as the guest speaker called the church and pastor back to the priority of total penetration of their area with the gospel through total participation of the membership in witness. The invitation was given for those who would ask the pastor to lead and equip them and join him in discovering and sharing Christ with every lost person in the church's area of ministry to come forward and kneel with the pastor. All the deacons, teachers, and leaders and most of the members were deeply moved by the Spirit and took that step. They were saying, "We are available."

After the service the pastor said, "I do not need to leave the church. I have not led them to do the first work. We have lost our first love. The problem is we just do not love Jesus and we do not love people." Thank God, that changed. During the next few years the pastor led the people to penetrate their area with the gospel through personal witness. The church experienced revival and grew. It was a leader in its city in reaching the lost.

Loving people is a major factor in reaching them for Christ. It makes the difference in breaking down the barriers that lost people often have toward the gospel and toward a witnessing encounter. Loving people causes the Christian witness to be sensitive to the lost—to their needs, concerns, and feelings. It will enable the witness to listen with understanding and share Christ at the point of the lost person's need. It will help the Christian witness discern the leadership of the Holy Spirit in moving forward with the presentation of the gospel and asking the person to receive Christ. Loving people will cause Christians to be sensitive to divine appointments. Loving people is Christlike.

Personal preparation must be made by the individual witness. Mental, emotional, and physical preparation is necessary. The witness for Christ must clearly know the content of the gospel. Scripture study and memorization is needed to be able to share Christ in a meaningful way. Care should be given to preparing the attitude to make sure condemnation, condescension, anxiety, and other negative emotions are not conveyed. Attention should be given to physical hygiene and manner and style of dress so as not to be offensive. If people are offended, let it be an offense at the gospel and conviction of the Holy Spirit and not the thoughtlessness of the personal witness.

Formal preparation is advantageous but not essential for witnessing. The newest convert is often the best soul-winner by simply sharing what he or she knows in the power of the Holy Spirit. However, to continue to grow in Christ and to utilize effective techniques in sharing Jesus is helpful. To equip every Christian to share Christ, the Evangelism Section of the Southern Baptist Home Mission Board has developed several tools to be used by local churches and individuals. Some of them are:

    WIN (Witness Involvement Now) School
    One day soul-winning seminar
    CWT (Continuing Witness Training)
    BWR (Building Witnessing Relationships)
    Friends Forever
    People Sharing Jesus
    WOW (Win Our World youth witness training)
    Lifestyle Witnessing for Women

Numerous witnessing booklets, tracts, marked New Testaments, and other tools are available to help Christians in presenting the gospel.[6]

Tools such as those noted above assist in the following important features related to formal training: 1) supervised preparation, especially that which uses on-the-job training (evangelism is caught more than it is taught); 2) continuing preparation, for we never learn enough about the Bible, Jesus, the work of the Holy Spirit, and the nature of humanity that the preparation is complete; and 3) simultaneous preparation, because we must be involved in witness as we prepare for witness. If we are not, preparation is meaningless. The people who plan to wait until they are fully prepared to start witnessing seldom do.

We must tell what we know about Jesus. This is obedience to Jesus' commission. The Holy Spirit will use the most feeble witness to accomplish great things. It is not our ability but our availability that God blesses and uses. Use what you are learning as you are learning it.

Planning for Personal Evangelism in a Local Church

Local churches are primary in the work of personal evangelism. Each local church is a witnessing body of Christ. Members individually and the body collectively are to bear witness to the Head of the body, the Lord Jesus Christ. As a church body experiences and functions with good spiritual health, evangelism will flow and the lost will be reached for Christ. Witness for Christ is the natural lifestyle of a Christ-filled body.

Priority planning is essential for a church to continue to maintain spiritual vitality and give priority to personal evangelism. Evangelism must be planned into the calendar, budget, and personnel assignments in the church. If not, the church will drift away from evangelism. Every kind of activity and involvement will consume the attention and resources of the church. Several steps need to be taken for effective personal evangelism.

First, leadership must prioritize personal evangelism. The pastor should give primary leadership. Effective lay leaders must help as well. The church could select an evangelism chairman or director to assist the pastor and to represent evangelism in the church council or leadership team. In a larger church the evangelism chairman would lead the evangelism council or committee. The evangelism council or committee will be made up of members responsible for leading in different areas of evangelistic work. This group will help ensure that evangelism is adequately planned into the calendar, budget, and personnel assignments of the church. It will assist in planning and preparing for the ongoing evangelistic thrust, evangelistic events, and equipping activities.

Create a climate for evangelism in the church. A church should vibrate with evangelistic concern. We are in grave danger of losing our sense of lostness. To reach lost people, we must see them through the eyes of his love and sacrifice for their salvation. Emphasis must repeatedly be given to the mission of the church to reach the lost, or it is soon forgotten. The church must have a mindset for growth! It can be done!

Three things will be helpful at this point. First, *lead the people to pray.* Pray for God to guide the church to be all he wants it to be to implement the mission of Jesus. Pray for the lost at every meeting. Emphasize reaching every lost person in the church's ministry area. Second, *seek the Lord for revival.* Lead the church in a study and prayer emphasis for spiritual awakening. Third, *lead the church to study and implement Total Church Life evangelism strategy* or a similar holistic approach to church evangelism. Total Church Life evangelism emphasizes the balance of healthy worship, unity, fellowship, organization, equipping the laity, and evangelizing the lost.

Lead the church to develop a specific focus for reaching the lost and unchurched. Define the specific area or areas of ministry and influence for which the church will accept primary responsibility to saturate with the gospel, discover every lost and unchurched person, and seek to reach him or her for Christ. Periodic saturation should be done every three to six months to create in the community a climate for evangelism, God-consciousness, and an awareness of the ministry of the church. Saturation can be done through telemarketing, direct mail, door-to-door witness and surveys, literature and Bible distribution, sharing in the marketplace, and publicizing through signs, billboards, and posters, etc. Saturation can be done in connection with church activities and evangelistic events. It will result in witnessing opportunities and a continuous flow of new people visiting the church services. Place information you gather about people in a "people to reach" file or computer list. Assign their names to members for periodic contact through witness visitation and for relationship building. Develop a report system for contacts made indicating responses. Lead church members to be sensitive to divine appointments for witness. Train members to give the names of the people they have discovered through their daily contacts. Continue the process until each lost and unchurched person has either been reached for Christ or has moved away.

Involve every member at whatever level he or she will be willing to participate in reaching the lost. Some will immediately be excited about witnessing, visitation, and personal soul-winning. Others will be reluctant but will participate in praying for the lost, using the telephone, helping with direct mail, ministering to people, and visiting as a team person with an experienced witness.

Develop an organized program of outreach visitation, but continue to emphasize lifestyle and marketplace witnessing. Both are important to the evangelistic witness of the church. The organized program is essential to continue the strong emphasis on personal witnessing and to equip and grow the involvement of lay members in reaching the lost. However, more will probably be reached through lifestyle and marketplace witnessing as relationships are developed. The two approaches are complementary.

Utilize the Sunday school to organize to evangelize.[7] Outreach is one of the primary objectives of the Sunday school. It is an excellent approach for enlisting and equipping members for witness. Through the organized outreach visitation involving the Sunday school, people-to-reach assignments can best be made. Sunday school classes can utilize a team approach in praying for the lost, visiting and witnessing to them, developing relationships, giving encouragement to one another, and providing a caring fellowship for those being reached. The fellowship factor is a key to reaching the lost. They need to become a part of a Bible study or fellowship group who will care for them, nurture and disciple them, and help them be assimilated into the life of the church.

Develop the church calendar with evangelism as a priority. Plan a three-year evangelism calendar. Scheduled activities should be communicated to the membership well in advance so they can plan to participate.

The three-year calendar should include:

1. Ongoing evangelistic activities such as weekly evangelistic visitation, regular evangelistic Bible studies, and other regular times of evangelistic activities.

2. Evangelistic events such as vacation Bible school, revival meetings, crusades, special harvest days, evangelistic concerts and special speakers, and other special activities should be scheduled periodically.

3. Periodic evangelistic equipping activities with a goal to train and equip every member for witness and soul winning. Depending on its size and rate of growth, a church should conduct an equipping activity every three to six months. Even the smallest church should do so annually. There are numerous valid approaches to equipping for personal evangelism. The particular method of equipping to be used is not an issue. The important thing is to *do it!* Jack Stanton, former director of the Personal Evangelism Department of the Home Mission Board, SBC, has said, "There is no bad way to lead people to Jesus."

The Passion for Personal Evangelism

God uses all kinds of approaches in reaching all types of people for Christ. But the approach is secondary to the passion that keeps Christians consistently sharing Jesus. Personal evangelism is implemented through methods that vary from developing relationships by spending time getting acquainted, sharing in social activities, and gently guiding a person to Christ to engaging a stranger in conversation and sharing the gospel in street witnessing. God uses both. It took three years of caring nurture to lead our neighbors Rose and Larry to Christ. They will be our friends forever. Taking whatever time is needed in relationship with lost people to lead them to Christ is worth it. It was a passion for our friends to be saved that kept us praying and seeking to share Jesus with them until they came to Christ.

On the other hand, the passing witnessing contact on the street may well be a divine appointment from God. A radiant lady shared that she had been on the streets for some time. She had recently been divorced. She was down and defeated. Someone approached her and witnessed to her. She accepted Christ, went back home, and now is living a joyful Christian life and is serving in her church. It was a passion for souls that led the person who shared with her to approach a stranger on the street.

Regardless of the method used to reach people, a passion for souls is the critical factor in personal evangelism. A passion for souls has as its source our experience of salvation and a deep love for the Lord Jesus Christ. Paul had the inner motivation of the love of Christ that compelled him to share the gospel (2 Cor. 5:14). He expressed his broken heart for the souls of the Jewish people and his willingness to pay any price to reach them for Christ.

"I am a follower of Christ, and the Holy Spirit is a witness to my conscience. So I tell the truth and I am not lying when I say my heart is broken and I am in great sorrow. I would gladly be placed under God's curse and be separated from Christ for the good of my own Jewish people" (Rom. 9:1-3, CEV).

Personal evangelism is a fire in the soul. It is the individual Christian's response to Christ's call to take up the cross and follow him. It is not brow-beating, arm-twisting, button-holing, and manipulating people with the gospel. It is the free, unhindered flow of the gospel from the life of a Christian to a lost person. If we love people, we cannot withhold the gospel from them. We will continue seeking to share Jesus with them until the Holy Spirit opens a way.

God has given your church the army that can reach your community for Christ. It is the army of lay people in the church service every Sunday. It is God's intention for every Christian to witness. Enlist them! Equip them! Engage them! Encourage them! God will empower them!

Endnotes

1. See G. Campbell Morgan, *The Great Physician: The Method of Jesus with Individuals* (Old Tappan, N.J.: Revell, 1937); Roy J. Fish, "Evangelism in the Gospel of John," *Southwestern Journal of Theology* (Fall 1988), 37–41. Roy Fish has impacted my life in a very positive way. The day after I surrendered to God's call to preach at age seventeen, Dr. Fish came to my home to invite me to preach my first sermon in his church. He was a role model for me as a young pastor, especially in evangelistic leadership as a pastor and in personal soul-winning.

2. See Darrell W. Robinson, *Total Church Life* (Nashville: Broadman, 1985), for a holistic development of this approach.

3. See Frank Harber, "An Examination of the Historical Development of the Ministry of the Evangelist within the Christian Church" (unpublished dissertation, Southwestern Baptist Theological Seminary, 1994), for a lucid and scholarly study of the biblical gift of the evangelist.

4. C. E. Matthews, *Every Christian's Job* (Nashville: Convention Press, 1951).

5. George E. Sweazey, *Effective Evangelism* (New York: Harper and Bros., 1953), 26.

6. Information about these materials can be gained by calling the Home Mission Board of the Southern Baptist Convention at 1(800)634-2462 and ordering the *Home Mission Board Resources Catalogue* (511-38F).

7. An excellent resource is Harry M. Piland and Arthur D. Burcham, *Evangelism through the Sunday School* (Nashville: Convention Press, 1989).

8
Passionate Proclamation:
The Eternal Effects of Evangelistic Preaching

O. S. Hawkins

O. S. Hawkins is pastor of the historic First Baptist Church of Dallas, Texas. Prior to this he was pastor of the First Baptist Church of Fort Lauderdale, Florida, a perennial leader in evangelism in that state. He is the author of several books, including Drawing the Net.

Simon Peter preached his first recorded sermon on the Day of Pentecost. Looking in on the scene, we see that participation in the finished work of Jesus Christ was affirmed by the baptism, sealing, and filling of the Holy Spirit, and by speaking in other languages (Acts 2:1-13). People in Jerusalem "were all amazed and perplexed, saying to one another, 'Whatever could this mean?' Others mocking said, 'They are filled with new wine' " (Acts 2:12-13, NKJV). Simon Peter stood and proclaimed to them, "Men of Judea and all who dwell in Jerusalem, let this be known to you, and heed my words. For these are not drunk, as you suppose, since it is only the third hour of the day. But this is what was spoken by the prophet Joel . . ." (Acts 2:14-16, NKJV). Peter opened the scroll and read from the prophet Joel (Joel 2:28-32). He proclaimed the gospel of Jesus Christ from that text as recorded in Acts 2:17-40. His message was an evangelistic proclamation rooted and grounded in the exposition of God's Word.

When such proclamation is presented in truth and power today, it continues to draw men and women to beseech the heavens with the heartfelt cry, "Lord Jesus, come into my heart, forgive me, and cleanse my heart of sin. I want to be your child. I trust Jesus Christ as my personal Lord and

Savior." This model of evangelistic preaching on the great and glorious birthday of the New Testament church was delivered by Simon Peter.

A Prepared Preacher

What Peter had been. This is the same Peter who a few days earlier had denied that he ever knew Jesus. He was a natural leader among the disciples. He was always enthusiastic about Jesus. At Caesarea Philippi, when Jesus asked who people said that he was, Peter responded, "You are the Christ, the Son of the living God" (Matt. 16:16, NKJV). Following that great encounter, Peter became boisterous. Once, when Jesus hinted he was going to die, Peter blurted out, "Far be it from you, Lord; This shall not happen to You!" (Matt. 16:22, NKJV). Another time Peter asked Jesus where he was going and added, "Lord, why can I not follow You now? I will lay down my life for Your sake" (John 13:37, NKJV). The night Jesus was arrested in the Garden, Peter drew a sword to defend his Lord. Later that night, Peter became a shriveling coward when he was identified as a disciple of Jesus. Peter lied and reinforced his lie by cursing as he denied his Lord three times. Only two months before the Day of Pentecost, Peter was a traitor! He was a Benedict Arnold! He was a turncoat! What was wrong with him?

Simon Peter was a true believer. He trusted in Jesus Christ (John 5:24) and was a child of God by divine authority (Greek, *exousia;* John 1:12). But something was lacking in exercising his right as a child of God. He kept falling short. When he denied Jesus, Peter realized what he had done. He went out and wept bitterly with tears of true repentance. Peter looked into his own heart and didn't like what he saw. He examined his life and found it to be short of any nobility. He had denied his Lord because he was relying on his own strength to carry him through his spiritual conflict.

Peter's life had similar disasters during the days following our Lord's resurrection. His enthusiasm and emotions overloaded his capabilities, and his behavior proved to be embarrassing. Before Pentecost, he lacked the power to perform his desires for God. He had not been divinely empowered to follow Christ. God's Word was not yet the authority on which he based his decisions and actions. As leader of the believing community, Peter was an abject failure! He needed something else, and everybody knew it.

What Peter had become. Something happened to Simon Peter on the Day of Pentecost. He was altogether different. This difference was dramatic.

Instead of being a bumbling braggart, Peter was the powerful preacher of the gospel. He had been transformed. What happened to Peter?

On the day Jesus ascended into heaven, he told his disciples, "It is not for you to know times or seasons which the Father has put in His own authority. But you shall receive power when the Holy Spirit has come upon you; and you shall be witnesses to Me in Jerusalem, and in all Judea and Samaria, and to the end of the earth" (Acts 1:7-8, NKJV). The word "authority" (Gk. *exousia*) is the same word used in John 1:12 to relate the "right" or "authority" believers have to become God's children. The word "power" (Gk. *dynamis*) indicates a "dynamic enablement" or "ongoing source of power." This was the promise of the Father.

In the ten-day interval following the Ascension, the disciples waited on and received the promise of the Father. On the Day of Pentecost, Peter was *baptized* with the Holy Spirit. The Holy Spirit immersed him into the body of Christ. He was *indwelt* by the Holy Spirit, like every other believer in this dispensation. He was *sealed* with the Holy Spirit. He was *filled* and *anointed* by the Holy Spirit. At Pentecost, Peter received power (*dynamis*) that would enable him to accomplish God's will and to proclaim the gospel. He was marvelously transformed by God the Holy Spirit. Something new was added to Peter's spiritual life. He had been transformed from a coward to a champion for Jesus Christ. Peter, the transformed fisherman, stood up and in the power of the Holy Spirit boldly proclaimed the Word of God.

Proclaiming God's Word was central on the Day of Pentecost, and it should be central in the church today. God's plan hasn't changed! It is still by the foolishness of preaching that men and women are drawn to repentance (1 Cor. 1:23-24). We may point fingers in many directions for the moral collapse and decay in American civilization today. Much of the blame should be placed in pulpits where preachers have ceased to proclaim the gospel of Jesus Christ. Many preachers have ceased to open God's Book to God's people. We are reaping the results of a generation of people who know nothing of the Word of God.

Bold proclamation of God's Word must rely on God's dynamic enablement rather than on programs, politics, or praise services. Many today replace proclamation with programs. Much of their worship services involves promoting of programs. Others replace preaching with politics. Politics have so entered the pulpit that some omit the exposition of God's Word except when they need a "proof text" for a subject or agenda. Some replace preaching with praise. Many churches have given praise and worship, rather than the exposition of God's Word, the central place in the worship experience. Yet to be together in love and unity, and to be filled with the Holy Spirit, believers need the proclamation of the Word of God.

God still draws people to repentance by the "foolishness of preaching." Great churches today are characterized by *preaching* the Word of God. Peter's Pentecost sermon provides many elements preachers and teachers need to understand about the proclamation of God's Word. These elements of proclamation are that it is *prophetic* (Acts 2:17-21, 25-29, 34-35), *plain* (Acts 2:22-23), *positive* (Acts 2:24, 32), and *personal* (Acts 2:22-23, 36). When these elements are present, the proclamation of God's Word should be *penetrating* and "cut to the heart" (Acts 2:37).

The proclamation of God's Word should be *persuasive* and cause hearers to ask, "What shall we do?" (Acts 2:37). It should be *pointed* and call hearers to repent (Acts 2:38). Peter's direct appeal didn't offer multiple-choice options. The proclamation of God's Word should be *pious* because it is based on an awesome fear of the Lord (Acts 2:39). Proclamation should also be *persistent* and conclude with an appeal: "And with many other words he testified and exhorted them" (Acts 2:40, NKJV). "Exhort" (Gk. *parakaleo*) means to "call alongside" or "encourage." Finally, proclamation of the gospel should be *productive* (Acts 2:41). People ought to be saved. At Pentecost about three thousand were saved and followed our Lord in believer's baptism.

The proclamation of the gospel has many elements. I would like to look into the *prophetic, plain, positive, and personal proclamation of God's Word.*[1]

Prophetic Preaching

Proclaiming God's Word is prophetic. Prophetic preaching must be biblical. It should emerge from the text of God's Word. Simon Peter preached the Bible, and not his own opinion. He used the Word of God from Joel 2:28-32 as the basis for his message (Acts 2:16-21). He illustrated his text by quoting Psalm 16:8-11; 68:18 and 110:1 (Acts 2:25-28, 34-35). Peter established a scriptural, biblical basis for what was happening and for what he desired his hearers to do in response. Like his, our preaching should be biblical and prophetic.

Many preachers today do not proclaim a prophetic word from the Bible. Recently I talked to a man I know who recently preached in another church in the Dallas area. He said four hundred to five hundred were in attendance. He said less than one-fifth of the people present had a Bible with them. Even more alarming, he reported, even the pastor didn't bring a Bible to the service. A preacher who doesn't use the Bible for his message is like a surgeon going into surgery without a scalpel. He is like a carpenter building a house without a hammer. God tells us through the prophet, " 'Is not My word like a fire?' says the LORD, 'And like a hammer that breaks the rock in pieces?' " (Jer. 23:29, NKJV). It is no wonder that many churches are empty and powerless today. Bold prophetic proclamation must be biblical.

Great God-blessed churches in the world today have one common characteristic. They insist on the trustworthy exposition of the authoritative Word of the living God. In their pulpits and Sunday school classes, preachers and teachers find a text in God's infallible and inerrant Word and proclaim it boldly. Peter took his text from the Old Testament prophet Joel, who prophesied that the Lord would come and visit his people and live in their midst. After this supernatural visitation, the Lord would "pour out of [his] Spirit on all flesh" (Acts 2:17, NKJV). Many people today still look for the fulfillment of Joel's prophecy. Peter was emphatic about it: "This is what was spoken by the prophet Joel." Joel's prophecy was unfolding before their very eyes (Acts 2:16).

The Word of God is alive and powerful (Heb. 4:12). When Peter proclaimed it, the people "were cut to the heart" (Acts 2:37, NKJV). The word "cut" is a compound term (Gk. *kata* and *nusso*) meaning "to pierce through." It is used of the soldier who "pierced" (Gk. *nusso*) Jesus' side (John 19:34). God's Word pierces our hearts. We have a word for that—*conviction*. It demonstrates the two sides of the proclamation of God's Word: our side and God's side. We are to speak God's prophetic word to people. God brings conviction (John 16:8). We must speak out on moral issues confronting society.

A newly elected school board near Dallas, Texas, facing all kinds of attacks, recently voted to "emphasize such principles in the Plano schools as determining right from wrong, honesty, sexual abstinence before marriage, love of country, and value of human life." Isn't it strange how liberal churches today can speak out on issues they endorse without an ounce of criticism from the media? But let a conservative speak about morality, and he will be attacked for violating the separation of church and state.

The preacher and teacher of God's Word must "speak the truth in love." This means we must speak out on moral issues confronting God's people. Like Elijah, the prophets of old, and John the Baptist, Simon Peter spoke the truth in love at Pentecost. They all spoke to the moral issues of their day.

Dallas recently had a visit from Joycelyn Elders, then the surgeon general of the United States. As official spokesperson for the president, she was seeking to force sex education in schools as early as kindergarten. About teenagers she said, "We taught them what to do in the front seat. Now let's teach them what to do in the back seat." For us who are interested in crisis pregnancy centers she advised, "Get over your love affair with the fetus." She called us "the unchristian religious right," and "a threat to America." She condemned the school board for its stand. She was wrong!

God stayed his judgment on Sodom and Gomorrah when Abraham made intercession because of Lot's family (Gen. 18:16-33). Lot was certainly no paragon of virtue, but he was God's child. God delayed judgment on his behalf. In our day, the only restraint on God's judgment of our decaying civilization is the presence of his people. As preachers and teachers of God's Word, our assignment is to proclaim, "This is that which was spoken by the prophet!"

Proclaiming God's Word is profitable. God's Word is the basis for proclaiming the gospel. This fact was relayed by Paul to his understudies in the ministry. Paul reminded them of the authority of God's Word when he wrote to Timothy: "All Scripture is God-breathed and is useful for teaching, rebuking, correcting and training in righteousness, so that the man of God may be thoroughly equipped for every good work" (2 Tim. 3:16-17).

God's Word is profitable for four things: *doctrine, reproof, correction,* and *training in righteousness.* Our preaching ought to do these four things as well. It ought to teach doctrine, reprove sin, correct false paths, and instruct in righteousness. God's Word is a road map for the Christian life. It teaches us about Jesus Christ and our salvation as we get started in the Christian life. Along the way, we may get off the path by acts of our own will. The Word of God reproves us of our sin. It corrects us when we wander away from sound doctrine and behavior. God's Word gets us back on track. It trains and instructs us in righteous living so we can be conformed to his image. Effective ministry of God's Word does all four things.

Some preachers and teachers go to seed on doctrine. They never reprove sin, correct false paths, or train in righteousness and Spirit-filled living. Their churches are dead and dying. Others go to seed on reproof. They think their God-given call is to reprove everybody about their sin and point fingers in accusation. They don't teach doctrine or train in righteousness, and they are puzzled that their churches don't maintain a membership. Still others go to seed on correction to the virtual exclusion of training in righteousness and Spirit-filled living. They busy themselves trying to correct everybody else. Many today have gone to seed on training in righteousness. All they talk about is praise and worship. They speak about the Spirit-filled life to the virtual exclusion of teaching doctrine. Their churches often split, and their members are often scattered to the four winds.

In Acts we see that the early church wasn't obsessed with correcting the Roman system of justice or denouncing social institutions. Early Christians didn't go about pointing fingers of accusation. They proclaimed the gospel of Jesus Christ. Hearts and lives were transformed from within.

Simon Peter's Pentecost sermon is the first recorded sermon of the early church. It contained all four elements. Peter proclaimed, "God has made this Jesus, whom you crucified, both Lord and Christ" (Acts 2:36, NKJV). He spoke throughout about the deity of Jesus Christ. He reproved sin, saying, "You, with the help of wicked men, put him to death by nailing him to the cross" (Acts 2:23). He corrected false paths and called for repentance (Acts 2:38). He also trained in righteousness by telling his hearers to be baptized, to get into God's Word, to break bread with one another, and to grow in the grace and knowledge of the Lord Jesus (Acts 2:38-46). Peter's message contained all four elements.

Paul also had a balanced ministry of the Word of God. His first recorded sermon was preached at Pisidian Antioch (Acts 13:13-41). Like Peter, Paul included all four of these elements. The proclamation of Jesus Christ from the pulpit and from the teaching lectern should be a balanced ministry of the Word of God. We ought to teach doctrine. We ought to reprove of sin. We ought to correct false paths. We ought to be training in righteousness. Peter's messages, Paul's messages, and the messages of the early church recorded in Acts provide us with models of a balanced ministry of the Word of God.

At First Baptist Church in Dallas, where I have been called as pastor, I follow in the trail of men who have proclaimed God's Word prophetically. Dr. George W. Truett preached the Word of God from the very same pulpit for forty-seven years. He was followed by Dr. W. A. Criswell, who over the past fifty years has proclaimed the Word of God from the very same pulpit with a Bible in his hand. It is a great privilege for me to preach God's Word in this church. But something of vital importance must be kept in view. This church, like any other church anywhere, will die if its preachers and teachers don't proclaim the Word of the living God in prophetic boldness. A church is great in the eyes of God when it has *prophetic proclamation of God's Word.*

Plain Preaching

A clear message. Peter's task was to present the plain truth about what was happening on the Day of Pentecost. He said, "Let me explain this to you; listen carefully to what I say" (Acts 2:14). Peter didn't make his message difficult or obscure. He made it plain: "Listen to this: Jesus of Nazareth was a man accredited by God to you by miracles, wonders and signs, which God did among you through him, as you yourselves know. This man was handed over to you by God's set purpose and foreknowledge; and you, with the help of wicked men, put him to death by nailing him to the cross" (Acts 2:22-23). There were no verbal gymnastics here. He laid out a plain proclamation of God's Word. He didn't make it difficult. He preached about sin. He preached about the mercy of God in Christ. He preached about the coming judgment. The people understood him. His message was plain.

Many preachers today make their messages obscure and difficult to understand. They seem to want people to be impressed with their brilliance, their learning, and their skill at turning a phrase. They miss the point of proclamation altogether. Preachers are the stewards of the gospel message, which must be plain enough for a child to understand (Luke 18:16-17).

Many preachers don't make an impact because they don't proclaim a plain gospel. People may attend their services for weeks, for months, and even years without knowing what they must do to inherit eternal life. They don't "preach" (Gk. *kerusso*) the gospel. Paul said, "God made him who had no sin to be sin for us, so that in him we might become the righteousness of God" (2 Cor. 5:21). We should be like Paul, who said, "My message and my preaching were not with wise and persuasive words, but with a demonstration of the Spirit's power" (1 Cor. 2:4).

Our proclamation must be plain. We may not have the opportunity to proclaim it at some other time or occasion. There is an urgency to it. We must use each God-appointed opportunity and make our proclamation plain.

A Christ-centered message. The plain preaching of the gospel should also be Christ-centered. Peter preached about Jesus in his incarnation, his suffering, death, burial, resurrection, exaltation, and his very presence with them by his Holy Spirit. Peter didn't preach theology. He used theology to proclaim Jesus. He simply exalted Jesus Christ before his hearers and told of his crucifixion for their sins. His hearers may have thought, *Who crucified Jesus Christ?*

This question has received various answers. Some say the Jews crucified him. Others say it was the Romans. In the final analysis, it was the sin of each of us. He was crucified because of your sin and my sin. In point of fact, however, no one took his life. Jesus said, "I lay down my life—only to take it up again. No one takes it from me, but I lay it down of my own accord. I have authority to lay it down and authority to take it up again.

This command I received from my Father" (John 10:17-18). No one took his life. He laid it down. He loved us so much that he gave himself so we could come to the Father through him. The Bible says, "But God demonstrates his own love for us in this: while we were still sinners, Christ died for us" (Rom. 5:8).

A complete message. The transparent truth of the Cross was no accident. It was no ill-conceived "Passover plot" concocted by Peter and others to cover up an accidental death of some misguided martyr. It wasn't a last-minute Band-Aid on a wounded world when everything else had failed. To these and similar charges, God's Word says, "No!" God crucified Jesus because he loves us. The crucifixion of Jesus Christ was determined and planned by God. It was the program and plan of God.

Peter said, "This man was handed over to you by God's set purpose and foreknowledge; and you, with the help of wicked men, put him to death by nailing him to the cross" (Acts 2:23). The term "set" or "determined" (Gk. *horizo*) carries the notion of "horizon" or "boundary." The word "purpose" (Gk. *boule*) is the strongest word used in the New Testament for "counsel" (KJV) or "definite plan" (RSV). It carries the notion of "irrevocable will, determination, purpose, design, or plan." God's set purpose may be carried out with or without specific human cooperation, response, or consent. Peter said the Crucifixion was the set purpose of God, and there is nothing you or I could do to stop or alter God's plan for the atonement of sin on Calvary. God was in control. Jesus was handed over by God's own set purpose.

Look at the love of God in operation here: "For God so loved the world that he gave his one and only Son, that whoever believes in him shall not perish, but have eternal life" (John 3:16). Peter's message was plain. His hearers didn't miss his point. They were conscience-stricken and responded by asking, "What shall we do?" (Acts 2:37). Their response of conviction demonstrates that they clearly saw their involvement in the rejection and death of Jesus. The plain proclamation by Peter brought conviction of their sin individually. So it is today. When we preach the plain gospel, men and women, boys and girls, come under conviction. God the Holy Spirit moves in individual hearts to bring people to Christ. Jesus said, "Just as Moses lifted up the snake in the desert, so the Son of Man must be lifted up, that everyone who believes in him may have eternal life" (John 3:14-15). Peter preached Jesus! His message was plain. A church is great in the eyes of God when it has *prophetic and plain proclamation of God's Word.*

Positive Preaching

Positive aspects of the gospel. The plain, prophetic proclamation of God's Word must be positive. Peter said, "but God raised him up from the dead, freeing him from the agony of death, because it was impossible for death to keep its hold on him" (Acts 2:24). He added, "God has raised this Jesus to life, and we are all witnesses of the fact" (Acts 2:32). The gospel proclamation ought to be positive. I don't mean positive in terms of a "pumped-up" mental attitude. I'm not talking about positive thinking or possibility thinking. It is positive in that it offers hope.

Peter proclaimed the resurrection of Jesus Christ. Jesus Christ is alive! That was the heart of Peter's message. God raised Jesus from the dead. The living Christ can meet any need. This should be the heart of every sermon. Our Lord Jesus is not dead! He is alive! He is here!

As the living Christ, he can meet our every need. This is the positive gospel. Every preacher and teacher of God's Word ought to study their preaching and teaching to see how much they have made of the resurrection of Jesus Christ. We should see how much we have made of the fact that Jesus Christ is alive and that he can meet every need in our lives. We ought not preach or teach a lifeless religion. Our gospel proclaims a living relationship with a living Christ.

Peter said, "We are all witnesses!" The disciples had seen the resurrected Christ. He had transformed their lives. Most of them would meet a martyr's death. They never would have died to perpetuate a lie. People don't die for a lie. Theirs wasn't some kind of pumped-up mental attitude. The Resurrection is at the heart of the gospel. The disciples had seen Jesus, and he was alive. That fact burned within their hearts, and it brought a positive note to them. That is where we get our positive thrust! Our Lord is alive! Our preaching should be positive. We should proclaim that there is not a single need in the human heart that the living Christ cannot meet. Ours is a positive gospel!

Practical implications of the gospel. As I was reflecting about this positive gospel, I thought about our daughter Holly. She recently graduated from high school and went off to college. As my wife, Susie, and I drove back from taking Holly to her first day in college, memories flooded our minds. We thought of when she was a little girl in a wheelchair. In those days we thought she had lupus. She was involved in a special medical program at Duke University Medical School in North Carolina. We had to take her there from Fort

Lauderdale for treatments. We have seen her through so many things, and our minds wandered through those memories as we drove home.

Finally, I thought back to the day she was born. It was early one hot June day in Ada, Oklahoma. I remember pacing the second floor corridor at Valley View Hospital. It was a special day as our little Holly was making her way into the world. I was in the waiting room when Dr. Stevens appeared at the nursery window and held that tiny package of love, wrapped in a pink blanket. He laid her in a bassinet and rolled her over by the window, where I could have a good look. I stood there alone for several minutes, thanking the Lord and watching that little red-faced beauty waving her arms, kicking her feet, and crying at the top of her lungs. Suddenly I noticed I was no longer standing there alone. A housekeeper with her mop bucket was looking over my shoulder.

"Is that your baby?" she asked.

"Surely is," I proudly answered.

"Well, it's no wonder she's crying, being born into the world she has been born into." Then she turned around and sauntered off down the hall, pushing her mop bucket as she went.

For a moment I thought, *She's right. If I believe everything I preach and teach, then it would be far better for my little girl to go on to heaven. After all, she wouldn't have to go through all the heartaches of life. She would never have that haunting longing that some moment could be lived over again.* I began to pray. It was an intimate moment with Jesus, Holly, and me. I often pray hymns during my private devotional time, and that morning the Holy Spirit began to pray through me the words of the song by Bill and Gloria Gaither:

> How sweet to hold a new born baby,
> And feel the pride and joy [s]he gives;
> But greater still the calm assurance,
> This child can face uncertain days because He lives.
> Because He lives, I can face tomorrow;
> Because He lives, all fear is gone;
> Because I know He holds the future,
> And life is worth the living just because He lives.[2]

That's the positive note of the gospel! Whatever our need today, life is worth the living just because he lives. Once we've encountered the risen Lord personally, we can face any trial and any test that comes our way. Even though the world around us may become hostile and threatening, we can face it because our Lord lives. A church is great in the eyes of God when it has *prophetic, plain, and positive proclamation of God's Word.*

Personal Preaching

The directness of God's appeal. The positive, plain, and prophetic proclamation of God's Word should also be personal. Although Peter preached to a crowd, he was speaking to individuals. This personal element demonstrates the marvelous "anointing" of God's Word as it is proclaimed. Isaiah said of the Word, "It will not return to me empty, but will accomplish what I desire and achieve the purpose for which I sent it" (Isa. 55:11). Biblical preaching is directed to those points where God's Word will bring the conviction of sin. Preachers need not evade nor avoid issues that are spoken of directly in Scripture. Those issues are as personal as they are plain.

Today many sermons are preached in the first person plural ("we") or in the third person plural ("they"). This is how preachers are taught. Peter's sermon did none of this. He used second person personal pronouns ("you"). He went directly to the personal level: "Jesus of Nazareth was a man accredited by God to *you* through him, as *you yourselves* know. This man was handed over to *you* by God's set purpose and foreknowledge; and *you*, with the help of wicked men, put him to death" (Acts 2:22-23; emphasis added).

Many preachers are afraid of offending deacons, elders, big givers, civic leaders, politicians, and various others. Their preaching avoids confrontation with individuals and with personal sin. Their proclamation isn't personal. It is indirect and nonconfrontational. It doesn't bring conviction of sin. It doesn't point men and women to their need of a personal Savior. The messages are aimed at the head, not at the heart. Charles Finney said:

> Preaching should be direct. The gospel should be preached to men, and not about men. The minister must address his hearers. He must preach to them about themselves, and not leave the impression that he is preaching to them about others.[3]

Peter called out, "You, you, you!" He confronted his audience for both their lack of involvement and their involvement. They lacked involvement when they didn't respond to the mighty accreditation of Jesus Christ, which God demonstrated in their experiences. They were involved when they actively participated in the rejection and crucifixion of Jesus. Peter didn't let them evade the charges. He didn't let them avoid their guilt. His preaching was personal.

God used Peter's sermon to prick the hearts of his hearers. When Peter did his part, God was bound to do his part. When we do our part, God binds himself to do his. When we team up with God, we will experience what Peter experienced: "When the people heard this, they were cut to the heart" (Acts 2:37). Peter preached, and God moved in the hearts of individuals who heard the message. In our own day, God speaks to individuals personally when his Word is proclaimed. A church is great in the eyes of God when it has *prophetic, plain, positive,* and *personal* proclamation of God's Word.

The desire of God's heart. Over the years, our family has sensed God's living presence many times. We recently experienced his presence as we began a second "empty-nest" experience. Our oldest daughter, Wendy, was already at college. Our youngest, Holly, was getting ready to go. The night before she left, she came into our bedroom and climbed up on our bed. We talked together and prayed together as we have so many times over the last eighteen years.

After a time of personal interaction and prayer, she went on to her bedroom. The next night she was in the freshman dorm at college, as Susie and I entered a new stage of our lives. First Wendy, and then Holly wouldn't be around anymore. We are full of pride because of the joy our kids have brought us. Wendy and Holly both love the Lord and have lived pure lives. They excelled in school and have lots of friends. Our minds are filled with wonderful memories, from comic books to commencements.

To be honest with you, however, there is a loneliness and a pain in our hearts. The morning after each of our daughters left home, Susie and I sat down for breakfast. We were together, but there was an empty place at the table. We faced an emptiness. Our lives are full. We're both active people. There are places to go and people with whom to be. There is plenty of responsibility. Plenty of everything. Plenty of everything except Wendy, and now except Holly.

Some have left home spiritually. When you think about it, God has plenty of children. He has plenty of singers. Plenty of doctors. Plenty of carpenters. Plenty of nurses. Plenty of preachers. Plenty of everybody—except you. All of them together can never take your place. There will always be an empty chair at his table when you are not home. If at times he seems to be crowding you a bit, it may be that he is longing to fellowship with you. You are his child. You are unique. No one else has a fingerprint or DNA like yours. He made you that way because you are indescribably valuable to him. Although he has millions of other children, you are unique with him. There is an empty place at the table if you aren't there. He wants you to come home. He calls out to you, "Come home!" A church is great in the eyes of God when it has *prophetic, plain, positive,* and *personal* proclamation of God's Word.

The message is *prophetic* and *plain.* The plain truth of the gospel is that without Jesus Christ there is no hope of eternal life, but with him, through him, and by grace through faith we can have eternal life. The message is *positive.* Our Lord Jesus Christ is alive! We can face uncertain days because he lives. The message is *personal.* Throughout the Bible prophets called for individuals to make a personal decision. It was so with Simon Peter. Joshua said, "Choose for yourselves this day whom you will serve" (Josh. 24:15). Elijah said, "How long will you waver between two opinions? If the LORD is God, follow him" (1 Kings 18:21). Jesus said, "Come, follow me" (Matt. 4:19). Finally, "The Spirit and the bride say, 'Come!' And let him who hears say, 'Come!' Whoever is thirsty, let him come; and whoever wishes, let him take the free gift of the water of life" (Rev. 22:17). If you have gone away, come home!

Endnotes

1. For further expansion of these and other principles of evangelism, see my book, *Drawing the Net: 30 Practical Principles for Leading Others to Christ Publicly and Personally* (Nashville: Broadman, 1993).

2. William J. and Gloria Gaither, "Because He Lives," 1971.

3. Charles Grandison Finney, *Lectures on Revival of Religion* (New York: Revell, 1835, 1968 reprint), 223.

9

Mass Evangelism for the 90s:
A New Look at an Old Approach

Kelly Green

Kelly Green is a vocational evangelist from Mobile, Alabama. He is a popular speaker at evangelistic crusades, revival meetings, and at major evangelistic meetings for youth and adults. He studied with Dr. Fish while earning his M.Div. at Southwestern Seminary.

The New Testament abounds with illustrations of mass evangelism.[1] John the Baptist preached to great crowds of people in the wilderness of Judea. Jesus spoke to great multitudes throughout his ministry. Matthew 13:2 refers to "large crowds." John 6:2 notes the "great crowd" of people who listened to him, with just the men numbering five thousand.

Peter's sermon at Pentecost presents a striking example of the effect of Spirit-anointed preaching: "Those who accepted his message were baptized, and about three thousand were added to their number that day" (Acts 2:41). The early apostles were said to have "filled Jerusalem" with their teaching about Jesus (Acts 5:28). Acts 8:4 reminds us that "Those who had been scattered preached the word wherever they went." The evangelist Philip "went down to a city in Samaria and *proclaimed* the Christ there. When *the crowds* heard Philip and saw the miraculous signs he did, they all paid close attention to what he said" (Acts 8:5-6, emphasis added).

Paul proclaimed Christ in Damascus, Salamis, Pisidian Antioch, Iconium, Lystra, Derbe, Perga, Philippi, Thessalonica, Berea, Athens, Corinth and Ephesus (Acts 9–19). Demetrius the silversmith's observation about Paul's ministry shows his far-reaching impact: "And you see and hear how this fellow Paul has convinced and led astray large numbers of people here in Ephesus and in practically the whole province of Asia" (Acts 19:26).

Other examples could be cited, but these suffice to make the point. As George Peters affirms, "Great-campaign evangelism was the methodological fountain which gave birth to the church of Jesus Christ."[2]

C. E. Matthews argues that there are only two timeless, biblical methods of evangelism: mass and personal. He says,

> Any soul that was ever won to Christ by another, regardless of time, place, or condition, was reached either through mass or personal evangelism. Neither of these methods can succeed without the other. They are Siamese twins. Without mass evangelism, personal evangelism loses its inspiration and its power. Mass evangelism is pulpit evangelism. It is God's method.[3]

In other words, while special approaches and tools can be applied to any given age or context, mass evangelism as a primary means of sharing the gospel transcends the passing of time.

Church history bears testimony to God's blessing on mass evangelism. Names such as Whitefield, Wesley, Edwards, Asbury, Finney, Moody, Smith, Chapman, Torrey, and Sunday bring to mind images of proclamation evangelism in settings as diverse as cathedrals, colleges, concert halls, coal mines, camp meetings, and cow pastures. In our own day, Billy Graham and Luis Palau are among the most prominent of a whole host of itinerant evangelists who are proclaiming the gospel throughout the world in large crusades, cooperative revival meetings, or single church evangelistic emphases.

Revival meetings have been an important tool in Southern Baptist life in helping churches maximize their opportunity to impact their community. Chuck Kelley, professor of evangelism at New Orleans Baptist Theological Seminary, states, "The strength of revivalism as a method of evangelism among Southern Baptists is undeniable."[4]

Bill Cathey calls attention to the correlation between revival meetings and the number of baptisms in a given year, noting that in the years when Southern Baptists used nationwide simultaneous revivals, including 1950, 1951, 1955, and 1964, baptisms increased significantly.[5]

Southern Baptists, with their practice of believer's baptism, have generally utilized baptism statistics as an indication of the number of conversions in that year. In the 1980s and 1990s Southern Baptists have conducted simultaneous revival meetings in 1986 and 1990 and plan to again in 1995. In 1986 and 1990, baptisms increased significantly across the convention, while the years following simultaneous efforts they fell. Revival meetings clearly have impacted the results of evangelism in the Southern Baptist Convention.

Current Situation and Challenges

As we enter the final few years of the second millennium, some are arguing that mass evangelism's days are numbered. Critics argue that rapidly changing culture, particularly in North America, has made this approach irrelevant. The fast-paced 1990s do in fact provide many more options for people to spend their time than did the 1950s. Furthermore, lost people do not attend religious meetings as readily as they did in the 1950s. The televangelist scandals have helped bring the public's opinion of evangelists to what may be an all-time low.

What are we to make of this? Clearly, the practice of mass evangelism is changing. The days of the two-week revival meetings are probably gone. Even eight-day meetings are rarely used anymore. Most venues are set up for Sunday through Wednesday, or perhaps Wednesday through Sunday. Many churches today are going to one-day "Harvest" events, while other churches have abandoned the local church revival meeting altogether. Yet as Bill Cathey argues, "The answer to the dilemma is not to forsake revival meetings *but to alter our approach in preparing for them.*"[6]

Mark Twain once noted, "The reports of my death have been greatly exaggerated." So too are the reports of the death of mass evangelism. Those who are predicting the end of evangelistic crusades when Billy Graham passes from the scene would do well to learn from the following quotation from Oswald Smith, the great Canadian evangelist from a previous era:

> Well, now, where in such a church is there room for an Evangelist? Why, he is simply crowded out, for that kind of programme doesn't need him. Think you the churches of today are pleading for evangelistic services? Could Crossley and Hunter persuade the worldly churches of this Laodicean age to close their doors and unite in a city-wide campaign? Can you picture the modernistic ministers of this generation sitting together on the same platform, lauding, praising and backing a Moody and Sankey campaign? Certainly not. Evangelism has been ruled out of court. It is no longer the order of the day. Nor will the churches ever again throw open their doors to travelling Evangelists, as they did a generation ago. That peculiar type of Evangelism has gone and gone forever.[7]

Oswald Smith was a great man, but he clearly wasn't a prophet. Just as Smith could not possibly foresee the rise of Billy Graham's worldwide ministry, so the prognosticators of our own day may find themselves looking rather foolish at their confident assertions about the future of revival meetings.

In the remainder of this chapter, we will look to the future of mass evangelism. As a foundation, we will first examine some of the benefits provided by mass evangelism.

Benefits of Mass Evangelism

One obvious benefit of mass evangelism is that it provides an occasion where the gospel can be heard by hundreds and even thousands of people. One evangelist can communicate the Good News of Jesus Christ to many persons at one time. Whether the preaching results in conversion or in the planting of gospel seeds, many persons are impacted. Numbers are significant because numbers represent people.

Another benefit is the general raising of "God-consciousness" in the area where a revival meeting is being held. Persons are reminded about the issues of time and eternity whether or not they attend any of the public meetings. This general awareness provides an excellent opportunity for believers to begin conversations with persons on spiritual topics.[8]

Training of believers in witnessing and follow-up is often a benefit of crusades. Many persons who have been Christians for years learn for the first time how to share their faith and disciple a younger believer. Through the training provided by the crusade, the goal of Ephesians 4:11-12 begins to be realized: "[God gave] . . . some to be evangelists . . . to prepare God's people for works of service."

Unity among churches and Christians is another benefit of mass evangelism, one that ultimately contributes to furthering the cause of reaching people for Christ. Did not our Lord tell us, "All men will know that you are my disciples, if you love one another" (John 13:35)?

Mass Evangelism in the 90s and Beyond

Importance of relevance. The apostle Paul's example must be taken seriously by all who desire to be effective in reaching others for Christ. Paul affirms:

Though I am free and belong to no man, I make myself a slave to everyone, to win as many as possible. To the Jews I became like a Jew, to win the Jews. To those under the law I became like one under the law (though I myself am not under the law), so as to win those under the law. To those not having the law I became like one not having the law (though I am not free from God's law but am under Christ's law), so as to win those not having the law. To the weak I became weak, to win the weak. I have become all things to all men so that by all possible means I might save some. I do all this for the sake of the gospel, that I may share in its blessings. (1 Cor. 9:19-23)

Are we willing to "become all things to all men" so that by all possible means we might save some? This does not mean compromise. There is a difference between relevance and compromise. Robert Mounce offers sound advice:

> Much modern talk about the necessity for relevant preaching misses the mark because it interprets relevancy as no more than a sort of friendly rapport with the spirit of the age. It deals with the Gospel and man's culture, not the Gospel and man's need. Its concept of what makes preaching relevant lies much too close to the surface of things. Just because a sermon is couched in the latest idiom and addressed to a contemporary situation does not make it truly relevant. To be genuinely relevant it must be addressed to man's ultimate spiritual need. It must deal with those questions that lie at the heart of human existence. It must answer man's predicament. It must deal with sin and offer salvation. Only the preaching of the Gospel is preaching that is truly relevant.[9]

The gospel must not change (Gal. 1:8-9). Our approach to sharing that message can and must change. What are some contemporary approaches to mass evangelism?

Special event evangelism. Churches in the 90s are increasingly turning to evangelistic events to reach the masses. This is especially true in urban and suburban settings. For example, some churches use musical artists who employ an evangelistic appeal; some will have a series of events aimed at the unchurched.

Other churches employ mass evangelism events related to special occasions. One church provided a Valentine's banquet for the couples of their area. A local personality shared his Christian testimony, which resulted in several placing their faith in Christ.

Block parties are another approach. A church may hold a neighborhood party, inviting people from the surrounding area to come for a meal and entertainment. The gospel is shared as a part of this experience. Several churches used this approach in Indianapolis prior to the Southern Baptist Convention meeting in 1992. As a result, almost one hundred people professed faith in Christ.

Using events such as these do not replace the necessity of preaching or the importance of the evangelist. They simply enhance mass evangelism by adapting it to particular contexts.

Affinity group evangelism. One approach receiving a great deal of attention today is known as "affinity group evangelism." Affinity evangelism means to reach out with the gospel of our Lord Jesus Christ to a group of people who have common needs, common interests, or common vocations, or who belong to a community or fraternity.[10] It is simply another way of saying we must "reach people where they are." Many evangelists, including Billy Graham, as evidenced by his recent crusades in Cleveland and Atlanta, are finding fertile fields in the 90s among young people.

Reaching Students with the Gospel in the 90s

Perhaps the most exciting and effective part of mass evangelism today relates to young people. It is increasingly difficult to get adults to come to crusade meetings. However, since most people come to Christ before they are twenty years of age, it is imperative to "strike when the iron is hot." In most revival meetings, the vast majority of decisions for salvation take place on a designated "Youth Night." Following a Sunday-through-Wednesday format, this is normally held on Tuesday evening.

The size of the church or meeting place has nothing to do with the success of Youth Night. Teens are the single most accessible group to utilize in bringing their lost friends to a "Harvest" event. The main reason for this is the school system. Students are daily surrounded with lost people. In Dr. Oscar Thompson's book *Concentric Circles of Concern*, he demonstrates how personal relationships are effective channels of evangelism. He remarks, "The gospel moves on continuous lines—on lines of relationship."[11]

Teenagers are willing to inconvenience themselves in reaching their peers. They will take risks to invite their friends to a crusade service. But this begs the question "How does an evangelist go about getting the students to actually bring their friends?" Obviously, the evangelist must possess a deep love for and an ability to communicate with youth. On a practical level, two things have worked well for me: 1) employing a youth associate; and 2) pizza.

The single most important element in my ministry is having a youth associate who travels with me weekly to the meetings. I realize that is not an option for all evangelists, but I can state without any reservation that he is the most valuable asset I have. His specific responsibility is Youth Night. He comes in on Saturday and gets acquainted with the youth minister. Sometimes on Saturday morning there is a youth visitation. Sunday morning the associate does a joint Sunday school rally with all the students. This introduces him to students, and normally there will be a number of decisions made during the rally.

Sunday afternoon we do a "Bring 'em Back Alive" emphasis to encourage the young persons to bring their friends to the Sunday night service. After the Sunday night service is over, the associate will meet all the teenagers in a designated area. He hands out pizza tickets and asks students to give them out to their friends.

Monday and Tuesday, the associate goes to the schools to speak to classes, address students at a full assembly program when possible, or just eat lunch with the students from the youth group. This "hands-on approach" brings great dividends.

The pizza "blast" provides a venue that is easy to invite someone to attend. Typically, for every ten tickets handed out, one student will visit. If five thousand tickets are distributed, normally your attendance will be between 350 and 500. Can you get excited about preaching the gospel to five hundred young people? I can!

Over the years there has been some legitimate criticism about "gimmicks." After evaluating several other options to use as incentives, I have found pizza still works the best at drawing a crowd of young people. Nothing else is even a close second. Yet in using this approach we must "advertise with integrity." We must make it clear that there will be a "religious service" following the pizza blast.

Regardless of the size of church, this is an effective vehicle to use. I have preached at nearly seven hundred Youth Nights, and I am convinced that the combination of a youth associate plus pizza is a winner for the '90s. If a youth associate is not used, you can still have the rally with the evangelist and involve the local schools. Any level of involvement will help.

I would like to share an illustration to put this approach in perspective. The value of one person in this process should not go unmentioned. Three months after a meeting, a woman who was an active member of a church's intercessory prayer ministry called one day to share a blessing. She had been in the prayer room when a call came in. At the other end of the phone was a scared, upset seventeen-year-old girl named Rebecca (name changed to protect her identity). She had been kicked out of her house because of an unplanned pregnancy.

This woman left the prayer room and drove across town to pick up Rebecca. She invited Rebecca to come to her home, which she did. After staying at the woman's home for a few days, Rebecca asked her why she had been so kind to her, a total stranger. The woman said that it was because of Jesus and the personal relationship she had with him. She had the privilege of leading Rebecca in a prayer of commitment to Christ as her Lord and Savior.

She then asked Rebecca how she knew to call the prayer room. Rebecca reached in her purse and pulled out a crumbled pizza ticket that was one of the twenty-two thousand the teenagers had handed out three months earlier. In my office I have a picture of a nine-month old baby boy (Rebecca's son) plus a letter of thanks. That was the result of one ticket! There are "Rebeccas" all over the world waiting for someone to share Jesus with them.

"Frontliners"—a balanced approach between mass evangelism, personal witnessing, and discipleship training.

Pastors have a legitimate concern about the productivity of summer revival meetings. Several years ago, we began something in our own ministry that literally revolutionized our summer meetings. Each year from mid-June until mid-August, we have youth groups join us in our crusades. They are called "Frontliners."

Here is how the concept works. Our revival meeting becomes their mission trip. For example, in Denver, Colorado, we did a multiple church crusade with about ten churches. What takes place once the youth group gets to the church field is awesome to behold. From the time they become a part of the crusade until they leave, the excitement is electrifying.

In the mornings we meet at about 9:00. From 9:00 until noon we have discipleship training. We use outstanding speakers to train the students in areas such as having a personal devotional life (quiet time), how to witness, and how to have a personal Bible study. The students follow along in their Frontliner manuals.

Each year we establish a theme. Recently our theme was moral purity. After the Bible study time, we have a contemporary worship service that is geared for students. At noon they eat lunch. From 1:00 until 4:30 in the afternoon, they go out to share their faith and hand out gospel tracts (we use Billy Graham's *Steps to Peace with God*) and pizza tickets. They go to malls, parks, swimming pools, bowling alleys, and anywhere else teens hang out.

The more mature youth are called the "Posse." They tackle the tougher areas in town. In one crusade in Nashville, these students (350 of them) made twenty-six thousand contacts. They lead backyard Bible clubs, conduct door-to-door surveys, or whatever the host church feels would be most beneficial.

In Las Vegas, the Frontliners were most effective doing backyard Bible clubs. In Denver they were most effective doing door-to-door surveys. The main idea is to get the students outside the walls of the church and face-to-face with lost persons, where in a loving, tactful manner they can share Jesus.

In Dothan, Alabama, one twelve-year-old boy witnessed to an eighteen-year-old bag boy at a local grocery store. The older boy said he was interested in the message, but he had to go back to work. The unusually bold twelve-year-old didn't stop there. He went to the manager's office and told him he was a "Frontliner" from Texas, visiting in Dothan. He asked the manager's permission to allow the bag boy a ten-minute break so he could share the gospel with him. The manager, who we later discovered was a Christian, graciously allowed his employee time off to sit down with this young man, who led him to Jesus.

In Clarksville, Tennessee, one church group went to a swimming pool to witness. When they finished, thirty-nine teens made a decision to follow Jesus as Savior and Lord. The beauty of Frontliners is not just the excitement and boldness. The teens on the mission trip grow spiritually as they learn to trust God in new areas of their lives.

Frontliners has worked in churches with three hundred in attendance and in areawide crusades with five thousand in attendance. The key is to take only as many with you as the local church or churches can house. A church that has three hundred members can probably only house about forty to fifty students; but an areawide crusade could perhaps house three hundred to four hundred students in the homes of members of the sponsoring churches.

Frontliners is a combination of discipleship training and personal witnessing merged with mass evangelism. It combines the excitement of a youth camp with practical methods of sharing one's faith. It helps the young people to become more grounded in the Word of God.

The effects of the Frontliners' ministry can linger for months. One youth minister wrote to me nine months after his students had participated and said their evangelism was up by 67 percent, an increase he directly attributed to the Frontliners experience.

Conclusion

Mass evangelism has a solid biblical and historical foundation. It has been greatly used by God to bring many lost persons into a saving relationship with Jesus Christ. While it is not the only method of evangelism, its importance should not be minimized. Those who proclaim God's Word must continually seek to adapt approaches to fit different times and cultures.

Our Lord pointed to the enduring aspect of proclamation evangelism: "And this gospel of the kingdom will be preached in the whole world as a testimony to all nations, and then the end will come" (Matt. 24:14). Mass evangelism that is culturally sensitive will be effective as long as there are masses to reach. In the words of Fanny Crosby, may we use whatever means we can, including mass evangelism, to "Rescue the Perishing":

> Rescue the perishing; care for the dying.
> Snatch them in pity from sin and the grave.
> Weep o'er the erring one; lift up the fallen.
> Tell them of Jesus, the mighty to save.
> Rescue the perishing;
> Care for the dying.
> Jesus is merciful; Jesus will save.
> Plead with them earnestly; plead with them gently.
> He will forgive if they only believe.
> Rescue the perishing; duty demands it.
> Strength for thy labor the Lord will provide.
> Back to the narrow way, patiently win them.
> Tell the poor wand'rer a Savior has died.[12]

Endnotes

1. This is not to say that these examples contain all the elements which characterize contemporary mass evangelism. However, they do point to the significance of proclamation evangelism to large groups of people in the biblical period. While some might make distinctions between the terms *mass evangelism, revival meeting, evangelistic campaign,* and *crusade,* they will be used as synonyms in this chapter.

2. George Peters, "Great-Campaign Evangelism," in *Crucial Issues in Missions Tomorrow,* ed. by Donald A. McGavran (Chicago: Moody Press, 1972), 206.

3. C. E. Matthews, *The Southern Baptist Program of Evangelism* (Atlanta: Home Mission Board, 1949), 9.

4. Charles S. Kelley, Jr., *How Did They Do It? The Story of Southern Baptist Evangelism* (New Orleans: Insight Press, 1993), 10.

5. Bill Cathey, *A New Day In Church Revivals* (Nashville: Broadman, 1984), 13.

6. Ibid., 5 (emphasis added).

7. Oswald J. Smith, *The New Evangelism* (Toronto: The Peoples Church, 1932), 10–11. The following illustration makes this same point for our day: "Some years back, two rather skeptical clergymen sat on the platform of a Billy Graham crusade. One of them said to the other, 'Why doesn't somebody tell this guy Graham that the day of mass evangelism is over?'

"Waving his hand across the overflowing stadium, his friend replied, 'Why doesn't somebody tell all these people?' " (See David Shibley, *A Force in the Earth: The Charismatic Renewal and World Evangelism* [Altamonte Springs, Fla.: Creation House, 1989], 87).

8. Richard Harris and Tom McEachin, "Planning Crusades in Single Churches," in *The Calling of An Evangelist,* ed. J. D. Douglas (Minneapolis: Worldwide Pub., 1987), 283–284.

9. Robert Mounce, *The Essential Nature of New Testament Preaching* (Grand Rapids: Eerdmans, 1960), 155–56.

10. Paul Cedar, "Affinity Groups in Evangelism," Seminar at the North American Conference for Itinerant Evangelists, Louisville, Kentucky, June 29, 1994.

11. W. Oscar Thompson, Jr., *Concentric Circles of Concern* (Nashville: Broadman, 1981), 22.

12. Fanny J. Crosby, "Rescue the Perishing," 1869.

10
The Personal Life of the Witness:
Coming Alive in Christ and Introducing Him to Others

Jack Stanton

Jack Stanton serves as director of the International Institute of Evangelism and the Jim Mellers Evangelism and Conference Center at Southwestern Baptist University, Bolivar, Missouri. He has pastored numerous churches and served several state conventions as director of evangelism. He was elected first vice president of the Southern Baptist Convention in 1986 and 1987. He has authored The Christian Witness *and* How to Have a Full and Meaningful Life.

Peter and John had just experienced the joy of sharing Christ effectively. Thousands became followers of Jesus. Unfortunately, the Sadducees were unhappy. They captured the two apostles for interrogation. Peter again boldly proclaimed the Gospel. Luke recorded two interesting observations at this juncture: The Jewish religious leaders recognized that the two had been with Jesus (Acts 4:13); and Peter declared to the leaders, "We cannot help speaking about what we have seen and heard" (Acts 4:20). These men had obviously been transformed through their relationship with Christ. As a result they gave a powerful witness to him.

The Christian witness is a person who through a personal experience with Christ knows or has seen something and is therefore competent to give evidence. The witness a Christian gives is a witness to Christ. It is not a witness to our goodness, to a certain plan, or to religious activities. This witness emerges from a Christ-redeemed and Christ-controlled life.

If we do not let others know that the abundant life we possess is from Christ, we will confuse those who seek such a life, and God will not receive the glory that should be his. It is of utmost importance to live right, and it is equally important to speak for Christ. To leave out either is like trying to fly a plane with one wing. Both wings of a plane are needed to fly the plane, and both a dedicated life and a verbal proclamation are needed for an effective witness for Christ.

Witnessing is not a set of hard, fast rules memorized and used. It is not a list of Scripture verses to be used to overpower a person into a decision. It is simply sharing with others what we know by experience to be true in and through Jesus Christ. Any Christian can do this, and every Christian is expected to do this: "You will be my witnesses" (Acts 1:8).

In order to tell others about Christ, we must know him in a very personal way.

The Personal Experience of the Witness

The apostle John wrote:

> We are writing to you about something which has always existed yet which we ourselves actually heard and saw with our own eyes: something which we had opportunity to observe closely and even to hold in our hands, something of the Word of life! For it was life which appeared before us: we saw it, we are eye-witnesses of it, and are now writing to you about it. It was the very life of all ages, the life that has always existed with the Father, which actually became visible in person to us. We repeat, we really saw and heard what we are now writing to you about. We want you to be with us in this—in this fellowship with the Father, and Jesus Christ his Son. (1 John 1:1-3, Phillips)

We cannot share what we do not have. Unless we have experienced new life in Christ and walk with him daily, we will have no message of hope to share.

In the beginning, God created human beings in his image. He gave to them will, intellect, and emotion. He walked and talked with them in fellowship. Becoming dissatisfied, they became openly disobedient—rebels against God. Romans 5:12 reveals, "Sin entered the world through one man, and death through sin, and in this way death came to all men, because all sinned." God did not forsake his creation, however, for Paul also wrote: "But God demonstrates his own love for us in this: While we were still sinners, Christ died for us" (Romans 5:8).

Jesus demonstrated this love by coming to earth "to seek and to save what was lost" (Luke 19:10). He came that we might have life and have it more abundantly. Humanity is now divided into two classes—the saved and the lost. Many words are used to describe the acquiring of this new life. Such terms as "born again," "converted," "saved," "accepted Christ," "believed on Christ," "trusted Christ," and "inherited eternal life" are used to describe the unique experience of becoming a Christian.

Nicodemus (see John 3:1-21) came to Jesus by night to inquire about this new life. He was a member of the strictest religious sect of his day, a religious and civil leader, and yet Jesus made it plain that unless he was born again he could not understand or participate in the kingdom of God.

The new birth is not acknowledging Jesus as a teacher come from God, for Nicodemus did this. Jesus is not the one who *shows* the way; he *is* the Way. Neither is the new birth the accumulation of enough good works to merit God's attention and redemption. No doubt Nicodemus had many good works to recommend him, but we are told, "For it is by grace you have been saved, through faith—and this not from yourselves, it is the gift of God—not by works, so that no one can boast. For we are God's workmanship, created in Christ Jesus to do good works, which God prepared in advance for us to do" (Eph. 2:8-10). Good works enter in, but they are a product of, and not a pathway to, salvation. Nor is church membership or religious activity the new birth. There is little question but that Nicodemus knew the Scriptures, tithed, and engaged in the various religious ceremonies of his religion, but these could never suffice for the new birth.

Sincerity is not the new birth, for a man can be sincerely wrong as well as sincerely right.

The Bible makes plain the way to be born again. It says, "For you have been born again, not of perishable seed, but of imperishable, through the living and enduring word of God" (1 Pet. 1:23). To be saved or born again is to ask Jesus, who died for you and was raised from the dead, to be the Lord of your life (Romans 10:9-13). This must be more than an intellectual assent to truth. It must be a total commitment, in which you turn your life over to him.

A young couple stands before a minister to be married. In answer to the minister's inquiry, "Will you take this woman as your wife?" the man responds, "I do." This is his confession with his mouth that he loves the woman by his side and will leave all others to live with her. As the young lady also responds in the affirmative, the minister pronounces them husband and wife. How they feel at this point will be determined by their emotional makeup and the surrounding circumstances. But how they feel will not alter the fact that they are married.

So it is with those who commit their lives to Christ in humble, simple faith. They do not know all the future holds, but their love for Christ and his love for them will sustain them in the days ahead. The strength we need to face the problems of daily living is found in Christ.

Do you remember when you made your commitment to Christ and experienced the new birth?

The Power of the Personal Testimony

The personal testimony has always been an invaluable part of a believer's witness. Scripture is replete with examples: the blind man in John 9, Paul in Acts 22 and 26, and so on. In our day, however, when many people do not share our high value of Scripture, our life and the change wrought by Christ becomes imperative. People today are keenly interested in spiritual matters. Sharing our experience with Christ can help demonstrate to others the reality of the Christian experience. Christianity is not a mere religion; it is a relationship!

Dr. Kenneth Chafin reminds us:

> The sharing of personal testimony is a wonderful way to witness. It is impossible to read the book of Acts without being impressed with Paul's use of his personal testimony. It is difficult to imagine Paul's speaking very long without sharing his experience with Christ. Every person who has come to know God through Jesus Christ has an experience to share. The sharing of this experience is a vital part of Christian witnessing.[1]

Your conversion testimony can play a vital role in witnessing. Perhaps you were converted as a child and think that your testimony is unimportant. Most testimonies we hear in public are of those who were involved in some gross sin in their past. Be assured, your salvation is as important to God as that of Paul, Billy Graham, or any other! Tell your story. Persons with whom you witness can identify with you as they hear your story. Here are some practical tips as you prepare to share your story with others:

1. Write out your testimony, seeking the Spirit's guidance.

2. Focus on three areas: your life before Christ, how you came to know Christ, and the difference knowing Christ makes today.

3. Give adequate but precise details showing how Christ became your Lord and Savior and how Christ meets your daily needs.

4. Use language the nonbeliever can understand.

5. Relive your testimony as you tell it. This will enable you to present it with loving enthusiasm.

6. Relate your testimony to the Scriptures, using pertinent verses as they are needed.

7. When you share the testimony, speak distinctly and in a natural tone, avoiding any mannerisms that might detract from the presentation.

8. Be brief (two to three minutes). People are interested in your testimony, but not your life story!

9. Ask the Holy Spirit to help you present Christ so that the unbeliever will want to know him and will come to know him personally.

10. Share your Christian testimony with other Christian members of your family, then with Christian friends, until it becomes a natural part of your daily conversation. Then share it with your lost friends and others.

The moment a person accepts Christ as Lord and Savior, he or she has the initial preparation necessary for witnessing. New believers have a story to tell! Now they can introduce the Christ they know and love to others who need him.

The woman at the well (see John 4) met Jesus and was so transformed by this experience that she left her water pot to hurry to the city to tell the people about Christ. It is recorded: "Many of the Samaritans from that town believed in him because of the woman's testimony" (John 4:39).

The man in the tombs (see Mark 5:1-19) is a vivid example of life without Christ and the changes that take place when Christ comes in. Possessed by an unclean spirit, he lived with the dead. The broken chains gave mute evidence of the binding of sin and the rebellious nature at war with everything and everyone.

Then Jesus came and changed everything. The man was suddenly seated, clothed, and in his right mind. Jesus had healed the fever of sin and clothed him with a robe of righteousness.

So much happened in this initial encounter with Christ that the Gadarene asked to join Jesus on his trip. However, Jesus said to him, "Go home to your family and tell them how much the Lord has done for you, and how he has had mercy on you" (Mark 5:19).

When I first became a Christian, I knew very little about the Bible, the church, or the Christian life. However, I did know that I had met Christ and that he had changed my life. Encouraged by the fact that the man who led me to Christ had only been a Christian for two days when he witnessed to me, I began to share with my friends and others what I had experienced through Jesus Christ. In spite of my feeble and sometimes crude attempts at witnessing, I was amazed and happy to see many of my friends commit their lives to Jesus Christ.

The basic step in preparation for witnessing is a vital life-changing experience with Christ. If we know his love and forgiveness, if in our daily life we find him to be our friend and guide, it will be natural to want others to know him. We gladly speak of those we love and unashamedly introduce our friends and loved ones to others. Genuine love for Christ will prompt us to share him with those who need his love and forgiveness.

Spiritual Preparation for Witnessing

We should never be content with remaining immature Christians. We must "like newborn babies, crave pure spiritual milk, so that by it you may grow up in your salvation" (1 Pet. 2:2), and continue to "grow in grace and knowledge of our Lord and Savior Jesus Christ" (2 Pet. 3:18).

There must be complete and continued consecration to Christ if we are to be adequately prepared to witness effectively. We must stay in constant communion with God. When sin breaks this fellowship, we must immediately confess and forsake it. John F. Crosby reminds us that "in confession we fight through our unworthy desires, our honest reservations, our limited commitment, our foolish decisions, our hasty remarks, our silence when we should have spoken."[2]

Is there unconfessed sin that hinders your witness? If so, confess it and know the joy of renewed fellowship and power. "If we confess our sins, he is faithful and just and will forgive us our sins and purify us from all unrighteousness" (1 John 1:9).

Most of us feel inadequate and weak. Is there power available that will make us the witnesses we ought to be? Jesus said, "Anyone who has faith in me will do what I have been doing. He will do greater things than these, because I am going to the Father" (John 14:12). Jesus prefaced the great commission with, "All power is given unto me in heaven and in earth" (Matt. 28:18, KJV), indicating that if the disciples would go with the gospel, he would supply the power.

There are many sources of power available to the alert Christian, but let me call your attention to four basic ones.

Be a student of the Scriptures

The Bible provides the basis for our assurance. "I write these things to you who believe in the name of the Son of God so that you may know that you have eternal life" (1 John 5:13).

We can believe God and trust his Word. The Bible is the basis for our authority. The early Christians turned to the Word of God as their source of life and faith. They used it as a textbook of education, and it helped them lay a solid foundation for a truly Christian family life.

God's Word, like God himself, is the same yesterday, today, and forever. It cannot lie, for its Author cannot lie. Its message speaks with eternal authority and in relevant terms to the great issues of life, death, and life after death. We are not left without a message from God, for God has spoken through his Word, the Bible.

What we believe about the Bible will determine the message we give to the world. The Bible is inspired—"God-breathed" (2 Tim. 3:16). This does not mean that it is inspired only as it inspires the mind of a person, but that the text is inspired. It remains true whether accepted or rejected. It is infallible. It never deceives or misleads and is trustworthy and reliable. We must never lose the anchor of the authority of the Bible, or we will drift into sentimentality and be thrown upon the resources of the human mind, which are not sufficient to meet the need.

A. M. Chirgwin quotes Chrysostom as saying:

> The worst thing about it . . . is that you believe that Bible-reading is purely a matter for monks. You say, I have to give my attention to public business; I carry on a trade; I must look after my wife and children and servants; in short, I am a man of the world, it is not my business to read the Bible; that is the business of people who have renounced the world and devote themselves to a lonely life upon the tops of mountains.[3]

The early Christians used the reading of the Bible to spread the faith. They appealed to the Scriptures even when dealing with pagans. This seems odd since the Bible meant nothing to pagans, and one would not expect them to be moved by arguments based on such documents. However, it was so effective that the Bible became the regular tool of their evangelism.

A prepared witness will be a sincere student of the Scriptures. Jesus said, "Study the Scriptures because you think that by them you possess eternal life. These are the Scriptures that testify about me" (John 5:39). The disciples in Berea were called noble because "they received the message with great eagerness and examined the Scriptures every day" (Acts 17:11).

A daily, systematic study of the Bible will enrich the life of believers and enable them to share their faith more effectively. Many wonderful tools are available to assist us in studying God's Word. Some students of the Bible find it especially helpful to take a Bible passage, outline it, and then summarize it in their own words. This enables them to have a good grasp of the scriptural truth and be able to explain it to a nonbeliever in language he or she will understand.

Another profitable study is to trace a certain subject through the Bible. It might be helpful to list subjects you are interested in on the blank pages of your Bible. As you find Bible verses related to these subjects, list the references under the appropriate subjects for later use.

Scripture memorization is very helpful in developing the life of the believer and in quickly providing scriptural answers to questions asked by interested inquirers. "I have hidden your word in my heart that I might not sin against you" (Ps. 119:11). An excellent way to do this is to write the passage to be memorized on a card and then go over it again and again until it is learned. Do not try to learn too many, or you may become discouraged. Perhaps one or two verses a week will do, at first.

In addition, devotional books can help your Bible study. The small group study *Experiencing God* (by Henry Blackaby) has been a significant tool to help believers get started in a daily, consistent devotional life. Oswald Chambers' *My Utmost for His Highest* is a classic in the field. Other tools are available. The key is to find a method of studying Scripture that is effective and that you will stay with.

Studying Scripture will greatly enhance your witnessing as well. John Pollard, a business executive, was asked the following question by an employee: "You know a lot about Christianity. I'd give anything in this world if you would tell me how to be saved." Unfortunately, Pollard hardly knew how to answer the man. Stumbling for a suitable reply, he picked up a small New Testament, which opened at Luke 18:13, where the publican prayed, "God, have mercy on me, a sinner."

The worker was saved, but John Pollard resolved at that moment to learn better how to use the Bible to show a person how to become a Christian. As a result he developed a marked New Testament that has helped many share Christ through the years.

Experience the power of the Holy Spirit

Jesus said, "It is for your good that I am going away. Unless I go away, the Counselor will not come unto you; but if I go, I will send him to you" (John 16:7). We are not left orphans; the Holy Spirit has come to help us. As you learn to listen to his prompting, he will aid your growth in Christ.

It is the Holy Spirit who applies the redemptive work of Christ to the individual life. We are born again by the Holy Spirit. Walter G. Harbin said, "The Holy Spirit finds us sin-enslaved orphans lost amidst the meaningless immensities: He redeems us and makes us Sons of God; heirs of everlasting life."[4]

H. E. Dana reminds us that "regeneration is the initiation of a life of witnessing. In it the Holy Spirit transforms the disposition, creates a new spiritual state, and implants a new attitude toward God thus preparing the believer for a life of service."[5]

The Holy Spirit ministers to our needs. *He gives assurance.* "This is how we know that he lives in us: We know it by the Spirit he gave us" (1 John 3:24).

He instructs us in the Word. "We have not received the spirit of the world but the Spirit who is from God, that we may understand what God has freely given us. This is what we speak, not in words taught us by human wisdom but in words taught by the Spirit, expressing spiritual truths in spiritual words" (1 Cor. 2:12-13).

He guides us. "Those who are led by the Spirit of God are sons of God" (Rom. 8:14).

He intercedes for us. "In the same way, the Spirit helps us in our weakness. We do not know what we ought to pray for, but the Spirit himself intercedes for us with groans that words cannot express. And he who searches our hearts knows the mind of the Spirit, because the Spirit intercedes for the saints in accordance with God's will" (Rom. 8:26-27).

The Spirit aids our witness. *He teaches us.* "But when he, the Spirit of truth, comes, he will guide you into all truth. He will not speak on his own; he will speak only what he hears, and he will tell you what is yet to come" (John 16:13). This does not mean God will place his Word in our mind without any effort on our part. But it does mean that if we conscientiously study, the Spirit will call things to our remembrance when they are needed. Since he knows the heart and mind of the nonbeliever, he can tell us whether we are to present the tender mercies of God, or reveal the judgment of God; whether we are to continue to press for a decision, or leave to return later.

He empowers us for service. When Peter and John were commanded not to speak in the name of Jesus, they prayed,

> *"Now, Lord, consider their threats and enable your servants to speak your word with great boldness." . . . After they prayed, the place where they were meeting was shaken. And they were all filled with the Holy Spirit and spoke the word of God boldly (Acts 4:29, 31).*

He dwells in us to make us more like Jesus. "Don't you know that you yourselves are God's temple and that God's Spirit lives in you?" (1 Cor. 3:16).

He convicts of sin. He will reprove the world of sin, and of righteousness, and of judgment. We cannot convict people by manipulation, threat, or a display of human wisdom. This is the work of the Holy Spirit, and he will accomplish it if we will present the gospel.

A sensitivity to the Holy Spirit is a mark of the prepared witness. The one essential in effective witnessing is the Spirit of God. Without him, we do not know where to go or what to say. There is no magic formula to be followed in witnessing; the Spirit must ever be our guide.

Many are dying without Christ because we often let the pressure of *good* things keep us from doing the *best.* We must constantly take advantage of every God-given opportunity to witness for Christ before it is forever too late. Will you, in quiet prayer, ask God to fill you with his Spirit, make you more Christlike, and help you to witness for Christ each day? He will help you if you ask.

Prevail in prayer

Prevailing prayer opens up the floodgates of God's presence and power to help prepare the witness. We are admonished to "pray without ceasing" (1 Thess. 5:17, KJV). Most of us wait until we faint before we pray even though Jesus said that we should "always pray and not give up" (Luke 18:1). The great saints of the past prayed for hours, sometimes spending all night on their knees. Jesus made much of prayer. He prayed early in the morning (Mark 1:35), in the evening (Mark 6:46), and all night (Luke 16:12).

It is very helpful to set apart a definite time each day for prayer. Let it be a quiet time alone with God, shut off from the everyday distractions of life. "But when you pray, go into your room, close the door and pray to your Father, who is unseen. Then your Father, who sees what is done in secret, will reward you" (Matt. 6:6). The practice of praying aloud in these "closet" prayer meetings has been very helpful to some.

Many prefer to pray early in the morning. They like to speak with God before they speak with others and find this gives help and strength for the day. Throughout the day, we should speak with Christ from time to time as naturally as we would with anyone else present with us and interested in our activities. A practical aid for many is journaling. Many saints, including John Wesley, Jonathan Edwards, and George Whitefield made use of a journal to record events, concerns, and prayers. In addition, many find using lists of prayer requests helpful.

We must pray for ourselves, for forgiveness, for strength, for guidance, for right attitudes, and proper motivation in witnessing. We must pray for our fellow believers, that they would be encouraged and strengthened. We must pray for the lost. In many of our churches, we are bold to pray for the sick by name, but hesitate to pray for the lost by name. We spend more time praying for sick bodies than we do for sick spirits, even though the body dies and the spirit lives on. Do not fail to pray for the lost by name. You may be the only one who cares enough to pray.

Before Elijah prayed the prayer that brought fire down from heaven and Israel back to God, he repaired the altar that was broken down (1 Kings 18:30). It may be that our lack of power speaks of "altars" that need to be repaired. Take inventory concerning the following hindrances to prayer:

Wrong motive: "You want something but don't get it. You kill and covet, but you cannot have what you want. You quarrel and fight. You do not have, because you do not ask God. When you ask, you do not receive, because you ask with the wrong motives, that you may spend what you get on your pleasures" (James 4:2-3).

Sin in the life: "Surely the arm of the LORD is not too short to save, nor his ear too dull to hear. But your iniquities have separated you from your God; your sins have hidden his face from you, so that he will not hear" (Isa. 59:1-2).

Idols in the heart: "Son of man, these men have set up idols in their hearts and put wicked stumbling blocks before their faces. Should I let them inquire of me at all?" (Ezek. 14:3).

Unforgiving spirit: "And when you stand praying, if you hold anything against anyone, forgive him, so that your Father in heaven may forgive you your sins" (Mark 11:25).

Selfishness in giving: "If a man shuts his ears to the cry of the poor, he too will cry out and not be answered" (Prov. 21:13).

Wrong treatment of spouse: "Husbands, in the same way be considerate as you dwell with your wives, and treat them with respect as the weaker partner and as heirs with you of the gracious gift of life, so that nothing will hinder your prayers" (1 Pet. 3:7).

Great revivals have always been preceded by great praying. A little invalid woman, shut up in a room in London, prayed for two years that Moody would come to England. God answered her prayers, and a revival swept over England under Moody's preaching. It was there he felt he received his "roving commission," which led him into an evangelistic ministry around the world. Before he died, he personally witnessed hundreds of thousands say yes to Christ.

Fellowship and worship with a local church

The New Testament reveals nothing of isolated Christians. To become a Christian was to identify with other Christians and worship and work with them. New Testament evangelism flowed out from the church and back into the church.

The church was not an afterthought with God; it was in his mind from the beginning. Jesus said, "I will build my church; and the gates of hell shall not prevail against it" (Matt. 16:18, KJV). When the critics of the church are gone, the church will remain, for it is the Lord's church, and he has promised to build it.

The church provides inspiration. Here we worship God and enjoy the greatest fellowship on earth. Here the battle-scarred warrior for Christ finds rest and renewal in the singing of the great hymns, the earnest prayers, and the reading and proclaiming of the Word of God.

The church promotes instruction. In the great commission, the church is told to teach everything Christ had commanded. By preaching, through teaching and training groups, and by missionary and evangelistic endeavor, the church seeks to carry out this mandate. The church plans for involvement of its people, and this produces understanding and an inner strength. This involvement relates, not only to the church services, but to all of life.

A life consumed by Christ demonstrates his compassion

The result of a growing relationship with Christ is the same compassion he demonstrated for the lost. Compassionate concern for the nonbeliever identifies the prepared witness. Method always follows motive. When we care enough, we find a way of expressing that love and concern. Our problem is not that we do not know enough to witness; our problem is that we do not care enough.

Perhaps we lack concern because we really do not believe all persons apart from Christ are lost and bound for hell. We look on the outside and see the appearance of respectability, but God looks on the inside and sees wickedness. When we read Luke 16:19-31 and Revelation 20:11-15 and 21:8, it is sobering to remember that these are experiences all who die outside of Christ must face.

Christlike concern will cause us to seek out the lost, make friends with them, and attempt to cultivate a relationship that will produce a sympathetic hearing for the gospel. How many nonbelievers are you really friends with? Can you list six? Why not make up a "Responsibility List" of nonbelievers and seek to express God's love for them through your genuine interest and friendship.

As we go with the gospel, God will help us be even more effective in our witness for Christ. Involvement means growth. Practice helps make perfect. Witnessing for Christ is not the same as selling shoes or soap, but we do know that the "gospel . . . is the power of God for the salvation of everyone who believes" (Rom. 1:16), and that God's Word will not return void. Walk with Christ, and allow him to use you for his glory.

Endnotes

1. *The Sunday School Witnessing Plan for a Church* (sponsored jointly by the Home Mission Board and Sunday School Department, 1966), 17.
2. John F. Crosby, *Witness for Christ* (Philadelphia: Westminster, 1965), 90–91.

3. A. M. Chirgwin, *The Bible and World Evangelism* (New York: Friendship Press, 1954), 24.

4. Walter G. Harbin, *Modes of the Heavenly Life* (New Orleans: Charles O. Chalmers, 1910), 6.

5. H. E. Dana, *The Holy Spirit in Acts* (Kansas City: Central Seminary Press, 1943), 63.

11
The Secret of Effective Follow-Up

Billie Hanks, Jr.

Billie Hanks, Jr. is president of International Evangelism Association and founder of Discipleship Lodge in West Texas. He is a graduate of Baylor University and Southwestern Baptist Theological Seminary. He is the author of Everyday Evangelism *and co-editor of* Discipleship: Great Insights from the Most Experienced Disciple Makers.

In my first course as a seminary student, my heart was greatly moved as Roy Fish taught about the importance of follow-up. He assigned *The Master Plan of Evangelism* by Robert Coleman as part of our reading. The message of this book provided fresh insight and challenged my presuppositions. Soon I found myself asking questions that searched my heart: *What should I be doing about follow-up? Is a traditional new member's class adequate to meet the spiritual needs of new believers?* The answers to those questions brought honest re-evaluation and positive change in my understanding of how good personal follow-up impacts evangelism.

When we understand that follow-up is a ministry of example, we see that the Scriptures have a great deal to say on the topic. Paul exhorted the Corinthian believers, "Follow my example, as I follow the example of Christ" (1 Cor. 11:1). This clear principle echoed Jesus' words to the disciples in Matthew 4:19: "Follow me . . . and I will make you fishers of men." The unmistakable emphasis of both invitations was to learn by observation. This principle, so common to life, was the cornerstone of early Christian education.

Spiritual instruction took place in a training environment where relationships were the primary means of personal growth. Over time this relational learning environment slowly changed as Christian education began to formalize. Gradually, individual friendship-based training was replaced by the greater convenience of teaching in a classroom setting.

The earliest new believers sought to spend time talking with the apostles and other seasoned disciples who had actually known and walked with Christ. This was their best source of understanding as they attempted to follow the Lord's teaching. In time, as the individual books of Scripture were brought together in the canon, the completed Biblical text greatly aided in the equipping process. However, early manuscripts were few in number, and a high percentage of new believers could not read.

The Christian faith flourished in the first century in spite of the fact that literacy was still the privilege of the educated minority. In this environment the gospel message was passed from one person to the next through verbal communication. Early Christians were taught to explain their faith verbally as they lived out the gospel message in everyday life.[1]

Paul said, "For our gospel did not come to you in word only, but also in power and in the Holy Spirit and with full conviction; just as you know what kind of men we proved to be among you for your sake" (1 Thess. 1:5, NASB).

Paul was basically saying, "We lived among you in Thessalonica, and we presented the message of Christ to you in word and deed. We sought to do this in the power of the Holy Spirit. Why? In order that you might believe our message and have a spiritual frame of reference for your faith."

The early church's equipping process focused on the ministry of example and relational growth. Love, integrity, truth, and even ministry skills were best transmitted in the caring context of a personal friendship. The environment was one of trust and mutual encouragement. Spiritual discipline was first observed then emulated by the original generation of new believers. The balance between teaching and training was so natural that it almost seemed to flow. Perhaps Philippians 4:9 best demonstrates this foundational principle: "Whatever you have learned or received or heard from me, or seen in me—put it into practice." What we *hear* equates to teaching, and what we *see* equates to training. Both means of communication are essential to the discipling process for personal growth.

The classic saying "More things are caught than will ever be taught" defines one important aspect of effective follow-up. Although many aspects of spiritual growth can be transmitted through a corpus of Christian literature, personality, enthusiasm, laughter, and the twinkle in one's eye cannot. These experiential aspects of communication are also indispensable components of a successful follow-up ministry. While the cognitive aspects of discipleship are many, there is an intangible quality of spiritual life that seems to flow through the friendship itself.

Why is follow-up the critical link in successful evangelism? Dr. Herschel Hobbs has wisely said, "The process of evangelism is not complete until the evangelized becomes an evangelist."[2]

A breakdown in the initial follow-up or foundational equipping process can short-circuit the tremendous potential of this cycle of evangelistic multiplication. Demas, who "forsook Paul for the love of this world," could not evangelize others for Christ. John Mark, who started out well, almost failed to reproduce spiritually because of his timidity. Satan's plan for all young believers is to see them live in daily defeat, and then eventually go to heaven empty-handed. He wants churches to grow slowly, labor for addition, and totally neglect the powerful ministries of spiritual multiplication and personal follow-up.

Reflect on compounding interest, the reproductive cycles of nature, and the world's biological population explosion. Soon it will be clear why multiplication is God's primary method for replenishing the earth. One unspayed female dog and her descendants can produce 4,372 puppies in just seven generations, and one unspayed cat and her offspring can produce 80 million kittens in ten years. This same fundamental concept of multiplication applies directly to the great commission. Billy Graham has said,

> One of the first verses of Scripture that Dawson Trotman, founder of the Navigators, made me memorize was, "The things that thou hast heard of me among many witnesses, the same commit thou to faithful men, who shall be able to teach others also" (2 Timothy 2:2, KJV). This is a little like a mathematical formula for spreading the gospel and enlarging the church. Paul taught Timothy; Timothy shared what he knew with faithful men; these faithful men would then teach others also. And so the process goes on and on. If every believer followed this pattern, the Church could reach the entire world with the gospel in one generation! Mass crusades, in which I believe and to which I have committed my life, will never finish the great commission; but a one-by-one ministry will.[3]

For the church, spiritual multiplication is the essential key for fulfilling Christ's missionary mandate to make disciples (Matt. 28:19-20). Through just one committed new believer who is growing consistently, sharing his or her faith naturally, and personally training others to do the same, the entire world can eventually receive the good news of Christ.

This amazing process of spiritual multiplication is personal, enjoyable, effective, and even inexpensive. Any church in the world can do it. It simply requires the vision and commitment to train disciplers who will personally work with every new believer and new member who joins the church. Through these Christ-centered friendships, those who are trained not only grow personally but also learn the "whys" and "hows" of discipling others. This cycle of follow-up, personal growth, and evangelism is the practical expression of 2 Timothy 2:2, which Billy Graham refers to as a "one-by-one" ministry.

You may be thinking, *If the world can be evangelized in one generation through multiplication, why hasn't it already happened?* Personal evangelism will not produce multiplication in isolation from effective follow-up. In other words, personal witnessing and personal follow-up must be seen as interlocking parts of a comprehensive and intentional discipling process. Ultimately, through this New Testament approach to evangelism, lifestyle witnessing can become as natural as praying. Acts 1:8 is not merely a commission for the few believers who are called by God to pastor or teach; it is to be the ministry of the entire church.

How can we build a new generation of spiritually qualified, reproducing witnesses? The answer is painfully obvious. The process begins with you and me. We must care enough to provide good follow-up and spiritual mentorship for each new believer. The nineteenth-century North American evangelist Charles Finney once said:

> When the hearts of converts are warm with their first love, then is the time to make them fully acquainted with their Saviour, to hold him up in all his offices and relations, so as to break the power of every sin. . . . Unless this course be taken, their backsliding is inevitable. You might as well expect to roll back the waters of Niagara with your hand, as to stay the tide of their former habitudes of mind, surrounded as they are with temptation, without a deep, and thorough, and experiential acquaintance with the Saviour. And if they are thrown upon their own watchfulness and resources, for strength against temptation, instead of being directed to the Saviour, they are certain to become discouraged, and fall into dismal bondage.[4]

When should follow-up begin? Experience has shown that a ministry of example and Christian friendship should begin as soon as a new believer makes the decision to receive Christ as his or her Lord and Savior. In one major study a church discovered that 90 percent of its new members successfully completed their ten-week personal follow-up process. The reason for this success was attributed to the fact that every new member was personally assigned to a trained discipler within seventy-two hours after making a spiritual decision. When that same opportunity was offered to other new members, just one week later, the ratio of completion dropped to 70 percent. And when that training was not offered until the third week, the number of graduates dropped to only 30 percent. This long-term test with approximately four hundred new members conclusively demonstrated that every effort should be made to offer immediate follow-up assignments.[5]

Concerned churches must consistently provide trained disciplers to protect their new believers from the multitude of worldly distractions and temptations that predictably erode spiritual devotion. The Lord's parable of the sower graphically illustrates this reality:

> Listen! A farmer went out to sow his seed. As he was scattering the seed, some fell along the path, and the birds came and ate it up. Some fell on rocky places, where it did not have much soil. It sprang up quickly, because the soil was shallow. But when the sun came up, the plants were scorched, and they withered because they had no root. Other seed fell among thorns, which grew up and choked the plants, so that they did not bear grain. (Mark 4:3-7)

The ministry of example is normative in the New Testament. Philippians 3:17 says, "Join with others in following my example, brothers, and take note of those who live according to the pattern we gave you." In the same spirit Paul wrote Timothy saying, "Don't let anyone look down on you because you are young, but set an example for the believers in speech, in life, in love, in faith and in purity" (1 Tim. 4:12). In a follow-up ministry, your life is your primary means of communication. Your character is the letter that can best be read by all those whom you disciple!

In today's nomenclature, personal follow-up is at the very heart of effective new member assimilation. It functions like a tutor pointing the way to the many other equipping and educational ministries of the church. To begin this process, the following insights may prove helpful. Field tests indicate that a church's disciplers should be trained to do the following:

Focus on building friendships
No matter what Bible study material you may select for follow-up, the discipler's personal friendship with the new believer will normally be more important than the curriculum.[6]

All new believers and new members need to feel accepted and loved as persons. Many of them will be hurting and will need to be assured that they are valuable both to God and to those who represent his church. This is where friendship plays such a vital role. Win Arn comments:

> Friendships appear to be the strongest bond cementing new converts or members to their congregation. If new converts do not immediately develop meaningful friendships in their church, expect them to return to their old friendships—and ways—outside the church. Seven new friendships are a minimum; ten, fifteen, or more would be better.[7]

The First Baptist Church of Houston, Texas, has been creating this awareness and closing its "back door" for several years. To assess their assimilation need, they conducted an "Exit Survey" with three hundred members who had left the church over the space of one year. The survey called for comments on worship, education, outreach, child care, and the many other ministries of the church. Each staff member feared that the survey might reflect a spiritual weakness in their personal area of leadership. To everyone's surprise, the survey revealed that 93 percent of those who moved to other churches did so simply because they could not make a friend. They liked the preaching, believed the doctrine, were blessed by the music, and supported the church's overall ministry, but an essential need was not being met. The survey revealed the same telling truth that has now been discovered again and again. People are not just looking for friendly churches; they are looking for true Christ-centered friendships. Today over 150 seasoned disciplers are meeting that need as new members join the church.

Gary McIntosh and Glen Martin clearly define today's attrition problem:

> The "back door" is the way people leave a church. Traffic flows out of a church's back door in three ways. The first way is through death. Each year many of God's saints are called home to be with the Lord. A church typically loses to death 1 to 2 percent of its total worship attendance each year. A second way people leave a church is through "transfer." As people transfer into one church, they are also transferring out of another. In general, a church loses 2 to 3 percent of its worship attendance through this means. A third way out is through "reversion." People slowly drift away from a church without uniting with another one. In North America "reversion" accounts for 2 to 6 percent of a church's losses in worship attendance.[8]

For example, a church with two hundred in worship attendance will likely lose four people through death, six people through "transfer," and up to twelve people through "reversion," for a total of twenty-two.

Be fun to be with!

Being positive is essential for building and maintaining strong relationships. Your attitude will either draw a new believer toward spiritual growth or cause him or her to question its importance. Legalism tends to kill good follow-up, so focus on the truth and depend on the Holy Spirit to produce real joy! The Lord said, "Until now you have not asked for anything in my name. Ask and you will receive, and your joy will be complete" (John 16:24). He wants his followers to experience inner peace and happiness.

As a young believer I had the privilege of being discipled by Grady Wilson of the Billy Graham team. Grady is remembered throughout the Christian world for his amazing wit, wisdom, and humor. Though he has been with our Lord for some years now, the indelible stamp of his life's verse rings in my memory: "Consider it pure joy, my brothers, whenever you face trials of many kinds" (James 1:2).

In today's world, every new believer will be dealing with some form of personal crisis or special need. Through you, he or she can learn the scriptural approach for successfully dealing with these problems. The Lord said, "In this world you will have trouble. But take heart! I have overcome the world" (John 16:33). As you share the trials you face as a believer, your new Christian friend can learn that hardship in life is normal and should actually be expected. He or she can also see how you bring each new trial to God in prayer and receive his peace and joy. The Lord assured us when he said, "My yoke is easy and my burden is light" (Matt. 11:30).

Come to the sessions spiritually prepared

Ask God to keep you fresh for the benefit of each new believer whom you disciple. He or she deserves your best!

If you have been a Christian very long, you will doubtless recognize that pastors, Sunday school teachers, and all other Christian workers face the tyranny of the urgent. For this reason, a daily quiet time is essential. It prepares our hearts and minds for ministry, and normally should take precedence over the many harried activities of the day. Your personal discipline in Scripture memory, prayer, and Bible study will not only provide a good example for the new believer; it will also leave you better prepared for your follow-up ministry. Paul said, "Discipline yourself for the purpose of godliness" (1 Tim. 4:7, NASB). Ultimately, there is only one person who can lead you to personal growth and discipline, and that is yourself. For this reason, I am personally encouraged by periodically meditating on Philippians 4:13, which says, "I can do everything through him who gives me strength." We are all called to succeed in the endeavors that God initiates. And he is faithful to bring his will to pass: "The one who calls you is faithful and he will do it" (1 Thess. 5:24).

Intercede for specific needs

Paul said, "And my God will meet all your needs according to his glorious riches in Christ Jesus" (Phil. 4:19). Ultimately, your new friend will need to learn this spiritual reality through personal experience. This realization often takes time and reinforcement. So, as you pray, seek to be very specific, and soon he or she will begin to see how God keeps his promises. Mark 11:24 (NASB) says, "Therefore I say to you, all things for which you pray and ask, believe that you have received them, and they shall be granted you."

Years ago, I was preaching at a Presbyterian church in Australia when the phone rang. The pastor interrupted the service and said, "Reverend Hanks, you have a telephone call from the United States of America." He made it sound so ominous and official that I was afraid a relative might have died. However, to my joy, I discovered that the phone call was from my discipler Grady Wilson, who was in North Carolina. He said, "Billie, I didn't mean to interrupt a worship service. I just wanted to know any specific needs that you might have as I pray for you." I was immediately reminded of Paul's attitude when he wrote, "Night and day I constantly remember you in my prayers" (2 Tim. 1:3). Grady continued, "It's been a long time since I've seen you, Billie. I'll be coming to Australia soon. Is there anything I can bring you?" It dawned on me that Grady's caring spirit was not unlike the demonstration of love seen in Paul's relationship with Timothy, his "true child in the faith" (1 Tim. 1:2, NASB). Initial follow-up and long-term equipping both require a patient spirit and a loving heart. This is why we must learn to depend upon God to carry out his follow-up ministry through us. "For it is God who is at work in you, both to will and to work for His good pleasure" (Phil. 2:13, NASB).

Affirm spiritual progress

If your new friend is excited, join in that excitement and celebrate his or her growth at every opportunity. This will be a source of real encouragement to both of you.

Several years ago, a budding young Christian M.D. was completing his internship at John Peter Smith Hospital in Fort Worth, Texas. He joined our church, and soon we became friends. He wanted to be discipled, so it was my privilege to meet with him for the period of about one year. We would study the Scriptures together and then work out at an area health club. From the beginning we determined to memorize two verses of Scripture each week and to quote them to one another. I was pleased when I discovered his unusual eagerness to grow—he had memorized not two but three verses the very first week!

As I complimented him for his faithfulness and encouraged him over the months, he continued to hide God's Word in his heart, share his faith, take sermon notes, and enjoy a consistent daily quiet time. Those meetings were rich investments of time for both of us. Now he can do the same for others.

Some new believers will require a great deal more time and encouragement than others. So remember Paul's words in Galatians 6:9, "Let us not become weary in doing good, for at the proper time we will reap a harvest if we do not give up." This race goes not to the swift, but to the steady.

Plan ahead for fellowship

After your Bible study and prayer sessions, always leave time to just enjoy the friendship. Some good ice cream, a brisk walk, or simply talking over a hot cup of coffee can say you care.

Low-fat frozen yogurt is my favorite dairy weakness. Scores of good follow-up sessions have been closed by going to an area ice cream parlor. The biblical idea behind this practice is not too difficult to recognize. The Lord sat quietly on the hillside with his apostles, and they often enjoyed seasons of quiet, or meals and fellowship together. It is this same spirit of relaxed communication and enjoyment that should permeate a contemporary discipling relationship. Completing a portion of the curriculum each time you meet is important, but always remember to include some unstructured activity. Seek to leave each session with a feeling of expectation about the next time you plan to meet together.

Always point to Christ

Keep him at the very center of your friendship! It is important to remember that, at best, we are highly imperfect models of spiritual excellence; so magnify Christ, because he alone will never disappoint the one whom you are discipling.

Your objective is to lead new Christians not to think and act like you, but to think and act in obedience to God's word. Gary Kuhne shares wise counsel on the subject of developing Christ-centered relationships:

> Having things in common is a good aid in developing a relationship, but when it becomes the center of focus of your relationship, you become limited in your circle of friends. In 1 John 1:3 John gives us the correct focus for lasting relationships: "We proclaim to you what we have seen and heard so that you also may have fellowship with us. And our fellowship is with the Father and with his Son, Jesus Christ."
>
> John gives Christ as the focal point of true fellowship. He claims that relationships should be developed around knowing Christ. This does not mean that it is wrong to have other things in common with a person you are following up. What it does mean is that often you are going to be put in a follow-up relationship with someone with whom you have little in common. This should not prevent you from having a meaningful relationship and friendship if Christ is at the center.
>
> How do you make Christ the focus? From the very beginning of follow-up with a new Christian, spend the bulk of your time on spiritual things. This doesn't mean lecturing that person, but it does mean devoting most of your time to spiritual communication, creating an atmosphere of spiritual sharing. Make it a natural thing to share with one another what God is doing and what God is teaching you through his Word.[9]

Recognize and develop spiritual gifts

Based on Ephesians 2:8-10, it is clear that every new believer is unique and brings a wealth of ministry potential into the Christian life.

Long live diversity! The Bible emphasizes the importance of each part of the Christian body (1 Cor. 12:14-26). Through your teaching, you can help a new believer understand and appreciate his or her own spiritual gifts. The secret of deep personal fulfillment comes from utilizing those God-given gifts for the Lord's glory. In an era of chronic low self-esteem, this understanding can literally change the quality of a new believer's life.

Focus on Christian character

In a world of pretense and eroding moral values, people are starved for a balanced expression of authentic Christianity. Superficial faith, hypocrisy, and extremism have taken their toll on our credibility in the secular community. The Lord said, "Let your light shine before men, that they may see your good deeds and praise your Father in heaven" (Matt. 5:16). More light is needed, and character is the spiritual reality that wins respect and penetrates the world's darkness. Said another way, your life will open or close the doors to your personal witness.

Years ago, while teaching a course on discipleship at a Christian university, a bright young student continually visited the class even though he was not registered for the course. His warm spirit, genuine enthusiasm, and good questions brought him to my attention. I soon discovered that he was in a summer training program being offered by The Navigators. However, because of his desire to be a pastor, he did not completely fit the mold of their training profile. After three weeks he asked if he could return to Texas and work as an intern while attending seminary. We prayed and both felt good about the idea. So I talked with the Navigator representative. I will always remember his wise counsel. He definitely felt the young man had the heart and dedication required to be a good minister. But he asked me to make a promise before leaving for Texas. He asked, "Will you focus on his character?" I assured him that I would, and soon the discipling process was under way. It was a good lifelong reminder.

It will be your privilege to teach your new friend that our skills, intelligence, and natural abilities mean little or nothing unless that knowledge is translated into character and a deep, honest love for God. It is our obedience that we give back to God in appreciation for his grace (John 14:15). Perhaps Christian character is best described as the sum of all that we do and say. If new believers are led to grasp this reality, they will never feel they have arrived spiritually or become highly critical of others. Why? Because in their hearts they will know that building character and Christlikeness is a never-ending process of grace, which will be completed only in heaven.

Present spiritual multiplication

When new believers truly discover that they have an important part to play in the great commission, suddenly two things happen. First, they see a tangible goal worth achieving. Second, they receive a challenge that is great enough to captivate their hearts.

New believers are usually teachable. Their lives are the pliable clay that God desires to shape. We dare not neglect this teachable moment. If they can observe your caring spirit and see you share your faith naturally, soon they will follow. And in that process they will be spared from years of timidity. They will observe that witnessing is natural, like a flowing stream. It need not be forced. By your example, they can develop a heightened sensitivity to God's leadership and learn how to fish for people (Matt. 4:19).

What happens when a church dares to follow the early church's example and grow through spiritual multiplication? Rev. Mike Lowery, pastor of Cana Baptist Church in Burleson, Texas, took that challenge eight years ago. When he came to his pastorate, there were sixty-nine people in Sunday school and one hundred in worship attendance. He was the only staff member; he didn't even have a secretary. As he prayed, the Lord spoke to his heart. Soon he became assured that he had all the ministry tools he needed to build a strong New Testament church. His mission was to apply the scriptural guidelines for multiplication faithfully and wait for God to build spiritual leaders.

He determined that each future leader should be committed to lifestyle evangelism and practice the disciplines of personal spiritual growth. He, his wife, and six other teachable couples agreed to build their lives around the principle of 2 Timothy 2:2. Each lady agreed to equip another lady at the end of the pastor's discipler training class, and each man agreed to do the same with a man. Just eight years later, the church has over one hundred trained disciplers who personally follow up and encourage new church members.

Today, Cana Baptist averages four hundred in Sunday school and five hundred in worship. Even more important, the membership is filled with Christian love. They experience the natural joy that comes from seeing those who find Christ grow in grace and spiritual maturity. When asked if spiritual multiplication still works, the pastor replied, "You bet it does! We just have to be patient and use God's plan."

In another much larger church, step one was simply closing the "back door." This needs to occur before you can expect reproducing growth. That church observed its attrition rate fall from 53 percent to only 3 percent in a brief span of twenty-four months. What made the difference? One hundred and ninety disciplers learned how to personally assist every new member who joined the fellowship. When love becomes tangible and fellowship becomes exciting, people simply want to stay and grow. Soon they begin telling others the Good News. The secret is Christ-centered friendship that has the clear spiritual objective of multiplication.

As your follow-up process creates an environment for prayer, spiritual discipline, and love, you can expect to see evangelism happen naturally. This process can begin the very first day your church's next new believer indicates his or her desire to "grow in the grace and knowledge of our Lord and Savior Jesus Christ" (2 Peter 3:18). This simple step of faith will be blessed!

Endnotes

1. See Michael Green, *Evangelism in the Early Church* (Grand Rapids: Eerdmans, 1970).

2. Herschel H. Hobbs, *New Testament Evangelism* (Nashville: Convention Press, 1960), 101.

3. Billy Graham, *The Holy Spirit* (Waco, Tex.: Word, 1978), 147.

4. Charles G. Finney, *Lectures on Systematic Theology,* ed. by J. H. Fairchild (South Gate, Calif.: Colporter Kemp, 1878, 1944 reprint), 477–78.

5. Billie Hanks, Jr., "Disciple Making and the Church," in *Discipleship: Great Insights from the Most Experienced Disciple Makers,* ed. by Billie Hanks, Jr. and William A. Shell (Grand Rapids: Zondervan, 1993), 100–101.

6. This does not mean, however, that curriculum is unimportant! Follow-up materials help guide the discipler to provide teaching and training in the areas where the new convert has needs. For a sample of follow-up materials that include detailed instructions for the spiritual mentor, see my *Call to Joy,* available from International Evangelism Association, P.O. Box 1174, Salado, Texas, 76571, (817) 947–3030.

7. Win Arn, "How to Use Ratios to Effect Church Growth," in *Church Growth: State of the Art,* ed. by C. Peter Wagner, Win Arn, and Elmer Towns (Wheaton, Ill.: Tyndale House, 1986), 97.

8. Gary McIntosh and Glen Martin, *Finding Them, Keeping Them: Effective Strategies for Evangelism and Assimilation in the Local Church* (Nashville: Broadman, 1992), 10.

9. Gary W. Kuhne, *The Dynamics of Personal Follow-up* (Grand Rapids: Zondervan, 1976), 57–58.

PART 3
"Revive Us Again": Spiritual Awakening

What is the relationship between spiritual awakening and evangelism? In this section, five writers deal with this general theme. Doug Munton reflects on the rich evangelistic heritage of spiritual awakenings in America. Preston Nix discusses the effects of the 1857–58 awakening on Baptists, the subject of Dr. Fish's own doctoral dissertation. Tim Beougher examines the 1970 revival at Southwestern Baptist Theological Seminary. Alvin Reid calls attention to the role of students in the history of awakenings. And Robert Coleman concludes with a note of optimism and hope for the prospect of revival in our time.

12
Igniting the Flame:
Spiritual Awakenings in America

Douglas W. Munton

Doug Munton is pastor of the First Baptist Church of Corinth, Texas, where he has served since 1985. He is also an adjunct professor at the Criswell College. Munton earned the B.A. from Wheaton College and the M.Div. and the Ph.D. with a major in evangelism at Southwestern Seminary. Munton was Fish's grader while in seminary.

There has always been a strong relationship between evangelism and the spiritual awakenings that have occurred throughout history.[1] As Dr. Roy Fish, professor of evangelism at Southwestern Baptist Theological Seminary, has said,

> The history of Christianity in the United States has been punctuated by periodic widespread revivals of religion. Traditionally, these have resulted in unusual numerical growth in evangelical churches and denominations and a general stimulation of religious interest throughout the country.[2]

These times of revival have been a fascinating part of religious history. America has been greatly influenced by these periods of spiritual awakening. The moral and religious renewal has changed the landscape of American faith. The story of Christianity in America is not complete without a careful study of the awakenings that have rocked the country. These revivals have not only stirred the religious community; they have led to great evangelistic harvests as well.

The evangelistic results of awakenings have been significant. The major revivals in American history have resulted in a large influx of new adherents to the faith. Also, a renewed interest in personal evangelism has marked all revivals in the history of this country.

While evangelism and revival are related, the two concepts are not synonyms. Evangelism refers to the winning of the lost to faith in Christ. Evangelism specifically deals with the process of leading the unregenerate to trust Jesus as Savior and then to begin to serve Christ as Lord. Revival refers specifically to the spiritual reawakening of a person who has already trusted Christ as Savior.

Evangelism is best seen, therefore, as the result of spiritual awakening. That is to say, a spiritual awakening always leads to evangelistic results. Charles G. Finney, in his famous work *Lectures on Revivals of Religion,* defined revival as "the renewal of the first love of Christians, resulting in the awakening and conversion of sinners to God."[3] Finney noted that evangelism was the result of a true revival.

Any true revival will necessarily lead to great evangelistic results. Churches will be strengthened. New churches will begin. The people of God will be burdened to bring the lost to faith in Christ. Believers will experience a renewed commitment to holiness. As a result, the lost will be convicted of sin and convinced of the claims of Christ. John Wesley White described evangelism as "invariably and inevitably the outgrowth of revival."[4] Earle Cairns took it a step further when he said evangelism is "both a product of revival and a stimulus to revival."[5]

It will help us to consider further the relationship between evangelism and spiritual awakenings. There has been much confusion about this relationship. J. Edwin Orr, the great historian of spiritual awakenings, helped to clarify this point:

> Revival is the return to activity from a state of neglect—primarily, the quickening of the spiritual life in believers who have become indifferent. By increasing the spiritual power of the Christians, Revival wins multitudes of sinners for Christ; consequently Revival is often confused with the results of revival, soul-winning.[6]

Part of the confusion over the relationship of spiritual awakenings and evangelism is semantical. In America, the term *revival* is used to refer to a series of special meetings, often evangelistic in nature. It would be more accurate to use the term "evangelistic campaign" or "crusade," or perhaps "a revival meeting" to describe this sort of spiritual or evangelistic methodology. Otherwise, one might find oneself in the contradictory position of saying, "We had a revival, but no one was revived!" Such could never be the case.

Due to this common misunderstanding of revival, Edwin Orr and others began to use the phrase "spiritual awakening" instead of "revival," especially in this country. This helped to make a distinction between a series of meetings designed to strengthen the church or reach the lost and a true reawakening of God's people that leads to evangelism.[7]

Defining Spiritual Awakenings

Several definitions of spiritual awakenings have been given, each with its own nuances. There have been two major schools of thought concerning the nature of spiritual awakenings. One is exemplified by Jonathan Edwards. Edwards emphasized the sovereignty of God in the sending of revivals. He believed revival came solely as a result of the will of God, not as a result of the work of man.[8]

Jonathan Edwards formulated a theology of revival that was a synthesis of Calvinistic theology and the experiences of genuine revival in his church and the surrounding area. Revival, he believed, was not something that could be worked up; it was an act of the sovereign God.[9]

A second school of thought is exemplified by Charles Finney. Finney emphasized the human role in spiritual awakening. He believed revival to be "a result we can logically expect from the right use of God-given means."[10] Further explaining this view, Finney stated,

> I said that revival results from the right use of means given by God. The means God has assigned to bring about revival no doubt naturally tend to produce a revival—otherwise God would not have appointed them. Yet these tools won't produce revival without God's blessings, any more than sown grain will produce a crop without God's blessing. God has as direct an influence or agency in producing a crop of grain as He has in producing revival.[11]

More about Finney's "right use of means" will be mentioned later.

It should be noted that while there are different emphases between the views of Edwards and Finney, there are similarities as well. Edwards did recognize the role of prayer and repentance to the coming of revival. Finney did believe that God was the ultimate Author of revival. Edwards emphasized, however, the sovereignty of God, while Finney emphasized our role and human responsibility. One should remember that Edwards wrote in reaction to the Arminianism of his day, whereas Finney reacted to a lifeless form of Calvinism.

Others have given helpful definitions of spiritual awakening. C. E. Autrey gave a definition of revival that recognized God's role in spiritual awakening while making a careful distinction between revival and evangelism. He stated,

> Revival is a reanimating of those who already possess life. Revival in the strict sense of the word has to do with God's people. It revives spiritual life that is in a state of declension. Revival is an instrument of evangelism. Evangelism is confronting the unregenerate with the doctrine of salvation. Evangelism embraces the reviving of the dead Christians as well as offering salvation to the lost. The prime purpose of revival is to revive the saved. When the saved are revived, it results in the salvation of the lost.[12]

J. Edwin Orr defined spiritual awakening as follows:

> An Evangelical Awakening is a movement of the Holy Spirit bringing about a revival of New Testament Christianity in the Church of Christ and in its related community. Such an awakening may change in a significant way an individual only; or it may affect a larger group of believers; or it may move a congregation, or the churches of a city or district, or the whole body of believers throughout a country or a continent; or indeed the larger body of believers throughout the world. The outpouring of the Spirit effects the reviving of the Church, the awakening of the masses, and the movement of uninstructed peoples towards the Christian faith; the revived Church, by many or by few, is moved to engage in evangelism, in teaching, and in social action.[13]

Dr. Roy Fish gave this definition of the term:

> Revival is a fresh touch from God, releasing his people unto fullness of blessing. It is a divine invasion of love, joy, peace, and conviction. It is an outpouring of the Holy Spirit on the church, empowering believers to love each other unconditionally, to rejoice in the Lord plentifully, to praise God appropriately, to serve him productively, to live lives that are godly, and to witness for him convincingly.[14]

Richard Owen Roberts called revival "an extraordinary movement of the Holy Spirit producing extraordinary results."[15] Cairns said revival is "the work of the Holy Spirit in restoring the people of God to a more vital spiritual life, witness and work by prayer and the Word after repentance in crisis for their spiritual decline."[16] A common theme among evangelical definitions of spiritual awakening is that there is a strong relationship between a spiritual awakening and evangelism. The relationship is so strong, in fact, that unless there is a resulting emphasis upon evangelism and an effectiveness in evangelism, a genuine revival has not occurred. This effectiveness can be seen in the major awakenings that have occurred in America.

Awakenings in American History

Many historians recognize four major awakenings in the history of the United States (or the early colonies), though there is no unanimity on this point. There are those, for instance, who divide what is commonly called the Second Great Awakening into two separate awakenings. Others discount the Revival of 1857–58 or regionalize the Revival of 1904–08 to Wales—or argue it was not as significant. Still others might add other periods of awakening to the list, such as the Awakening of the 1950s and the Jesus movement.

Some have suggested an analogy at this point to wars. This country has been in many wars. There have been major wars, like World War II. At other times, this country has been involved in lesser wars, but wars nonetheless. There have been times of spiritual awakening that have had an impact on only parts of society. There have been others that have impacted in greater ways. Some awakenings have been relatively brief. Others have lasted for many years.

This author believes that there have in fact been four major awakenings in this country. While there have been other awakenings of importance, these four periods stand out. The four awakenings may be titled the First Great Awakening, the Second Great Awakening, the Awakening of 1857–58 and the Awakening of 1904–08. Each of these was an awakening of major importance to the life of the church in America and to the well-being of the country as a whole. Additionally, each of these awakenings was significant in many other parts of the world. A brief examination will be made of each of these awakenings, with special attention given to their evangelistic impact.

The First Great Awakening

The First Great Awakening began in the colonies in approximately 1726 and had run its course within about thirty years.[17] Revival reached its peak from the mid-1730s through the 1740s.

Leaders of this revival include George Whitefield, one of the greatest preachers in history. Whitefield made several successful evangelistic visits to the colonies from his native England. His itinerant preaching attracted vast crowds and produced lasting results. Especially effective in the First Great Awakening was his preaching tour of the colonies from 1739–41.[18]

Jonathan Edwards, scholar, pastor, educator, and author, experienced significant revival in his church in Northampton, Massachusetts. Three hundred were converted there between December 1734 and May 1735. Edwards contributed his vast intellectual skills to defending the importance and authenticity of revivals. His support of the revival movement added considerable weight to the First Great Awakening. He proved to be an able defender of revivals through the written word.[19]

Gilbert Tennent aroused opposition with a fiery sermon delivered in 1740 entitled "The Danger of an Unconverted Ministry." But while preaching in Boston in the winter of 1740–41, Tennent saw six hundred converts. A student at the Log College, the forerunner of modern seminaries begun by his father, Tennent was a passionate preacher and a capable revival leader.[20]

Complete records of the First Great Awakening do not exist. The churches of the colonies, however, flourished. Anglicans, Congregationalists, Presbyterians, and the Dutch Reformed churches were most numerous and reaped the greatest benefits from the awakening. Baptists, however, illustrate well the momentum gained by the churches of this era. In New England in 1740, there were only twenty-one Baptist churches. Fifty years later the number had increased to two hundred and sixty-six, an increase of well over one thousand percent.[21]

The Second Great Awakening

The Second Great Awakening covered a number of decades. Some, like Orr and Cairns, prefer to see this as two separate times of revival. Most, however, believe this to be one extended period of the ebb and flow of revival. Probably the best dates for this awakening are approximately 1790 until the mid-1840s.[22]

There were three phases to the Second Great Awakening. The eastern states and colleges were impacted. The camp meetings of the West drew great attention. And Charles Finney brought a renewed vigor and effectiveness to revival with his conversion and subsequent ministry.

Many mark the revival at Hampden-Sydney College, 1787–90, as the beginning of the Second Great Awakening. Revival also came to Yale while Timothy Dwight, grandson of Jonathan Edwards, was president from 1795–1817. Williams College was significantly awakened during what is sometimes referred to as the "Haystack Revival." Other colleges also experienced awakening, as did many churches of the East.[23]

The West experienced revival in the camp meeting. James McGready led powerful revivals in Logan County, Kentucky, and the surrounding area. Cane Ridge, Kentucky, became the scene of a large camp meeting. The camp meetings tended to be somewhat boisterous and sometimes long-lasting affairs. The people sang and enjoyed fellowship, and various preachers would exhort the gathered audience. What the western preachers lacked in education, they made up for in passion.[24]

Also a part of the western revival was the circuit rider typified by Peter Cartwright. Cartwright was a fearless and tireless Methodist circuit rider who helped to rapidly multiply the Christian faith in the frontier regions.[25] Circuit riders advanced the spread of the faith over large areas, making up for a lack of trained pastors.

A third phase of the Second Great Awakening is seen in the life of Charles Finney. Charles Grandison Finney cast a giant shadow in the history of American religion. He is rightly seen as a watershed figure in the theology and practice of revival meetings and evangelism.[26]

Finney was a lawyer who was converted in 1821. Life immediately and radically changed upon his salvation experience. Speaking of the morning after his conversion, Finney said, "I had the impression, which has never left my mind, that God wanted me to preach the gospel, and that I must begin immediately."[27] And preach he did.

Charles Finney witnessed occurrences of revival throughout New England. He was used to continue the movement known as the Second Great Awakening. Finney saw thousands profess faith in Jesus Christ.[28] Churches flourished under this new wave of revival. Finney's work did not occur, however, without controversy.

Many called into question Finney's use of "new measures" such as his use of an "anxious bench," protracted meetings, and especially his bold preaching. Much of the criticism was theologically based. Some did not like, for instance, Finney's emphasis on immediate conversion. Finney described many of these critics as "hyper-Calvinists" who failed to see man's role in trusting God's grace.[29]

The Second Great Awakening was an extremely important time to the history of Christianity in America. Churches continued their westward expansion, paralleling population shifts. New methods found ready acceptance in these frontier churches. But the established Eastern Seaboard was blessed as well. The renewal on college campuses brought a new crop of eager pastors and missionaries. All in all, this extended period of revival was as significant as any event in American religious history.

The Awakening of 1857–58

The third major time of awakening in America was the Awakening of 1857–58.[30] This revival is among the most unique ever recorded. Orr, speaking of this awakening, stated,

> Having studied all recorded revival-awakenings occurring in the past 250 years, reading the most critical as well as commendatory opinions, I have come to the conclusion that, in comparison with all other movements of the kind, the Awakening of 1857–58 was the most thorough and most wholesome ever known in the Christian Church.[31]

These are strong words from the leading evangelical authority on the history of spiritual awakenings.

Careful documentation can be given for this awakening. It can be stated with authority, based on the records of the various denominations, that in America alone, one million people professed to trust Christ as Savior during this brief period of revival.[32] This was during a time when the entire population of the United States was only thirty million people. One is able to see, therefore, the great evangelistic effect of this revival time.

Many mark the beginning of this revival with the Union Prayer Meetings begun by Jeremiah Lanphier. Lanphier came to the North Dutch Reformed Church in New York City as the city missionary. While there, he began a noon prayer meeting. Attendance went from six men who were late for the first meeting to thousands gathering each day within a few months. The noon prayer time began to spread to other cities, where a phenomenal interest in the things of God grew.

This revival was effective in all parts of the country and beyond. Interestingly, it was not led by any particular evangelists or pastors. But it certainly had an impact on those in Christian ministry.[33]

Revival times have often had an impact upon the calling and effectiveness of evangelists. Dwight L. Moody, for example, was greatly affected by the Awakening of 1857–58. Edwin Orr recounted the following anecdote:

> I talked to a leading church historian and told him that I was engaged in fresh research into that (1858) great awakening, and he asked, "Who started that? Moody?" "No," I told him, "Moody did not start the '58 Revival. The '58 Revival started Moody."[34]

D. L. Moody was unquestionably one of America's greatest evangelists. His evangelistic campaigns were highly successful in America and Great Britain. His meetings drew large crowds and tremendous response. He greatly influenced the methodology of revival meetings.[35] These methods were learned to some extent from the Awakening of 1857–58. Orr called Moody the "greatest single product" of the revival.[36]

In many ways, the Awakening of 1857–58 paved the way for the coming of the great evangelists like Moody, J. Wilbur Chapman, and Reuben A. Torrey.[37] Their methods and expectations of revival were molded by what they learned from this revival period. The impact of this awakening lasted far beyond 1859 through the influence of these evangelists and other leaders who sought to bring revival to the land.

The Awakening of 1904–08

The Awakening of 1904–08 was called by Orr "the most extensive Evangelical Awakening of all time."[38] And yet, many regrettably relegate this revival to only the country of Wales. In fact, this revival impacted numerous countries and crossed many other barriers. During the two years of its greatest impact in each country, Orr estimated that more than five million people were won to evangelical faith.[39]

The Welsh Revival, which began in 1904, was certainly a major part of this important awakening. Wales, within a few months of the outbreak of revival, reported more than one hundred thousand professions of faith. Under the leadership of men like Evan Roberts, Joseph Jenkins,[40] and Seth Joshua, this revival had a wholesome effect on the people and churches of Wales.

Evan Roberts spoke often, during the revival in Wales, of the four great tenets of revival. First, he said, you must put away any unconfessed sin. Second, you must put away any doubtful habit. Third, you must obey the Spirit promptly. Fourth, you must confess Christ publicly.[41]

One contemporary author commented on the relationship of the Welsh Revival to evangelism. He said, "The outward and visible sign of the coming of Spring in the history of the nation is a great revival of religious earnestness—a sudden and widespread outburst of evangelistic fervor."[42] Evangelistic efforts were intense during the course of the revival.

Edwin Orr dedicated an entire book, *The Flaming Tongue: Evangelical Awakenings 1900–*, to show the worldwide impact of the Awakening of 1904–08. The revival concerned much more than Wales alone. While the awakening did not begin here, the United States experienced a powerful revival during this time. All across the country revival was reported. Many different denominations and various regions of the country were affected. A surge in evangelistic intensity and effectiveness was reported by pastors, evangelists, and laymen.

An example of the results of the awakening is the fact that the formation of Southwestern Baptist Theological Seminary was influenced by the revival. Throughout 1904 and 1905, the *Baptist Standard,* news magazine for Texas Baptists, carried stories about revival taking place in various places such as Houston, Waco, and Marshall. Noting the factors that contributed to the foundation of the seminary, L. R. Scarborough mentioned the impact of "great revivals."[43] Southwestern Seminary began during a period of revival.

The years of revival and following saw the work of many outstanding evangelists. R. A. Torrey and J. Wilbur Chapman continued their success. Billy Sunday rose to great heights of fame with his spectacular meetings. Sam Jones, Gipsy Smith, Mordecai Ham, and George Cates led remarkable campaigns. An interest in evangelism grew rapidly in these years.

It is unfortunate that many only know of the Welsh Revival without seeing the fuller impact of this awakening. The world was blessed by the Revival of 1904–08. America was impacted as well. It is hoped that more will come to recognize the importance of this revival time to the life of this country and the Christian community throughout the world.

The Evangelistic Impact of Awakenings

The revivals of history have greatly influenced evangelism. These wonderful periods of God's movement among his people have resulted in many conversions. Revival and evangelism work together.

Several conclusions about the relationship between spiritual awakenings and evangelism may be offered. First, it should be noted that when revival truly comes, evangelism will always follow. An awakened church is an evangelistic church. An awakened believer is an evangelistic believer.

One may not say he or she is fully submitted to the Lord Jesus Christ and not have Christ's concern for the lost. When believers live in obedience to God, they will take seriously God's commission to make disciples.

Revival brings with it a commitment to evangelism. There is a new concern for reaching the lost. Jesus told believers to pray for more harvesters for the whitened fields. Revival results in more harvesters ready to reach the lost. Compassion for the unsaved permeates the church as renewed believers seek to obey their Lord's directives.

Revival often results in new methods for evangelism. Charles Finney and D. L. Moody are but two examples of the changes that often occur. Every generation must bring the unchanging gospel message to a changing culture. An openness to new ideas and methods that impact the culture without compromising the gospel is characteristic of spiritual awakenings.

Revival meetings and invitations are two of the enduring methods spurred by revivals to help the church fulfill her mandate. Itinerant evangelistic ministries, citywide evangelistic campaigns, and the common use today of evangelistic music were likewise spawned out of past awakenings. Methods with more limited appeal which nevertheless have been used mightily by God include field or open-air preaching (Whitefield and Wesley) and camp meetings (the Second Great Awakening).

Other methods will be utilized as the church works to impact the community. While the message remains constant, the methods will constantly change. Every culture is unique. Methods are merely ways in which the church can relate the life-changing message of God's grace to people in their cultural setting. However, the most effective and enduring evangelistic methods have been birthed during a time of revival.

A renewed emphasis on the biblical office of the evangelist is common during the coming of revival. Many evangelists of history were greatly influenced by revival. They often played a great role in the revival itself. Evangelists many times found themselves on the cutting edge of spiritual awakenings.

The role of the evangelist is often heightened and magnified during revival times. At a time when the biblical office of the evangelist is often denigrated, it is a healthy reminder to see how God has worked through these men and women in history.

Spiritual awakenings often resulted in the calling of great numbers of young people to involvement in missions and evangelism. The evangelistic intensity extends to other countries and cultures as many of the finest young people are called to serve as missionaries, evangelists, and pastors.

Probably the most important reason for an increase in evangelistic efforts and effectiveness during a spiritual awakening has to do with a renewed emphasis by God's people to use God's power to win the lost. Revival causes God's people to turn to prayer as never before. They rely on the power of the Holy Spirit to minister and evangelize.

The power of God, available at all times, is appropriated by believers during revival. Christians do God's work in God's strength, not their own. Prayer becomes more than a formality; it becomes the lifeblood of the church. The Holy Spirit becomes more than a figurehead. He becomes a dynamic part of the believer's life.

Much of modern evangelism emphasizes methodology to the exclusion of spiritual power. Spiritual awakenings remind us that methods are secondary to the presence and power of the Holy Spirit in the life of believers. The finest methods in the world cannot replace the power of God working through his people. Church leaders today have emphasized methods, but many have lost touch with the Source of power. While methods are important, they are important secondarily. Spiritual power in the life of Christians is primary.

Spiritual awakenings influence evangelistic efforts because there is a renewed interest in reaching the lost, matched with a renewed dependence on the power of God to accomplish the goal. This combination of the passion of God and the power of God enables evangelistic efforts to blossom.

Those who care about evangelism should care about revival. Revival will sharpen the focus of the church on a lost world. Revival will deepen the effectiveness of the church in sharing the gospel. Both personal evangelism and the broader efforts of church and crusade will benefit from a genuine touch of God in spiritual awakening. May the Lord grant that this generation and the one to come may experience the powerful working of God which stirs believers and reaches a lost and needy world.

Endnotes

1. For the purposes of this chapter, the terms "spiritual awakening" and "revival" will be used synonymously. Some authors make a distinction between the two phrases. J. Edwin Orr, for instance, made a distinction between these two phrases near the end of his life in certain publications. See Orr, "Revival That Rocked the World," *Moody Monthly,* June 1986, 68–71, and Orr, *The Outpouring of the Spirit in Revival and Awakenings and Its Issue in Church Growth,* (Pasadena, CA.: By the author,

1984), 3–6 and 6–7. Orr stated that a revival "rejuvenates the family of God," while an awakening "rocks the surrounding community." See Orr, "Revival That Rocked the World," 68.

2. Roy Fish, "The Effects of Revivals on Baptist Growth in the South," in *The Lord's Free People in a Free Land,* ed. William R. Estep (Ft. Worth: Faculty of the School of Theology, Southwestern Baptist Theological Seminary, 1976), 99. I would like to thank Dr. Fish for inspiring me not only through his teaching and insights, for he also exemplifies an evangelistic fervor and a heart for the things of God that has greatly influenced my life. I am thankful to have such a hero.

3. Charles Grandison Finney, *Lectures on Revivals of Religion* (New York: Revell, 1835, 1968 reprint), 14.

4. John Wesley White, Foreword to Earle E. Cairns, *An Endless Line of Splendor: Revivals and Their Leaders from the Great Awakening to the Present* (Wheaton, Ill.: Tyndale House, 1986), 13.

5. .Cairns, *Endless Line of Splendor,* 15.

6. Orr, *Can God? 10,000 Miles of Miracle in Britain,* 7th ed., (Grand Rapids: Zondervan, 1935), 119–20. For further study of Orr, see Douglas W. Munton, "The Contributions of J. Edwin Orr to the Field of Spiritual Awakenings," Ph.D. dissertation, Southwestern Baptist Theological Seminary, 1991.

7. Unfortunately, many use the terms *revival* and *revivalism* interchangeably. See, for instance, Timothy L. Smith, *Revivalism and Social Reform in Mid-Nineteenth Century America* (New York: Abingdon, 1957); William Warren Sweet, *Revivalism in America: Its Origin, Growth and Decline* (New York: Charles Scribner's Sons, 1944); and William G. McLoughlin, Jr., *Modern Revivalism: Charles Grandison Finney to Billy Graham* (New York: The Ronald Press Company, 1959).

8. For more on Edwards, see Sereno E. Dwight, ed. *The Complete Works of Jonathan Edwards,* 2 vols. (Edinburgh: The Banner of Truth Trust, 1834); Perry Miller, *Jonathan Edwards* (New York: William Sloane Associates, 1949); and Ola Elizabeth Winslow, *Jonathan Edwards: 1703–1758* (New York: William Sloane Associates, 1940).

9. See Cairns, *Endless Line of Splendor,* 45–46.

10. Finney, *Lectures on Revivals of Religion,* 13.

11. Ibid., 14.

12. C. E. Autrey, *Revivals of the Old Testament* (Grand Rapids: Zondervan, 1960), 13.

13. Orr, *The Fervent Prayer: The Worldwide Impact of the Great Awakening of 1858* (Chicago: Moody Press, 1974), vii.

14. Roy Fish to Douglas W. Munton, July 31, 1994, transcript in the hand of Doug Munton.

15. Richard Owen Roberts, *Revival!* (Wheaton, Ill.: Tyndale , 1982), 16–17.

16. Cairns, *Endless Line of Splendor,* 22.

17. For more information on the First Great Awakening, see Edwin Scott Gaustad, *The Great Awakening in New England* (New York: Harper and Bros., 1957); and Alan E. Heimert and Perry Miller, eds., *The Great Awakening: Documents Illustrating the Crisis and Its Consequences* (New York: Bobbs-Merrill, 1967).

18. See, for instance, Arnold E. Dallimore, *George Whitefield: The Life and Times of the Great Evangelist of the Eighteenth Century Revival,* 2 vols. (London: Banner of Truth, 1970).

19. Edwards' writings on revival include his *Faithful Narrative; Thoughts on the Revival of Religion in New England; A Treatise on Religious Affections;* and *A Humble Attempt to promote Visible Union. . . .*

20. See Sweet, *Revivalism in America,* 139–44; Cairns, *Endless Line of Splendor,* 42–43. For more on the Log College, see Archibald Alexander, *The Log College,* reprint (London: Banner of Truth, 1968).

21. Albert H. Newman, *A History of the Baptist Churches in the United States* (Philadelphia: American Baptist Publication Society, 1898), 271.

22. For more on the Second Great Awakening see Orr, *The Eager Feet: Evangelical Awakenings, 1790–1830* (Chicago: Moody Press, 1975); John B. Boles, *The Great Revival 1787–1805* (Lexington: University of Kentucky Press, 1972); and Keith J. Hardman, *Charles Grandison Finney, 1792–1875: Revivalist and Reformer* (Syracuse: Syracuse Univ. Press, 1987).

23. See the chapter by Alvin Reid elsewhere in this book.

24. See Boles, *The Great Revival;* Catherine C. Cleveland, *The Great Revival in the West* (Chicago: University of Chicago Press, 1916); and Charles A. Johnson, *The Frontier Camp Meeting* (Dallas: Southern Methodist Univ. Press, 1955).

25. See Charles L. Wallis, *Autobiography of Peter Cartwright* (Nashville: Abingdon, 1956).

26. Bill J. Leonard, "Getting Saved in America: Conversion Event in a Pluralistic Culture," *Review and Expositor* 82 (Winter 1985): 119, suggested that "no single person influenced the way nineteenth-century Americans understood conversion more than the famed evangelist Charles Grandison Finney."

27. Finney, *Memoirs of Rev. Charles G. Finney* (New York: Revell, 1876), 25.

28. Richard Ellsworth Day, in *Man of Like Passions,* 2d ed. (Grand Rapids: Zondervan, 1942), 78, stated that as many as five hundred thousand people came to salvation as a result of the revival preaching of Finney.

29. See Hardman, *Finney,* 133–149 for a discussion between Finney and his detractors.

30. See also the chapter by Preston Nix elsewhere in this book.

31. Orr, *The Awakening of 1857–58 in North America* (Privately printed, 1983), 10. Orr, citing Perry Miller, referred to it as "The Event of the Century."

32. Orr, by looking at the membership totals of all the denominations, estimated that there were one million conversions during the two-year period of revival. See Orr, *America's Great Revival* (Elizabethtown, PA: McBeth Press, 1957), 28–29.

33. Orr, "Revival and Evangelism," *World Evangelization* (March 1985), 6.

34. Ibid.

35. For more information on Moody, see Richard Ellsworth Day, *Bush Aglow: The Life Story of Dwight Lyman Moody, Commoner of Northfield* (Philadelphia: The Judson Press, 1936); and J. C. Pollock, *Moody: A Biographical Portrait of the Pacesetter in Modern Mass Evangelism* (New York: The MacMillan Co., 1963).

36. Orr, *The Second Great Awakening in America* (London: Marshall, Morgan and Scott, 1952), 154.

37. Smith, *Revivalism and Reform,* 74.

38. Orr, *The Flaming Tongue: Evangelical Awakenings 1900–,* 2d ed. (Chicago: Moody Press, 1975), 191.

39. Ibid.

40. See the chapter by Alvin Reid elsewhere in this book.

41. See Orr, *The Flaming Tongue,* 26.

42. W. T. Stead, ed., *The Story of the Welsh Revival* (London: Fleming H. Revell Company, 1905), 26.

43. L. R. Scarborough, *A Modern School of the Prophets: A History of the Southwestern Baptist Theological Seminary* (Nashville: Broadman, 1939), 56.

13
The "Third Great Awakening" in America:
The Prayer Revival of 1857–58

Preston L. Nix

Preston Nix is pastor of the Eastwood Baptist Church in Tulsa, Oklahoma. Prior to that, Nix served as pastor of the Ridglea Baptist Church in Fort Worth, Texas. Nix earned an M.Div. and a Ph.D. in evangelism at Southwestern Seminary.

Beginning fifty years prior to the Revolutionary War, God brought revival to the emerging nation that would soon become the United States of America. This powerful revival in Colonial America has come to be known as the First Great Awakening. At the outset of the 1800s, as this country was expanding westward, she once again experienced a genuine "visitation from on high," termed appropriately the Second Great Awakening. God sent yet another "wave of refreshing" across the land toward the middle of the nineteenth century, immediately preceding the Civil War, and the Prayer Revival of 1857–58 was born. Although this was truly an extraordinary movement of God, which "probably permeated the religious life of . . . [this] country more than any other awakening," it is the least-known revival which has occurred in the United States.[1] This phenomenal Third Great Awakening and its subsequent effects on Baptists in this country are the subjects of this chapter.

Unexpected Beginning of the Revival

The two decades preceding the Civil War were years of geographical expansion and internal conflict for the United States of America. The nation at that time was experiencing phenomenal growth not only in population but also in geographical boundaries due to vast land acquisitions. The country was also growing economically and experienced "an unprecedented and undreamed of expansion of material prosperity" that was stimulated to a large degree by the development of the telegraph and the railroad.[2] The internal conflict was precipitated by the problems created from mass immigration into the country and controversy regarding the issue of slavery. The nation was seriously torn by these political questions. In the midst of that time period, religion declined. The conditions of mid-nineteenth-century America did not appear to be conducive for a national spiritual awakening.

Spiritual condition of the nation

From its inception around 1800 to the early forties, the influence of the Second Great Awakening continued for almost half a century. However, toward the middle of the century, revivals almost totally ceased throughout the country. This greatly affected the churches, as most denominations experienced decline:

> For several years, from 1843 to 1857, the accessions to the churches scarcely equaled the losses sustained by death, removal or discipline, while a widespread indifference to religion became prevalent.[3]

For fifteen years the nation was gripped by a serious spiritual drought.

There were three major reasons for this spiritual decline in mid-nineteenth-century America. The first of these was economic. The newfound economic prosperity of many turned their thoughts away from God. They became indifferent to the claims of faith and religion. The second reason for spiritual decline was political. The slavery-abolitionist struggle was at its height and consumed people's energy. The pulpit began to be used to denounce or defend the institution of slavery, and the preaching of the gospel suffered.

Surprisingly enough, the third major reason for spiritual decline in this country was religious. It resulted from the eschatological extremes of a misguided but zealous believer by the name of William Miller. Captain Miller, a veteran of the War of 1812, was licensed to preach by a Baptist church in 1833. Being untrained in biblical and theological interpretation, he endeavored to calculate the return of Christ from passages in the books of Daniel and Revelation. He decided that the Lord's return would occur on April 23, 1843. Many ministers and a great number of laymen were won over to his views.

As the time drew near, excitement in several localities became intense. Great meetings were held, people disposed of their material possessions, and ascension robes were prepared. Many were on the hilltop with Miller on April 23 to see the return of Christ, but the day passed without incident. Undaunted by the disappointment, Miller took a different approach to the prophecy of the seventy weeks of Daniel 9:24, utilizing the Jewish year for his new calculations. He set the second date for March 22, 1844, but nothing special happened on that day either. Subsequent dates were set, but they too were proved wrong, causing many to lose confidence not only in Miller's arithmetic but also in religion in general.[4]

Contributing factors to the awakening

The above-mentioned circumstances that helped to promote a spiritual decline in this nation would appear to be unfavorable preparation for an extensive religious awakening. In 1857, though, when things seemed the darkest, the tide began to turn. At least five factors contributed to the unexpected beginning of this great movement of God.

First, during the latter part of 1856, but especially in 1857, a number of churches in both the North and the South began to experience powerful revivals. Two of these revivals occurred in churches in Massachusetts, while two others occurred among congregations in South Carolina.[5] A fifth noteworthy revival sprang up outside of the borders of the United States, in Canada, among the Methodists in the city of Hamilton, in the province of Ontario, then known as Canada West.

J. Edwin Orr contended that this was the actual beginning of the Prayer Revival of 1857–58.[6] Walter and Phoebe Palmer, a physician and his wife, saw hundreds of converts in this and other camp meetings in Ontario as well as Quebec during the fall of 1857. Attendance at their services ranged from five to six thousand. Accounts of this extraordinary awakening created a desire in the hearts of the Methodists in the States for a similar blessing of God.

A second factor came from the Presbyterians, many of whom yearned for a fresh touch from God. On December 1, 1857, a convention was called in Pittsburgh for the express purpose of discussing religious revival. An address to the churches was drafted with the request that ministers read it from their pulpits and conduct meetings for their church officers to discuss the topics that had been considered at the convention, to plan systematic visitation to the families in their parishes, and to urge the people to pray for revival. Preachers were encouraged to preach on the subject of revival on the first Sunday of the New Year, and the first Thursday was observed as a day of prayer and fasting. A similar conference was held in Cincinnati shortly thereafter, with much the same agenda. The convention became a great prayer meeting, and the participating churches were stirred. It was not long afterward that revival came to the entire city of Cincinnati and spread to the West.

A third factor was the effort by many evangelical churches to aggressively enroll as many new people as possible in their Sunday school programs. Beginning in September 1856, the New York Sunday School Union urged upon churches of all denominations the responsibility of visiting in homes to enlist people in Bible study. The Union was especially burdened by the fact that there were fifty thousand unevangelized children in New York City alone.[7] Their program called for the organizing of mission Sunday schools in neglected areas of the city. The plan was also followed in Hartford, Detroit, Buffalo, and Boston, which all later came to be centers of revival. Many seeds were sown in these Sunday school outreach efforts, which became part of the great reaping of the harvest of 1858.

While the preceding factors certainly set the stage for the onset of an awakening in this country, most historians point to the inception of the union prayer meetings begun in metropolitan New York City as the actual start of the Revival of 1857–58. The downtown churches in New York City were experiencing decline. Membership in the churches was dropping as people and churches were moving to the suburbs as a result of the encroachment of trade and commerce into the inner city.

This difficult situation confronted the old North Dutch Reformed Church. However, instead of seeking a more inviting location, the church decided to employ a lay missionary to try to reach the people in that section of the city. They selected an energetic, forty-year-old businessman by the name of Jeremiah Calvin Lanphier. He had been converted in 1842 in a tabernacle built by Charles G. Finney but had no experience in religious work. He quickly left his mercantile business and enthusiastically began the duties of his new position on July 1, 1857.

He set out to reach the unchurched masses in that section of the city by calling on everyone that he could. He passed out many Bibles, tracts, and church brochures, attempting to attract people to the church and to Christ.

He met with some success, but the burden of the work was enormous. As he faced the problems of this downtown ministry, he continually prayed, "Lord, what wilt Thou have me to do?" Then one day the answer came. Since he had found great comfort in prayer, it occurred to him that it might be profitable for others, especially those engaged in business pursuits, to retire from their activities during the day for a brief time of communion with God. He had noticed on his rounds many businessmen "hurrying along their way, often with careworn faces, and anxious, restless gaze."[8] He saw the noon hour as the most feasible one, and distributed a handbill in many offices and warehouses, publicizing the initial noon prayer meeting. The handbill contained the following message along with the time, place, and format of the gathering.

> *How Often Shall I Pray?*
> As often as the language of prayer is in my heart; as often as I see my need of help; as often as I feel the power of temptation; as often as I am made sensible of my spiritual declension or feel the aggression of a worldly spirit. In prayer we leave the business of time for that of eternity.[9]

At twelve noon, September 23, 1857, the room on the third floor of the Consistory Building, in the rear of the North Dutch Church on Fulton Street, was opened for prayer. At the appointed hour Lanphier was the only one present, and for thirty minutes he prayed alone. Then at 12:30 P.M. a step was heard on the stairs, and the first person appeared. Soon others came, and there were finally six men at this inaugural gathering of the Fulton Street prayer meeting. On the following Wednesday, the six had become twenty; and on the third Wednesday, October 7, there were forty men praying at the noon hour. A decision was then made to hold the meeting daily instead of weekly. On October 14, over one hundred people attended the meeting. The attendance grew so rapidly that before the end of the second month, all three lecture rooms of the church were filled. Meanwhile, the flame was spreading, and almost simultaneously prayer meetings began to spring up all across the city. Churches began prayer meetings, many times without any knowledge of other meetings having begun. Within six months, fifty thousand people were gathering daily to pray in New York City, and tens of thousands more from all walks of life could be found at similar meetings in other cities across the nation.[10]

The final factor was a sudden and very severe financial panic in the autumn of 1857. It was precipitated by "excessive railroad building, over-speculation and a wildcat currency system."[11] When the crash came, thousands of merchants, along with the railroads, went bankrupt. The banks failed, factories shut down, and vast multitudes were out of work. All classes of people were affected by the financial panic, which reached crisis proportions on October 14, 1857. As the economy fell, many began to search for a more solid foundation for living: "Stripped of their self-dependence, and in despair, men again found time to think on their need of God."[12]

The Phenomenal Spread of the Revival

The revival spread with unbelievable rapidity throughout the nation. Prayer was the common denominator in the awakening as it emerged across the nation. News of the Fulton Street experience and other daily union prayer meetings prompted men to establish immediately similar meetings in their own cities to promote the Christian faith and to reach people with the gospel. Preaching services were held to further this great revival, but the union prayer meetings were the mainstay of the movement. Beginning in the Middle Atlantic states it appeared that "three streams of blessing" flowed out from there: one northward to New England; another westward along the Ohio River Valley; and a third southward as far as Texas.[13] An observer in a leading secular newspaper wrote,

> The Revivals, or Great Awakening, continue to be the leading topic of the day . . . from Texas, in the South, to the extreme of our Western boundaries and our Eastern limits; their influence is felt by every denomination.[14]

Newspapers throughout the country reflected this same view.

Awakening in the mid-Atlantic region
It was in the middle Atlantic states, particularly in New York City, that the revival first gained prominence. The revival began in prayer, and as news of the phenomenal prayer meetings spread, new meetings multiplied. Even theaters and public halls were opened to accommodate the crowds. Roy Fish estimated that more than 150 union prayer meetings were established in the city, with more than fifty thousand New Yorkers praying daily.[15]

The prayer meetings were without hype or hysteria. There was simply a hunger in the hearts of thousands of people to pray:

They felt impelled, by some unseen power, to pray. They felt the pressure of the call to prayer. So a place of prayer was no sooner opened, than Christians flocked to it, to pour out their supplications together.[16]

Even the secular *Journal of Commerce* recommended for its readers to "steal awhile away from Wall Street and every worldly care, and spend an hour about mid-day in humble, hopeful prayer."[17]

The effect of the noonday prayer meetings flowed over into weeknight services in many of the churches and flowed out into towns and villages across the state. Surrounding states including New Jersey and Pennsylvania began to feel the effects of the Prayer Revival.

Awakening in New England

The New England states also received divine visitation. A total of 150 towns in Massachusetts reported revival, with more than five thousand converted by the end of March of 1858.[18] Morning, noon, afternoon, and evening meetings were attended by great crowds in Portland, Maine, where the church bells daily summoned thousands to prayer. Providence, Rhode Island, saw revival in 1858 like she had never previously experienced. Revival swept through the state of Connecticut in an unprecedented way. It was reported that in one town in Connecticut not a single unconverted adult could be found.[19]

Awakening in the Midwest

In early 1858 the revival movement spilled westward over the Appalachian Mountains. Within only two months, 480 towns in the Midwest reported fifteen thousand professions of faith in their churches. Revivals broke out in most major cities, including Cincinnati, Cleveland, Louisville, Indianapolis, Detroit, Chicago, St. Louis, and Dubuque.

One of the most moving stories of the power of prayer during this revival came out of a prayer meeting in Kalamazoo, Michigan:

At our very first meeting someone put in such a request as this: "A praying wife requests the prayers of this meeting for her unconverted husband, that he may be converted and made a humble disciple of the Lord Jesus." All at once a stout burly man arose and said, "I am that man. I have a pious praying wife, and this request must be for me. I want you to pray for me." As soon as he sat down, in the midst of sobs and tears, another man arose and said, "I am that man; I have a praying wife. She prays for me. And now she asked you to pray for me. I am sure I am that man, and I want you to pray for me."[20]

Several other convicted husbands requested prayer, and the power of Almighty God fell upon the meeting. In a short while there were over four hundred conversions in the town. News of the prayer meetings in New York and Philadelphia motivated businessmen in the city of Chicago to organize their own union prayer meetings. Attendance was high, and the city was blessed with revival. Many Chicago churches experienced incredible growth in 1858.

It was in the YMCA noon prayer meetings that the life of young Dwight L. Moody was impacted by the revival. Here he received his challenge to work for Christ's kingdom. He wrote to his mother in New England to tell of his faithful attendance and joy at the services:

> I go every night to meeting—Oh, how I do enjoy it! It seems as if God were here Himself. Pray that this work may go on until every knee is bowed. I wish there could be a revival in Northfield, that many might be brought into the fold of Christ.[21]

Moody soon converted his inspiration and enthusiasm into service for the Lord. It was during the hot summer in 1858 that Moody gathered together a group of boys off the street and held his first Sunday school class at the beach on Lake Michigan. Thus, the great worldwide ministry of Dwight Lyman Moody began during the Prayer Revival of 1857–58 in Chicago.

Awakening in the South

Although there has been sharp disagreement among authorities as to how powerfully the revival affected the South, it appeared that the results of the revival in the south were "in proportion to the population, greater in the South than any other section."[22] Even in the North it was reported that revivals were sweeping Baltimore, Richmond, Nashville, Memphis, Mobile, Savannah, Augusta, Columbia, and New Orleans. The revival had an effect as far south as Texas, in the cities of Waco and Galveston, and reached as far west as the state of California. The revival even extended into the armies of the North and South during the Civil War, but especially had dramatic results among the Confederate troops:

During the long conflict which followed there was an extensive revival in the Confederate armies which, beginning in the army of Virginia, became so widespread as to be designated the great revival in the Southern Army.[23]

Awakening on the sea

The power of the Prayer Revival of 1857–58 was not confined to the land. Even at sea, ships nearing American ports came under the influence of the awakening: "Ship after ship arrived with the same story of sudden conviction of sin, and conversion among both passengers and crew."[24] It was as if there was a "definite zone of Heavenly influence" surrounding the Eastern Seaboard.[25]

A remarkable incident took place on the old battleship *North Carolina.* More than a thousand crewmen manned the ship. Four young sailors were granted permission to hold a prayer meeting in the lower part of the ship. As they prayed, the Spirit of God so filled their hearts with joy that they burst into song. The ungodly crew came to mock their religious shipmates. Miraculously, they fell under conviction, eventually kneeling humbly in repentance and faith. Night after night the prayer meeting was held, and conversions occurred on the vessel daily. They sent ashore for ministers to come help with the work.

The *North Carolina* was a receiving ship from which men were constantly transferred to other vessels. As a result, converts from the unusual movement of God, upon completion of their training, were sent out to other ships throughout the Navy. Revival fires were kindled everywhere that American naval vessels sailed because of the "rejoicing converts" from the *North Carolina.*[26]

Peculiar Features of the Revival

The Prayer Revival of 1857–58 was a remarkable event in its inception, its spread, and its influence. As one historian put it, "The characteristics of the Great Revival were such as to make it absolutely unique. It stands apart both in its method and its aims from every other great awakening."[27]

The revival commenced unexpectedly:

> Instead of being anticipated and watched for, as the outpourings of the Spirit often are, this advent was so sudden and unheralded, that ministers were in many cases taken by surprise, and scarcely able to realize that awakening and

new-creating influences were breathing on the hearts of their congregations. Like the rushing mighty wind of the day of Pentecost, it was unpreceded [*sic*] by prognostics.[28]

The most obvious feature of the revival was its emphasis on prayer, hence its name: "The Prayer Revival." The primary agency for its spread was the union prayer meetings. Every major city and many towns and villages organized such meetings. A man from Omaha, Nebraska, reported in one of Charles Finney's meetings in Boston that while traveling eastward, "I have found a continuous prayer meeting all the way. We call it two thousand miles from Omaha to Boston; and there was a prayer meeting about two thousand miles in extent."[29]

These prayer meetings were held anywhere there was room for people to gather. The meetings were very simple and followed much the same pattern as the Fulton Street meeting.[30] There was hymn singing, Scripture reading, short exhortations, but most of all requests for prayer and intercession on the behalf of the participants. Requests were mailed or telegraphed to meetings from all across the country. Concern for souls caused Christians to bring lost friends, family members, or business associates to the meetings, and "by personal witness in an atmosphere bathed with intercessory prayer, many were persuaded to repent."[31]

A third feature of the revival was the great participation of laymen. Some call the awakening a "lay revival" or "laymen's movement."[32] Some were reported to have taken leave from their jobs for personal soul-winning.[33] This revival marked the rise of laymen to greater involvement in the work of the church and participation in affiliated movements, such as the YMCA.

The interesting character of the converts provided the fourth feature. By this time many churches had almost lost faith in adult conversion. In 1857–58, a number of adults were won to the Lord as revival swept the nation. One writer spoke of the "large proportion of mature minds reached and won to Christ."[34]

Almost every age, ethnic group, and class of society was touched by the awakening. Whole families of Jews came to know Christ as their Messiah.

Another surprising feature was that there were no emotional excesses displayed during the course of this movement of God. It was free from swoonings, fallings, shakings, and such "religious exercises." These phenomena had led to the discredit of earlier revival meetings by some and created controversies among believers. The Prayer Revival of 1857–58 was characterized by a quiet type of solemnity. Enthusiasm as well as spiritual conviction and intensity were expressed, but in an atmosphere of order and restraint.

The revival also featured a strong spirit of cooperation among all Christians throughout its duration. There was no denominational rivalry, and no one group tried to dominate any of the meetings. No man or denomination tried to push a particular doctrine or further a particular cause. There was great unity of heart and soul among believers as they tried to bring the lost to salvation.[35] *Union* was the term used to describe the hundreds of prayer meetings so characteristic of the revival. Even at the original prayer meeting on September 23, 1857, at the Fulton Street Church, four different denominations were represented by the six men present.[36]

One of the most remarkable features of the revival was the unanimous approval it received from almost everyone. It was difficult to find anyone who had an unkind word about it. Never before or since has a religious event received such positive acclaim from the secular press. When the revival was at its height, the *New York Herald* and other newspapers published "Revival Extra" sections, giving the latest news of the revival from various parts of the country.[37] In fact, news of the revival replaced other news and held premier place for several months.[38]

The Prayer Revival of 1857–58 knew no bounds of any kind. It was not confined to one geographical area or any one denomination. All classes of people were touched by its pervasive influence. It "extended over the Northern states, from the Atlantic to the extreme west. It affected persons of every class, men and women, young and old, merchants, mechanics, clerks" and touched whole communities as it spread.[39] The awakening did not stop in America. It crossed the ocean and spread to Northern Ireland, England, Scotland, Wales, South Africa, Scandinavia, Switzerland, and Germany.

Significant Results of the Revival

The Prayer Revival of 1857–58 produced a number of significant results, which greatly affected life in this country. A principal result of the revival was the conversion of many souls and the addition of great numbers to the churches. Virtually all denominations experienced a numerical gain in their memberships. The total harvest has been estimated between three hundred thousand and one million converts.[40] Muncy revealed that in 1850, the ratio of church members to the total population was 15.5 percent, but by 1860 had increased to 22.7 percent.[41] In addition to new members, there was a corresponding increase in the number of churches in this country as a result of the awakening.

Beyond the participation of laity mentioned earlier, many young men were stirred in their hearts to dedicate their lives to God for full time vocational Christian service as well. The Prayer Revival of 1857–58 gave rise to a large increase of students for the ministry. Enrollment figures at seminaries, Bible schools, and colleges began to climb. As schools and seminaries became crowded, virtually every major denomination began making plans for new campuses. In addition, many colleges and universities experienced revival.[42]

The quality of the moral life of America was raised by the Prayer Revival of 1857–58. In several places the effect on the morals of the citizens was felt immediately. People began to pay their debts, and bartenders got out of their sinful businesses. There seemed to be a greater respect for the Lord's Day. The revival gave rise to church social work among the dispossessed and downtrodden. City mission centers sprang up dramatically in the cities in 1859–60. Out of the revival came the introduction of the YMCA and impetus to the creation of the Christian and Sanitary Commissions and Freedmen's Societies that were formed in the midst of the Civil War.[43] Even the awareness that slavery was morally wrong seemed to have been heightened as a result of the awakening.[44]

The character of this movement helped bring about a more open attitude toward revival meetings in this country. Such meetings began to be welcomed and encouraged by all major denominations. The type of spontaneous revivals experienced during this third great awakening helped pave the way for the later evangelistic work of Dwight L. Moody, Reuben A. Torrey, and J. Wilbur Chapman.[45] Many of the methods used by Moody were learned from this awakening, and J. Edwin Orr believed that Moody himself was the "greatest single product" of the revival.[46]

Finally, the Prayer Revival of 1857–58 was a providential preparation of this country for the Civil War.[47] The revival gave the church strength to go through this trying time of struggle. Thousands of Federal and Confederate soldiers who would soon die were converted in the revival and therefore prepared for eternity.[48] Churches would continue to minister to their soldier boys on the battlefields through financial gifts, literature, tracts, Bibles, and the rendering of spiritual as well as medical assistance. The revival hastened the day of national reconciliation and helped in the difficulties of Reconstruction.[49]

Impact of the Revival on Baptists

Evangelical Christianity in this country was greatly affected by the Prayer Revival of 1857–58. Virtually all denominations experienced a significant numerical gain in their memberships as a result of it. Baptists also enjoyed significant growth during this marvelous movement of God and were strongly influenced by the revival in various other ways.

Evangelistic results. In his dissertation on the effects of the Awakening of 1858 on Baptists, Roy Fish calculated that a total of 188,000 individuals were baptized into Baptist churches between 1857 and 1859.[50] This was the first time in their history that Baptists in the United States had baptized over 100,000 converts in a two-year period. The accelerated growth experienced by Baptists can be seen in a percentage comparison of the number of baptisms between 1857 and 1858. Baptist churches in the South baptized 43 percent more converts in 1858 than they did in 1857, while those in the North showed an incredible 150-percent increase in baptisms from 1857 to 1858.

Highly significant overall is the fact that of the one million souls converted as a result of the Prayer Revival of 1857–58, almost 20 percent of them chose to join the ranks of those who called themselves Baptists. No doubt this surge of growth strengthened a relatively new branch of Baptists who had organized the Southern Baptist Convention in Augusta, Georgia, in 1845, which would later become the largest non-Catholic Christian denomination in the world.

New churches. Baptists witnessed the addition of 650 new congregations to their denomination in 1858. This was the largest increase in the number of Baptist churches over any previous year. Of the total number, 308 were in northern states, while 342 were in states affiliated with the Southern Baptist Convention. In 1856 there were 354 new congregations, while the number was 455 in 1857.[51]

Mission work. There was much anticipation, as indicated in Baptist missions publications of the day, that the Prayer Revival of 1857–58 would be a significant catalyst to further the cause of missions throughout the world. It was believed that the Baptist missionary enterprise would be strengthened because more individuals would be called by God to serve as missionaries, and financial contributions to all mission causes would greatly increase. Although Baptist mission work did make progress following the revival, two factors made it difficult to determine to what degree the expectations were fulfilled. One factor was that many young men who were potential future missionaries enlisted to fight in the Civil War. Another factor was the financial panic of 1857, which even at the height of the revival caused a sharp decrease in gifts to missions.[52] When the effects of the financial panic had subsided, however, mission giving reached an all-time high, indicating "that a definite beneficent effect [for missions] was felt as a result of the revival of 1858."[53]

Baptist churches both in the North and in the South performed mission work during the Civil War among the soldiers on the battlefields. Southern Baptists were so committed to missionary efforts among the Confederate troops that they withdrew 150 missionaries from the field in order to focus their evangelistic energies on the soldiers in the southern armies. Giving to army missions by Southern Baptist churches far exceeded any amount given to previous mission enterprises. Fish concludes: "This missionary effort on the part of both southern and northern churches was undoubtedly an effect of the revival of 1858."[54] One historian drove home this point with a question as he referred to the missionary efforts during the Civil War: "Who will dare affirm that such great things would have been possible if the revival of 1858 had not preceded the war?"[55]

In addition to the effects mentioned above, the Prayer Revival of 1857–58 affected Baptists in various other ways. Baptist laymen began to take a more active role in the ministries of their own churches.[56] Many of those converted in Baptist churches felt called of God into Christian ministry and began to prepare themselves educationally for the Lord's service. Revival was experienced by several Baptist schools, such as Brown University, Richmond College, and Baylor University.[57]

One rather interesting effect of the revival on Baptists came about as a result of the conviction among members of many denominations that immersion was the only true biblical method of baptism. This became a great advantage for Baptists because not only did many members of other denominations forsake their infant sprinklings to join Baptist churches, but also several ministers left those same denominations to unite with Baptist churches through believer's baptism.[58] Fish reported that due to the Prayer Revival of 1857–58, when the War between the States began, Baptists in this country were stronger than they had been since the formation of the Southern Baptist Convention in 1845.[59]

Conclusion

The "third great awakening" in America, which began in prayer and spread through prayer, was indeed a powerful movement of God. J. Edwin Orr, a leading authority on spiritual awakenings, said that it was the greatest revival that he had ever studied.[60] In a chapel service at Southwestern Baptist Theological Seminary in 1983, attended by this writer, Orr concluded his lecture on the Prayer Revival of 1857–58 with these words:

> What I've told you [today] has been a case where the Lord said, "Stand aside for a little while and I'll show you what I can do." And perhaps that will happen again before the coming of our Lord and Savior Jesus Christ. So be it.[61]

The desperate spiritual condition of America today should cause all believers to cry out in fervent prayer to God for such a spiritual awakening in this land. If God chooses to send awakening to this nation again as he did in 1857–58, so be it!

Endnotes

1. Roy J. Fish, "The Awakening of 1858 and Its Effects on Baptists in the United States" (Th.D. diss., Southwestern Baptist Theological Seminary, 1963), iii. The author wishes to acknowledge Fish's extensive dissertation research on the Prayer Revival of 1857–58. He diligently compiled the records of approximately six hundred Baptist associations from across the United States for the period of 1853–60 in order to give a thorough and accurate statistical analysis of the effects that this revival had on Baptists in this country. I also want to thank Dr. Fish personally for the inspiration, support, and example that he gave to me not only as a student but also as a minister striving to "do the work of an evangelist."

2. Fred W. Hoffman, *Revival Times in America* (Boston: Wilde Company, 1956), 106.

3. Frank G. Beardsley, *Religious Progress Through Religious Revivals* (New York: American Tract Society, 1943), 39–40.

4. C. E. Autrey, "The Revival of 1858," *Southwestern Journal of Theology* 1 (October 1958): 10.

5. For a fuller account of these "preparatory" revivals, see Fish, "Awakening of 1858," 12–14.

6. J. Edwin Orr, *The Second Evangelical Awakening in America* (London: Marshall, Morgan, and Scott, 1952), 23.

7. Fish, "Awakening of 1858," 15.

8. Samuel Irenaeus Prime, *Prayer and Its Answer* (New York: Scribner, 1882), 24.

9. Talbot W. Chambers, *The Noon Prayer Meeting of the North Dutch Church* (New York: Board of Publications of the Reformed Protestant Dutch Church, 1858), 42.

10. Fish, "Awakening of 1858," 18–19.

11. Frank G. Beardsley, *A History of American Revivals* (New York: American Tract Society, 1904), 216.

12. Hoffman, *Revival Times,* 108–09. Although the Bank Panic of 1857 in the providence of God was a factor in the beginning of the revival movement, it was by no means the cause of the awakening as some historians have proposed. See J. Edwin Orr, *The Fervent Prayer* (Chicago: Moody Press, 1974), 5.

13. Orr, *Awakening in America,* 31.

14. *National Intelligence* (Washington), 20 March 1858, as quoted by Orr.

15. Fish, "Awakening of 1858," 18–19.

16. Samuel Irenaeus Prime, *The Power of Prayer* (New York: Scribner, 1859), 26–27.

17. *Journal of Commerce* (New York), 26 November 1857, as quoted by George W. Van Vleck, *The Panic of 1857* (New York: Columbia Univ. Press, 1943), 107.

18. William C. Conant, *Narratives of Remarkable Conversions and Revival Incidents,* with an introduction by Henry Ward Beecher (New York: Derby and Jackson, 1858), 429.

19. *Presbyterian Magazine,* June 1858, as quoted by Orr, *Awakening in America,* 47.

20. Chambers, *Noon Prayer Meeting,* 196–97.

21. William R. Moody, *The Life of D. L. Moody,* (Chicago: Revell, 1900)

22. Warren A. Candler, *Great Revivals and the Great Republic* (Nashville: Publishing House of the M.E. Church, South, 1904), 216–17. See also Orr, *Fervent Prayer,* 29–30. For opposing views see Charles G. Finney, *Memoirs of Charles G. Finney* (New York: Revell, 1876), 444; and Beardsley, *History of Revivals,* 227–28.

23. Beardsley, *Religious Progress,* 49.

24. Hoffman, *Revival Times,* 114.

25. John Shearer, *Old Time Revivals* (Fort Worth: Potters Book Store, n.d.), 45.

26. Ibid.

27. Beardsley, *History of Revivals,* 228–29.

28. David N. Lord, ed., "Thoughts on the Revival of Eighteen Hundred and Fifty-Eight," *The Theological and Literary Journal* 11 (July 1858–April 1859): 197.

29. As quoted in Harold A. Fischer, *Reviving Revivals* (Springfield, Missouri: Gospel Publishing, 1950), 173.

30. For a full description of the proceedings at the prayer meetings, see Chambers, *Noon Prayer Meeting,* 45–68.

31. Autrey, "Revival of 1858," 13.

32. Beardsley, *History of Revivals,* 230; *Religious Progress,* 48.

33. Francis Wayland, "The Revival in America," *The Baptist Magazine* 50 (August 1858): 470.

34. "The Revival of 1858," *The Freewill Baptist Quarterly* 7 (1859): 60.

35. Smith said, "Unity in evangelism had routed sectarian controversy." See Timothy L. Smith, *Revivalism and Social Reform in Mid-Nineteenth Century America* (New York: Abingdon, 1957), 71.

36. Beardsley, *Religious Progress,* 48.

37. Ibid., 49.

38. Orr, *Awakening in America,* 107.

39. Wayland, "Revival in America," 467.

40. Beardsley, *History of Revivals,* 236; see also Grover C. Loud, *Evangelized America* (New York: Dial Press, 1928), 223. Beardsley argued that five hundred thousand was the most probable figure. Candler and Orr, however, argued for the one million figure. See Candler, *Great Revivals,* 215–16; and Orr, *Awakening in America,* 64.

41. W. L. Muncy, Jr., *A History of Evangelism in the United States* (Kansas City, Kans.: Central Seminary Press, 1945), 114.

42. Orr, *Fervent Prayer,* 11.

43. William Warren Sweet, *Revivalism in America: Its Origin, Growth, and Decline* (New York: Scribner, 1944), 160–61.

44. Fish, "Awakening of 1858," 247.

45. Smith, *Revivalism and Reform,* 74.

46. Orr, *Awakening in America,* 154.

47. Beardsley, *History of Revivals,* 238.

48. Candler, *Great Revivals,* 225.

49. Autrey, "Revival of 1858," 20.

50. Fish, "Awakening of 1858," 228. The total number of baptisms in the Baptist churches during the revival period represented a baptismal ratio of one baptism for every 10.8 members.

51. Ibid., 228–229.

52. Ibid., 249–250.

53. Ibid., 6. For an analysis of the differences in mission giving between churches in the North and the South, see Ibid., 251–55.

54. Ibid., 258,

55. Candler, *Great Revivals,* 228.

56. Greater lay participation in the denomination was actually encouraged by Baptist ministers as they "caught the vision of what a consecrated laity could accomplish." See Fish, "Awakening of 1858," 231.

57. See Ibid., 238–245.

58. Ibid., 233–235.

59. Ibid., 6.

60. J. Edwin Orr, *The Prayer Revival of 1857–58,* taped lecture at the Second National Conference on Prayer for Spiritual Awakenings, cassette TC 9136, Home Mission Board, n.d.

61. Orr, *Revival of 1858,* taped lecture of Theological Fellowship Chapel, cassette TC 9803, Southwestern Baptist Theological Seminary, 1983.

14

Times of Refreshing:

The Revival of 1970 at Southwestern Baptist Theological Seminary

Timothy K. Beougher

Timothy K. Beougher serves as assistant professor of evangelism at Wheaton Graduate School and associate director of the Institute of Evangelism at the Billy Graham Center. Beougher studied under Fish during his M.Div. at Southwestern Seminary, and Fish served as a reader on his Th.M. thesis on the 1970 Awakening's impact on Southwestern. Beougher also holds a Ph.D. in historical theology from Trinity Evangelical Divinity School.

Revival has been defined by Stephen Olford as "that strange and sovereign work of God in which he visits his own people, restoring, reanimating and releasing them in to the fullness of his blessing."[1]

During the third week of March 1970, Southwestern Baptist Theological Seminary in Fort Worth, Texas experienced an outpouring of this sovereign work of God. Students spontaneously met together for prayer, confession of sin, and public testimonies of what God was doing in their lives. The revival touched not only individuals, but the seminary community as a whole. Its impact not only reached area churches but was felt throughout the Southern Baptist Convention.

This chapter seeks to tell the story of this relatively recent revival.[2] In a day when the cries for awakening[3] grow louder and louder, seeing how God has worked in the past provides both instruction and encouragement for prayer in the present.

The editor of the outstanding book on the 1970 Asbury Revival, *One Divine Moment*,[4] chose not to use individual's names in the account of that revival, wanting instead for the emphasis to be placed where it is deserved—on the work of the Holy Spirit. This author desires that the Holy Spirit receive no less credit for what took place at Southwestern. Revival *always* comes from God. But while the author shares this concern, he also realizes one of the aspects of revival sometimes overlooked is that God uses people—warts and all—as instruments of revival. Therefore, people's names will be used throughout this account.[5]

To understand conditions prior to the 1970 revival, we begin with a brief examination of the late 1960s in America.

The Historical Setting Preceding the Revival

To refer to the decade of the 1960s in America as "turbulent" surely seems like an understatement. It was an era filled with drugs, sex, violence, tear gas, shootings, arson, bombings, the Vietnam War, riots, assassinations, etc. Colleges and universities were the scene of frequent demonstrations, many resulting in the destruction of property. Conditions grew so bad that by 1970, several schools canceled commencement services because of fear of violence.

Religion and church life were also in decline. The cover of *Time* magazine for April 8, 1966 wondered, "Is God Dead?" The question was not only being asked by liberal theologians. America seemed to be falling apart at the seams. Where was God? Churches faced sagging attendance, enrollment fell at seminaries, and religious book sales lagged.

But in the midst of the bad news, signs of hope were appearing. Thus, *Time* magazine's last cover of 1969 asked, "Is God Coming Back to Life?"

One such sign of hope was the Jesus movement, a name coined to describe the spiritual awakening in the United States that occurred in the latter 1960s and early 1970s, mainly among young people.[6] Another was the revival at Asbury College and Seminary during February 1970.[7] One observer describes the situation in Wilmore, Kentucky:

> While many students across America were burning down buildings and rioting in the streets, students in this college community were strangely drawn to their knees to pray. It was as if the campus had been suddenly invaded by another Power. Classes were forgotten. Academic work came to a standstill. In a way awesome to behold, God had taken over the campus. Caught up in

the wonder of it, a thousand students remained for days in the college auditorium—not to demand more freedom or to protest the Establishment, but to confess their sin and to sing the praises of their Saviour.[8]

The Asbury revival began in a college chapel service in Hughes Auditorium on February 3, 1970. Following a time of testimonies,

> a mass of students moved forward. . . . There was not room for all who wanted to pray at the altar. Many had to kneel in the front seats of the auditorium. Their prayers were mingled with heartfelt contrition and outbursts of joy. It was evident that God was moving upon his people in power. The presence of the Lord was so real that all other interests seemed unimportant. The bell sounded for classes to begin but went unheeded.[9]

Classes were canceled for the remainder of the day as students continued to testify and pray.

The revival spread to the seminary campus during its chapel service the next day, following the same format of open confession of sin and desire for a fresh touch from the Holy Spirit. Day after day this continued, until classes finally resumed on February 10.

This movement of God at Asbury caused persons to desire this same experience for themselves. As news of the revival spread, people from other campuses called to ask for prayer for their schools. Soon Asbury students were traveling all over the nation to tell what God had done on their campus and in their individual lives. By the summer of 1970 at least 130 colleges, seminaries, and Bible schools had been touched by the revival outreach, and Asbury students continued to go to other schools and local churches.[10] Schools influenced included Azusa [Pacific] College, Taylor University, Spring Arbor College, Roberts Wesleyan College, Oral Roberts University, and Greenville College, just to name a few.[11]

The Revival at Southwestern

Southwestern Baptist Theological Seminary, located in Fort Worth, Texas, consistently boasts the largest student enrollment of any evangelical seminary in the world.[12] The school was not isolated from problems during the tumultuous years of the 1960s. No riots ensued and no buildings were burned, but there was student unrest and rebellion, some of which focused around a controversial new president's mansion.[13] An underground student newspaper started circulating on the seminary campus which was highly critical not only of the proposed president's home but of the administration in general, conveying an "ugly" spirit.[14]

Another manifestation of discontent were the so-called open forum chapels. When students demanded a forum to voice their complaints and concerns, Dr. Robert Naylor, Southwestern's president at the time, proposed that one chapel service a month be given to let students "air their grievances."[15] Microphones were placed around the auditorium so students wanting to speak could be heard. A panel composed of administrators, faculty, and usually a trustee and student representative were seated on the stage to respond to questions and comments.[16] The tone of these chapels was very ugly, with comments often filled with hatred and unbelief.

These and other events were merely the visible manifestations of the underlying critical spirit that seemed prevalent on campus. Yet as in the broader picture of the nation as a whole, signs of hope were appearing amid the negative backdrop. A key event occurred in December 1967, when Dr. Jack Gray was asked to review J. Edwin Orr's new book, *The Light of the Nations* for the *Southwestern Journal of Theology*. Orr's book traced the history of spiritual awakening and its impact on the advance of the church. Gray tells what reading that book did for him:

> The Lord used it as a remarkable instrument to conscript me into prayer for personal, seminary, denominational, and national spiritual awakening. I was overwhelmed by the burden he gave me and by his enabling me to respond and to pray for awakening.[17]

Gray sensed the Lord leading him to create a means by which faculty and students could unite together to pray for revival. Several began meeting weekly to pray for a spiritual awakening on Southwestern's campus. Other prayer groups sprang up around the campus as well, most with a burden for revival.

For some two years, people prayed without seeing the revival for which they longed. In February of 1970, Southwesterners heard of the Asbury revival, many through Billy Graham's "Hour of Decision" broadcast of Sunday, February 15, 1970.[18] The news brought great encouragement to those praying for revival at Southwestern, and students began to enlist others to pray with them.[19]

When Dr. Roy Fish heard that Asbury students were going to other schools to share about the revival, he prayed about them coming to Southwestern. After talking to persons involved with the Asbury revival, Fish called President Naylor to ask him about having Asbury students come and share at Southwestern. When Naylor gave his approval, the invitation went to Asbury for students to come to Southwestern's campus to give their testimonies.

Fish learned at about noon on Friday, March 13, that three Asbury students were coming. A service was planned to let them share on campus on Monday afternoon, March 16. When one student heard they were coming, he said, "Let's don't wait until the Asbury students get here. Let's have a prayer meeting tonight."[20] The student put up a poster in Fort Worth Hall and Barnard Hall (the men's and women's residence halls) saying there would be a prayer meeting for revival at 8:30 P.M. in the Student Center West.

Between twenty-five and thirty students gathered to pray. A remarkable spirit of openness and concern developed in the meeting. Burdens were shared, sins were confessed, and praise was lifted to God both in song and in prayer.

At about eleven o'clock, Dr. Jack Gray closed the meeting with a prayer of dedication for the meeting at 4:00 on Monday. When Gray got up to leave, he noticed three young men whom he did not know. He went over to them and asked, "Are you students here? I do not think I know you." They said, "No, we are from Asbury. When we arrived on campus we saw a notice about a prayer meeting, so we came over to join in. But we might as well go home. Revival is already here!"[21]

The three students were Darius Salter, an Asbury College senior; Parks Davis, an Asbury Seminary senior; and David Perry, a first year student at Asbury Seminary.[22] They had left Wilmore, Kentucky, on Friday evening after a prayer time in Dr. Robert Coleman's living room. They spent the night in Memphis, Tennessee, and then drove the rest of the way to Fort Worth on Saturday.

Despite their initial feeling that they were not needed at Southwestern, they stayed in Fort Worth through the next week. Dr. Roy Fish had made arrangements to have the students speak in area churches that Sunday. Persons were touched and relationships healed in churches in Mesquite; Wilshire Terrace Baptist Church, Euless; and Travis Avenue Baptist Church in Forth Worth.[23] The next day, numerous Southern Baptist pastors were touched by God's Spirit at an associational meeting where the Asbury students testified.[24]

Monday afternoon brought the Asbury students back to the seminary campus for the scheduled testimony time in Scarborough Preaching Chapel.

This chapel, located in the lower level of the theology building, is a miniature of a church sanctuary designed for teaching and preaching. By four o'clock Monday afternoon it was full. Dr. Roy Fish recalls that there were about two hundred gathered together, despite the difficulty of getting the word out to students.[25]

Fish introduced the three Asbury students. David Perry and Darius Salter gave brief testimonies about the February 3–10 revival at Asbury, and how it impacted the seminary, the college, and them personally. Parks Davis was scheduled to be the keynote speaker, but when he was introduced, he did not move. After a few moments, he stood and simply said, "The table is set; come and dine."[26] Then he sat down.

This was followed by one or two minutes of awkward silence. Then students and spouses began to rise and come to a microphone to share what God had been saying to them.[27] There were confessions of sin, painful and humiliating pleas for forgiveness, and earnest calls for help in prayer.[28]

One of the most powerful moments in the service came when a young wife rose and said:

> I was born and reared in a preacher's home. Now I am married to a preacher. I've gone to church all of my life just because it was the thing to do. But it has never meant much to me. I've resented the time the church has demanded of my husband. And now I know why! I've just asked Jesus to come into my heart, and he has![29]

Gary Maroney was one of the students who shared during this time. He recounts,

> I have never been in a place where the presence of the Spirit of God was so overpowering. It was like electricity going through the room. The Lord was really dealing with my heart. I knew the Lord; I was a Christian; I knew his calling in my life, but I knew that I was not up to date in my relationship with him. I was not experiencing his fullness in my life.
>
> I wanted to do what the Lord wanted me to, but there was a war going on. I wanted to be what God wanted, but I was afraid of what the consequences might be. I finally came to the place where I said, "All that really matters is that I must be right with You, Lord." I went down to the front and knelt. I began to weep before him and to confess my sin to him.

After a while, I got up. As I was praying, it was like there were waves of his love just flowing over me. There was a cleansing and a purging in my life.

I left and walked across campus. It was raining. The refreshment of the drops of rain mirrored the joy in my heart. I kept thinking over and over, *I'm clean; I'm clean before the Lord.*[30]

Henry Liginfelter remembers the atmosphere in the meeting:

The Holy Spirit's presence was overpowering. Everybody was just bent over pews, praying and confessing. I didn't know if there was anybody up speaking or not—it didn't make any difference. Most of us were bowed so low we couldn't have got up if we'd wanted to.[31]

Dr. Jack Gray summarizes what the participants experienced: "God was so mightily present we could all but touch him. It was awesome. . . . We were meeting God in all his majesty!"[32]

The meeting finally ended about 1:00 A.M. Many had stayed the entire time. Some had left to go and bring back wives and friends to the chapel. Some students left the meeting to go make relationships right with others.

The following day, Tuesday, the Asbury students shared all day in various classes on Southwestern's campus. When they shared, once again students were moved to prayer and confession. Many knelt on the floor beside their desk to pour out their heart to God. Dr. Jack Gray recalls:

In classes throughout the day, the moment one gave his testimony, the Spirit of God would fall on us and elicit spontaneous, slow, deliberate searching of God and response to him. I was seeing what I had never seen in my life—the sovereign work of the Spirit of God without counsel from anybody—just a testimony of one in whom he had worked. Then the Holy Spirit would take it and use it to search and probe the hearts of everyone present.[33]

At 3:00 that afternoon, another voluntary service was held, this one in the larger Truett Auditorium. Again many lives were touched with the service continuing until 6:30 P.M.[34]

That evening, Dr. Trozy Barker, dean of men, called a meeting in Fort Worth Hall at 10:00. Barker recalls,

I felt the Spirit moving on campus and called a meeting of the fellows in the dorm here to let them share. . . . Mrs. Barker and I stayed there until 1:30 A.M. I know it went on until at least 3:00 A.M., when two fellows went to the room of another fellow to apologize to him for some attitudes they had towards him.[35]

Gary Maroney remembers a student telephoning his father:

There was a young man in the dormitory who went and called his father after he had gotten his heart right with the Lord. They had a strained relationship— he called his father to ask him to forgive him. On the telephone he was weeping. The Lord worked in his father's heart, and the relationship was restored.[36]

A student had called President Naylor on Tuesday evening to see if the Asbury students could share in chapel the next day. Naylor said the chapel speaker was already scheduled, but that the students could have the twenty-minute coffee break time.[37]

The speaker for chapel that Wednesday morning was Dr. LaCoste Munn, professor of New Testament at the seminary. Word had spread that the Asbury students were going to share and the auditorium was packed. After Munn finished his message, President Naylor told those who wanted to remain that they could. He turned the platform over to Dr. Fish, who introduced the Asbury students. The students shared what had taken place at Asbury and how it had impacted their campus. When David Perry ended his testimony, he raised three fingers into the air and boldly proclaimed, "Jesus is Lord!" Dr. Gray tells what happened next: "The Spirit of God began immediately to draw out of those present confessions, burdens, reconciliations, pleas for help in prayer, and glorious testimonies of victory."[38]

After a time of sharing, the bell rang. President Naylor moved slowly to the podium and noted that the bell had rung for class. Dismissing those who had class,[39] he encouraged those who did not have class to feel free to stay. About two to three hundred stayed, while others came and went. It was a time of open confession and testimony of victory.[40] At 2:45 that afternoon, that meeting was brought to a close.

The effects were felt in area churches that night, as Southwestern students went to Wednesday evening prayer meetings. Dr. Fish notes, "Wherever they shared, without exception, somebody was saved. No, they gave no invitation, but people heard and listened, and where they were sitting, openly invited Jesus Christ to come in."[41]

Dr. Gray summarizes the aftermath of the Wednesday meeting:

> Through the rest of the week we found ourselves walking in a sense of reverent awe, our minds racing with questions, our wills painfully adjusting to the demands of what God had wrought, our hearts reaching out in eager desire to tell others, and our souls lifted in glorious joy, praise, and new dimensions of loving adoration of the Lord.[42]

Indeed, many lives had been changed during the week, but that was only the beginning. The concentric circles of impact began to widen in ever-increasing fashion.

The Aftermath of the Revival

The following week was spring break, when students scattered all over the country to preach revivals under the banner of "Pioneer Penetration." Dr. Jack Gray recalls, "More than usual glowing reports of revived churches and larger than usual ingatherings of the lost were brought back as classes resumed the following week."[43]

Ben Loring recalls the impact the Southwestern Revival had on the ministry of those who went out that week, noting, "I saw things happening that I knew were not from me. People were saved left and right; church members were renewed."[44]

Dr. Gray, speaking in chapel in December of 1970, had the following to say:

> Revival is in our nation. Revival is in our seminary. I did not say our nation is in revival. There is a difference. I did not say our seminary is in revival. The kingdom was at hand before many were in it.[45]

That fall, several chapel speakers shared what God was doing in their churches or their own personal lives. Two testimonies that stood out as particularly memorable were given by Joe Ann Shelton and Frank Stovall, both of whom had undergone personal revival during this time period.[46]

The ongoing campus effects are likewise evident in an excerpt from a letter written by Dr. Jack Gray in September 1970:

God continues to declare his presence at Southwestern. Evidences of God's spontaneous work of revival across our nation have come to us this fall in the person of many profound young Christians with more contagious joy, and faith, and hunger for more of the Lord than I have ever seen in any previous assembly of new students. The carry-over of revival from last year in former students is strong and healthy. New students and former students are mutually contributing to each other and toward revival this year.[47]

Jim Elliff recounts:

I don't think I have really seen as consistently as that time the depth of movement in those meetings. Even though we were really green . . . we had a message of revival to share. Getting right with God and getting right with others was pretty much the theme we carried.

We saw remarkable things happen in those churches. There was real brokenness; individuals would be getting right with each other and would confess things publicly during church services. Sometimes it was accompanied with a great number of people being saved.[48]

The Fact of "Recoil"

Before highlighting further examples of how individuals and churches were influenced by the revival, honesty demands our looking at another factor in revival—the fact of "recoil." Not everyone who was revived has "stayed with the stuff." Robert Coleman reminds us,

We should remember, too, that there are still obvious human limitations among those who are revived. Regrettable as it may seem, spiritual renewal does not make one any less a man. Ignorance, emotional instability, personality quirks, and all the other traits of our fallen humanity, are very much in evidence. Though the revival is not responsible for these shortcomings, it has to bear their reproach.[49]

This was evidenced in the revival at Southwestern. Two students who were actively involved in the revival have since left the ministry, both due to moral reasons.[50] This underscores the principle that even if one has a life-changing experience, he or she cannot live merely from that experience. There has to be a continued daily obedience to the Lord.

Subsequent Ministry

The revival did not solve all problems—revival never does. But even a cursory examination of some of the subsequent ministry God allowed those who experienced revival at Southwestern to have should end all doubt that the Southwestern revival of 1970 did have a substantial impact. The following testimonies speak for themselves:

Immanuel Baptist Church in Altus, Oklahoma. "The very next Sunday evening service [after the week of revival], I was back up in my home state of Oklahoma, and I shared what took place at Immanuel Baptist Church in Altus. I just shared in a way very uncommon to myself. I tend to be dramatic in preaching—this was low key for me—but I shared the story, and the invitation began and lasted for an hour. The Spirit of God just moved in a way totally beyond anything else I have seen since.

"People embraced one another, weeping; reconciliation came about; and all that had to be totally of the Spirit of God. It wasn't anything that was prompted or manipulated. The service lasted the whole length of time, and nobody was up front telling anybody to do anything."[51]

First Baptist Church, Perry, Georgia. "I went back to First Baptist Church, Perry, Georgia, as their youth director for the summer. I came into a very rebellious youth group. I began almost immediately sharing what God had done in me at the revival at Southwestern. At a youth retreat early in the summer . . . God just began breaking those young people. It was not an emotionally charged thing. The Lord just broke those young people and saved them.

"The pastor was touched. He got up in front of the church that Sunday and said, 'If I ever get in this pulpit again without the power of God, I pray he'll strike me dead.' He then turned the service over to the young people.

"These kids were so turned on that they wanted to share it. We began getting invitation after invitation to share in Baptist churches in the area. They would just call and say, 'Can you bring your young people to tell us what has happened?' We would rent a bus and go. That was my youth program for the summer.

"I would just get up and introduce these kids. They would sing and share their testimony. Almost everywhere we went, the same thing would happen. The kids would finish, and the people of the church would begin to confess."[52]

Town of Buena Vista, Colorado. "The following August, four of us went up to a little church in Colorado. My brother Jim was one of them. The meeting wasn't sponsored by any church, but all the churches were involved.

"The place was absolutely packed. In one service, over half the high school was saved. You could walk down the street and see lights on in the middle of the night due to people staying up to study the Bible.

"One night eighty people came forward and trusted Christ in less than a minute. Hundreds were saved in those days."[53]

Liberia, Africa. "The revival had ripples that went out everywhere. I went to Liberia, Africa, and ministered to a group of missionaries there. A real spirit of division had developed among some there. I shared the testimony of what God had done at Southwestern, and God fell on that group of missionaries. The same thing happened: confession of sin; brokenness; one after another standing to share. The two leaders of the faction went to one another and made things right. The mission may have been headed for a split, but the Lord healed things there. That was worth more than all my preaching while I was there."[54]

A church in central Florida. "In the summer I went to a small town in central Florida to preach a revival. You can hardly separate the fact that God was doing some unusual things through our ministry at this time.

"The church was so dead that it had been using its baptistry as a storage room. And here on Sunday morning was a young seminary student preacher. Almost in spite of that, the movement of God began to happen. When we gave the invitation people began to come from everywhere. . . .

"I found out later that a dear lady had been praying for revival for twenty-two years every Tuesday at noon in the front of the church."[55]

This chapter has only scratched the surface of the effects of the revival. Because of the multiplying effect through people's lives, it soon becomes impossible to trace the path of awakening. One can confidently assert that the influence of the Southwestern Revival certainly continues even today.

Conclusion

How should the Southwestern Revival be evaluated? How are we to interpret what took place? While much more could be said, four points deserve special mention.

First, contrary to popular thought, the Southwestern Revival did not begin at Asbury. Dr. Robert Coleman says,

> What the Asbury students did was simply encourage and give some focus to what they [Southwesterners] had been praying for on their campus over the years. The Asbury influence was essentially an encouragement to the burden of revival they had already been feeling. It gave the impetus to a movement that was already underway. So with the prayer that had already gone on at Southwestern, it fueled the flames.[56]

Second, the history of the Southwestern Revival reinforces the truth that no one can continue to live a consistent Christian life from a one-time experience. Unfortunately, some of those who were touched by the revival have since fallen away from a vital walk with Christ. As was pointed out earlier, each and every believer must make a new pledge of obedience daily.

Third, one can readily see that the Southwestern Revival was not of the magnitude of a "Great Awakening." Despite many individuals being deeply touched, the fact that things basically went on as normal at the seminary shows it did not deeply affect the entire campus. Michael Gott argues, "Some of the potential of the stirring of God was never realized. I'm not sure I would call it a revival. I would call it a stirring that never really took off in all of its potential."[57]

Yet having acknowledged this, one must finally recognize that it did have far-reaching effects. Dr. Robert Coleman, who was at Asbury during the 1970 Revival, says:

> The Southwestern dimension of the Asbury revival has had an influence across the Southern Baptist Convention because of the strategic position of the seminary. In my opinion, in terms of the outreach, the single most significant impact of the Asbury revival was upon the Baptist ministry through Southwestern. I think time has proven that to be the case. No one knows exactly how many churches were touched, but I expect there were thousands, considering the second, third, and fourth generation ripples. Finally the ripples get so far removed that you can hardly trace them back.[58]

Because of these "ripples," a few of which were highlighted in this chapter, the Southwestern Revival of 1970 deserves serious merit as a genuine awakening. Call it what you want, but ask God to do it again!

Endnotes

1. Stephen F. Olford, *Heart-Cry for Revival* (Westwood, N.J.: Revell, 1962), 17.

2. This chapter is condensed from the author's master's thesis entitled: "The Revival of 1970 at Southwestern Baptist Theological Seminary: A History and Evaluation." Unpublished Th.M. thesis, Trinity Evangelical Divinity School, 1987. Since little written material is available on the revival, the documentation has been taken primarily from personal interviews with selected administrators, faculty, and students who were at Southwestern in 1970.

3. There is no commonly accepted vocabulary to describe movements of revival. Some make a distinction between the terms "revival" and "awakening," using "revival" to mean a large movement of God's Spirit, while using the term "awakening" to refer to smaller movements (e.g. J. Edwin Orr, *The Light of the Nations: Evangelical Renewal and Advance in the Nineteenth Century*. No. 8, *The Paternoster Church History*, ed. by F. F. Bruce. [Exeter, Eng.: The Paternoster Press, 1965], 264). This author uses the terms "revival" and "awakening" as synonymous.

4. Robert E. Coleman, ed., *One Divine Moment* (Old Tappan, N.J.: Revell, 1970).

5. An individual's inclusion or exclusion in this account is not meant to suggest the degree of his/her involvement at the time of his/her current spirituality. In the Spring of 1970 there were over two thousand students enrolled at Southwestern; less than thirty have been interviewed by the author. Those who are quoted in the paper are those whose names were given to this author by more than one individual as someone who should be interviewed. The reader should also remember that many years have passed since the revival took place. Even the best of memories fade somewhat with the passage of time. Effort has been made to check and cross-check every item to help insure its accuracy. Still, someone's remembrance of an event may vary with what is recorded here.

6. See the chapter by Alvin Reid elsewhere in this book.

7. This has been well documented in the work edited by Coleman, *One Divine Moment*.

8. Ibid., 13–14.

9. Ibid., 17–19.

10. Ibid., 55.

11. Tom Carruth, "Special Report No. 4," Department of Prayer and Spiritual Life, Asbury Theological Seminary, February 11, 1970. *Christianity Today* also ran an article describing the impact of the Asbury revival on other campuses. See John Nelson and Janet Rohler, "Asbury Revival Blazes Cross-Country Trail," *Christianity Today*, (13 March 1970): 46–50.

12. For a comprehensive history of the school, see Robert A. Baker, *Tell the Generations Following: A History of Southwestern Baptist Theological Seminary, 1908–1983* (Nashville: Broadman, 1983).

13. "Letters to the Editor: Protest Seminary Home," *Baptist Standard*, (7 January 1970): 2.

14. Telephone interview with Dr. Felix Gresham, Fort Worth, Texas, 12 February 1987.

15. Interview with Dr. Robert Naylor, president emeritus, Southwestern Baptist Theological Seminary, Fort Worth, Texas, 13 February 1987.

16. A picture of one such panel is found in *Southwestern News* (December 1968): 3.

17. Telephone interview with Dr. L. Jack Gray, professor of missions, emeritus, Southwestern Baptist Theological Seminary, Fort Worth, Texas, 1 July 1986. His review can be found in the *Southwestern Journal of Theology* (Spring 1968): 108–109. Two of Gray's statements stand out: "He [Orr] repeatedly links prayer meetings as causes of revivals"; and "The significant point is made that the 'Revivals' were not 'frontier phenomena' but began in colleges of settled communities and great cities. Thus, evangelical awakenings, now as then, are still possible."

18. A typewritten news release from Asbury dated February 17, 1970, stated: "Billy Graham shares the Asbury revival with more than 25,000,000 on his popular radio program 'Hour of Decision.' "

19. Telephone interview with Dr. Gary Galeotti, professor, Criswell Center for Biblical Studies, Dallas, Texas, 10 February 1987. Danny Vance remembers, "When we heard about the Asbury revival, it had a tremendous effect on us! We realized it was not in the realm of the theoretical anymore, but that revival was a reality that was happening now. We wanted it to happen here." Telephone interview with Rev. Danny Vance, director, University Ministries, Southwest Baptist University, Bolivar, Missouri, 10 February 1987.

20. Telephone interview with Dr. L. Jack Gray.

21. Ibid. See also David Perry, *Rolling with Jesus* (Nashville: Broadman, 1971), 27. Perry recalls, "We walked into revival . . . revival was right there. What we had come to tell them about was already happening!" Telephone interview with Rev. David Perry, pastor, Emmanuel Church, Macon, Georgia, 22 February 1987.

22. The April 1970 issue of *Southwestern News* has a picture of David Perry on page 11.

23. Telephone interviews with Rev. Parks Davis, pastor, Jonesboro United Methodist Church, Jonesboro, Georgia, 12 March 1987; Dr. Fred Lowery, pastor, First Baptist Church, Bossier City, Louisiana, 9 February 1987; Dr. James Coggin, Fort Worth, Texas, 13 February 1987; and Rev. David Perry. See also Perry, *Rolling with Jesus,* 27.

24. Telephone interview with Rev. David Perry.

25. Dr. Roy Fish, "Spiritual Awakening at Southwestern," Chapel Service at Southwestern Baptist Theological Seminary, 20 September 1977. Southwestern does not have Monday classes because many of its students pastor churches several hours away from the seminary campus. This made getting word out especially difficult.

26. Perry, *Rolling with Jesus,* 21.

27. Fish, "Spiritual Awakening at Southwestern."

28. L. Jack Gray, "Revival at Southwestern Baptist Theological Seminary, Fort Worth, Texas," (typewritten), 1970, 7–8. It was at this service that an indiscreet confession of sin took place. A student publicly confessed lusting towards a female student. Dr. Roy Fish admonished the group, "Let the circle of your confession be only as big as the circle of your sin."

29. Ibid., 8.

30. Telephone interview with Rev. Gary Maroney, pastor, Scenic View Baptist Church, Portland, Oregon, 5 March 1987.

31. Telephone interview with Rev. Henry Liginfelter, Alcoa, Tennessee, 5 March 1987.

32. Gray, "Revival at Southwestern Baptist Theological Seminary," 8.

33. Interview with Dr. L. Jack Gray.

34. Perry, *Rolling with Jesus,* 28.

35. Telephone interview with Dr. Trozy Barker, supervisor, men's residence hall, Southwestern Baptist Theological Seminary, Fort Worth, Texas, 17 February 1987.

36. Telephone interview with Rev. Gary Maroney.

37. Chapel services at Southwestern traditionally run from 10:00 A.M. until 10:30 A.M. The twenty minutes between the end of chapel and the bell at 10:50 calling students to their 11:00 classes was commonly known as "coffee break time."

38. Gray, "Revival at Southwestern Baptist Theological Seminary," 8.

39. Most of the participants interviewed by this author felt like it was a mistake not to cancel classes. David Perry, looking back in retrospect, says "At the Wednesday coffee break, I believe the Holy Spirit was grieved or quenched. He was doing the same thing in that coffee break that he was doing at Asbury a month earlier and the choice was in the hands of the administration. I am not in any way being critical, but the way I see it, Dr. Naylor had to make a choice whether to continue classes or dismiss classes. I believe he made the wrong decision. When the decision was made to continue classes, there was a sense of sorrow and grief. There was a simple awareness that we were on the very edge. God is sovereign and I trust God, but I look back and wonder what impact Southwestern—with the size and the scope, all the things you can see on the human level—could have had in the nation and in the world if we had just released the Holy Spirit, canceled classes, and let God really get through to those he had there—his called people.

Now, I wasn't in his shoes, and now, seventeen years later, I am an executive, I have to make tough decisions, and they are not always right. But I have never wavered from that basic conclusion." (Telephone interview with Rev. David Perry)

But as others pointed out, the administration did approve of the students coming, speaking in classes, and ultimately being given the coffee break time. Darius Salter comments, "Today I would be able to identify with those who did have some apprehension. Even for those with apprehension, it took a great deal of charity and faith to allow us to share." (Telephone interview with Dr. Darius Salter)

40. Interview with Dr. Roy Fish.

41. Fish, "Spiritual Awakening at Southwestern."

42. Gray, "Revival at Southwestern Baptist Theological Seminary," 9.

43. Ibid. A picture of some of the students who went out in March of 1970 can be found in *Southwestern News* (April 1970): 16.

44. Telephone interview with Dr. Ben Loring, pastor, First Baptist Church, Lawton, Oklahoma, 17 February 1987. See also David Reid, "Revival at Southwestern: Fifteen Years Later," n.d. (typewritten), 3–4.

45. L. Jack Gray, "Revival Is Here!" chapel service at Southwestern Baptist Theological Seminary, December 1970.

46. Joe Ann, though not on the faculty when she shared in chapel, had previously been a professor in the School of Church Music. Joe Ann's story is told in greater detail in the book by Bonnie B. O'Brien, *So Great the Journey: An Inspirational Profile of Joe Ann Shelton* (Nashville: Broadman, 1980). Frank Stovall was professor of voice at the time. Frank Stovall, "A Personal Testimony of What Christ Has Done for Me," chapel service, Southwestern Baptist Theological Seminary, Fort Worth, Texas, December 1970. This is one of the most moving personal testimonies this author has ever heard.

47. Dr. L. Jack Gray, personal letter to Dr. Thomas A. Carruth, September 11, 1970.

48. Telephone interview with Rev. Jim Elliff, North Little Rock, Arkansas, 10 March 1987.

49. Robert E. Coleman, *Dry Bones Can Live Again* (Old Tappan, N.J.:Revell, 1969), 16.

50. Telephone interviews with Dr. Felix Gresham and Dr. Cal Guy, distinguished professor of missions, emeritus, Southwestern Baptist Theological Seminary, Fort Worth, Texas, 28 February 1987.

51. Telephone interview with Dr. Gary Galeotti.

52. Interview with Carol (Proctor) Machen, Wauconda, Illinois, 30 January 1987. For a newspaper account of the "awakening" among the youth in Perry, see Maxine Thompson, "A Happening in Perry," *Home Journal,* July 1970.

53. Telephone interview with Rev. Tom Elliff, pastor, First Southern Baptist Church, Del City, Oklahoma, 10 March 1987.

54. Interview with Dr. Billie Hanks, Jr., president, International Evangelism Association, Fort Worth, Texas, 14 February 1987.

55. Telephone interview with Rev. Doug Tipps, pastor, River Oaks Baptist Church, Houston, Texas, 10 February 1987.

56. Interview with Dr. Robert Coleman, director, School of World Mission and Evangelism, Trinity Evangelical Divinity School, Deerfield, Illinois, 16 March 1987.

57. Telephone interview with Rev. Michael Gott, Jacksonville, Texas, 3 March 1987. Gott continued by maintaining, "We [Southern Baptists] are too programmed. What I believe killed the revival was that we had a predetermined program that was more important than anything else. We are too programmed—we really don't have room for revival."

58. Interview, Dr. Robert Coleman.

15
The Zeal of Youth:
The Role of Students in the History of Spiritual Awakening

Alvin L. Reid

Alvin L. Reid is the founding John Bisagno Chair of Evangelism and assistant professor of Christianity at Houston Baptist University. Prior to this he served as state evangelism director for the State Convention of Baptists in Indiana. He earned his M.Div. from Southwestern Seminary, and then a Ph.D. with a major in evangelism. Fish served as Reid's supervisor for his dissertation on the Jesus movement.

The place was Tiananmen Square, Beijing, China. An anonymous university student stood frozen before the imposing phalanx of tanks. The frail young man impudently faced down the mechanical behemoths. If the first tank moved left, he followed. When it lurched to the right, he stepped that way. This student stood in defiance of the might of the most populous nation on the earth, and the world was watching.[1]

You might not remember the date or where you were when this event occurred. But if you saw this scene in May 1989 on the evening news, you will never forget it. Such a demonstration reminds us of the zeal of youth and the impact one student can make.

The purpose of this chapter is to isolate and emphasize the vital but often overlooked role of students[2] in the history of spiritual awakening.[3] Specifically the author will argue that students have played a larger role in the origin, continuity, and effects of revival than has generally been recognized.[4] The study will be limited to the modern era and the more recognized examples of historic revival.

During the eighteenth century, three major manifestations of spiritual awakening emerged: Pietism on the European continent (which can actually be traced to the late 1600s), the First Great Awakening in the American colonies, and the Evangelical Awakening in the British Isles, led by the Wesleys and George Whitefield. Each of these affected the other to some extent, but also had unique features that separated them. In every case the role of students was important.

Pietism

Most historians date the beginning of Pietism with the publication of Philip Spener's *Pia Desiteria* ("Pious Desires") in 1675.[5] Spener, called the father of Pietism by many, emphasized the personal nature of the Christian experience. He secured the appointment of A. H. Francke at the new University of Halle in 1692. Under Francke's leadership, Halle became "a pietistic center of higher education and revivalism."[6]

Nikolaus Ludwig von Zinzendorf (1700–1760) studied at Halle from 1710–16 and organized prayer groups among the students while at the university.[7] From Halle, Zinzendorf went to the University of Wittenberg, where he formed the Order of the Grain of Mustard Seed in 1718. In 1722 he acquired an estate which became a safe haven for persecuted members of the Hussite church. It was from this group that the "Unitas Fratrum" (Unity of the Brethren), or Moravians, were born. A particularly powerful movement of the Spirit came at a Communion service on August 12, 1727. Following this, a continuous prayer structure developed, and a missionary enterprise began, which resulted in one missionary for every sixty Moravians. Zinzendorf's impact can be traced to his early years at Halle.

The First Great Awakening

The role of youth became abundantly clear in the First Great Awakening, which generally includes the period from the 1720s to the 1740s. Jonathan Edwards, one of the greatest theologians, practitioners, and writers in the annals of spiritual awakening, wrote his *Faithful Narrative* to give an account of the powerful revival that arose in 1734–35 in and around Northampton, Massachusetts, where he was pastor. Edwards prefaced the account by noting five powerful revivals during the long tenure of his predecessor and grandfather Solomon Stoddard. Edwards recorded that in each of the five movements Stoddard had stated the majority of young people were affected. Commenting on the revival in 1734–35 under his leadership, Edwards referred to the role of the youth in its origin: "At the latter end of the year 1733, there appeared a very unusual flexibleness, and yielding to advice, in our young people."[8] This came after Edwards began speaking against their irreverence toward the Sabbath. The youth were also affected greatly by the sudden death of a young man and then of a young married woman in their town. Edwards proposed that the young people should begin meeting in small groups around Northampton. They did so with such success that many adults followed their example. The revival surfaced following a series of messages on justification by faith.

Concerning the revival's effect on the youth, he commented:

> God made it, I suppose, the greatest occasion of awakening to others, of anything that ever came to pass in the town. . . . News of it seemed to be almost like a flash of lightning, upon the hearts of young people, all over town, and upon many others.[9]

The revival spread quickly to neighboring towns up and down the Connecticut River Valley.

When the First Great Awakening came in full force in 1740–41, Edwards wrote a treatise entitled *Some Thoughts Concerning the Present Revival of Religion in New England*. Edwards remarked further on the role of youth in this revival, while indicting older believers for their indifference:

> The work has been chiefly amongst the young; and comparatively but few others have been made partakers of it. And indeed it has commonly been so, *when God has begun any great work for the revival of his church; he has taken the young people,* and has cast off the old and stiffnecked generation.[10]

Another consequential feature of the First Great Awakening in relation to students was the Log College of William Tennent. Tennent, a Presbyterian, built a log house to provide ministerial training. Three of his sons and fifteen others were the early students.[11] George Whitefield recorded the following in his journal after visiting the Log College:

> The place wherein the young men study now is in contempt called The College. It is a log house, about twenty feet long and near as many broad;

and to me it seemed to resemble the school of the old prophets, for their habitations were mean; . . . From this despised place, seven or eight worthy ministers of Jesus have lately been sent forth; more are almost ready to be sent, and the foundation is now laying for the instruction of many others.[12]

From the Log College advanced several who would be leaders in the First Great Awakening. These included sons Gilbert, the most prominent revival leader among Presbyterians; John; and William, Jr.; along with Samuel Blair. In addition, many graduates established similar log colleges of their own. The Log College, which ultimately evolved into the College of New Jersey (now Princeton University), has been called "the forerunner of modern seminaries."[13] Thus the rise of seminaries, such a mainstay of ministry training in our day, can be traced to students in this awakening.

The Evangelical Awakening in England

John Wesley (1703–91) and George Whitefield (1714–70) are credited as being the leaders of the Evangelical Awakening in England during the eighteenth century. Wesley's experience as a college student at Oxford is probably best remembered by the "Holy Club," which involved both John and his brother Charles, Whitefield, and a handful of others. Whitefield was converted during those days. The fact that Wesley was not actually converted until years after his time at Oxford does not minimize the impact made on his subsequent ministry by the Holy Club.[14]

The Holy Club at Oxford is significant because it was this experience at the university which forged relationships between the men who figured prominently in the awakening in England and the American colonies. Wesley's oft-quoted conversion in 1738 led to a remarkable ministry which, along with Whitefield's influence and Charles's hymn writing, affected the spiritual life of the entire nation. While Wesley never sought to sever ties with the Church of England, the Evangelical Awakening resulted in the formation of the Methodist church. By John Wesley's death in 1791, there were seventy-nine thousand Methodists in England.

Beyond his impact in England, Whitefield made seven trips to the New World. His itinerant ministry across the colonies fanned localized revival fires into a spiritual inferno. What makes this more impressive is that Whitefield was only twenty-six years old in 1741, when the Great Awakening was at its peak!

The Second Great Awakening

At the turn of the nineteenth century, the Second Great Awakening instilled a fresh passion for God in the emerging nation. A major precipitating factor in this movement was the outbreak of revival on college campuses. Skepticism and infidelity characterized the colleges. During this period immediately following the birth of the United States, the colleges in the east were often greatly influenced by European thinkers in the Enlightenment.[15]

The campus of Hampden-Sydney College in Virginia became the first in a series of college revivals. Four young men—William Hill, Carey Allen, James Blythe, and Clement Read—were instrumental in the beginnings of revival at Hampden-Sydney in 1787 and the years following. Because they feared severe antagonism from the irreligious student body, the four young men began meeting secretly in the forest to pray and study. When they were discovered, they were greatly ridiculed by fellow students. President John Blair Smith heard of the situation and was convicted by the infidelity on the campus. He invited the four students and others to pray with him in his parlor. Before long, "half of the students were deeply impressed and under conviction, and the revival spread rapidly through the college and to surrounding counties."[16] Hill later chronicled the revival's impact:

> Persons of all ranks in society, of all ages . . . became subjects of this work, so that there was scarcely a Magistrate on the bench, or a lawyer at the bar but became members of the church. . . . It was now as rare a thing to find one who was not religious, as it was formerly to find one that was. The frivolities and amusements once so prevalent were all abandoned, and gave place to singing, serious conversations, and prayer meetings.[17]

In addition, subsequent revival movements came in 1802, 1814–15, 1822, 1827–28, 1831, 1833, and 1837.[18]

The Yale College revival began under the leadership of president Timothy Dwight, the grandson of Jonathan Edwards. Dwight came to the school when it was filled with infidelity. He began to preach against unbelief in the college chapel, and by 1797 a group of students formed to improve moral conditions. After more time passed, characterized by prayer, a powerful spiritual movement came through the school in the spring of 1802. A third of the student body was converted. Goodrich wrote of the change in attitude on campus:

The salvation of the soul was the great subject of thought, of conversation, of absorbing interest; the convictions of many were pungent and overwhelming; and "the peace of believing" which succeeded, was not less strongly marked.[19]

The movement spread to Dartmouth and Princeton. At Princeton three-fourths of the students made professions, and one-fourth entered the ministry.[20]

A group of students at Williams College in Massachusetts made a tremendous impact on missions. Samuel Mills entered the college during a time of awakening there between 1804 and 1806. He and four others began to pray regularly for missions. In 1806, at one particular meeting they had to seek refuge from a downpour in a haystack. During this "Haystack Meeting," Mills proposed a mission to Asia. This event was a precipitating factor leading to a major foreign missions enterprise. The first missionaries included Adoniram Judson and Luther Rice.[21]

Bennett Tyler collected twenty-five eyewitness accounts of pastors during the Second Great Awakening. No less than twenty revival reports described the integral role played by young people. Ten accounts noted that the revivals commenced with the youth, and five documented that the revival in their area affected young people more than any other group. Only one account out of twenty-five asserted that there were no youth involved.[22]

The 1857–58 Prayer Revival

The Prayer Revival of 1857–58 was characterized by its wide appeal.[23] Several colleges experienced revival during this time. J. Edwin Orr documented revival movements at Oberlin, Yale, Dartmouth, Middlebury, Williams, Amherst, Princeton, and Baylor.[24]

One pivotal feature of this revival in relation to young people was the bearing it had on Dwight Lyman Moody when he was only twenty years old. In 1857, Moody wrote his impression of what was occurring in Chicago: "There is a great revival of religion in this city. . . . [It] seems as if God were here himself."[25] Biographer John Pollock wrote, "The revival of early 1857 tossed Moody out of his complacent view of religion."[26] Moody went on to make a marked impact for Christ during the rest of the nineteenth century.

An aspect of Moody's influence which cannot be overlooked regarding students was his leadership in the Student Volunteer movement. Although this movement's roots have been traced ultimately to the Second Great

Awakening and the Haystack Meeting of 1806, it was Moody who invited 251 students in Mt. Hermon, Massachusetts, for a conference in 1886. As a result of these meetings, highlighted by A. T. Pierson's challenging address, one hundred students volunteered for overseas missions. In 1888 the Student Volunteer movement was formally organized, with John R. Mott named chairman. Over the next several decades, literally thousands of students went to serve as foreign missionaries.[27]

The Revival of 1904–08

At the turn of the twentieth century, fresh winds of the Spirit again began to blow. The most visible example of the period was the Revival of 1904–08. This included the Welsh Revival and other occurrences as well in the United States and abroad. Some features of the period were controversial, such as the birth of modern-day Pentecostalism in 1901 and the subsequent Azusa Street revival.[28] It is interesting to note that one of the key occurrences given for the outbreak of Pentecostalism occurred with students at a Bible school Charles Parham began in Topeka, Kansas, in 1900.[29] W. J. Seymour, the catalyst for the Azusa Street revival in Los Angeles, was influenced greatly in 1905 at another Bible school in Houston set up by Parham.[30]

The Welsh Revival refers specifically to the movement that began in 1904 in the tiny country of Wales. Orr cites a key place of origin of the movement in Wales to a church in New Quay, Cardiganshire, where Joseph Jenkins was pastor. During a testimony time in a service, Jenkins asked for responses to the question "What does Jesus mean to you?" A young person, fifteen-year-old Florrie Evans, only recently converted, rose and said, "If no one else will, then I must say that I love the Lord Jesus with all my heart."[31] Her simple testimony caused many to begin openly surrendering all to Christ, and the fires of revival fell.

The revival spread as young people went from church to church, testifying. An itinerant preacher named Seth Joshua came to New Quay to speak and was powerfully impressed by the power of God evident there. He then journeyed to speak at Newcastle Embyn College. The next week he spoke at nearby Blaenannerch. While speaking there a young coal miner named Evan Roberts, who was a ministerial student at the college, experienced a powerful personal revival. He felt impressed to return to his home church in order to address the youth there. Seventeen heard him following a Monday service. He continued preaching, and revival began.[32] The revival spread across the country, and news of the awakening spread worldwide.

Colleges reported revival, such as the one at Denison University in Ohio.[33] Incidentally, it was during this period that Southwestern Baptist Theological Seminary was born.

Campus Revivals in the Mid-Twentieth Century

While there has been no revival that one could call a "great awakening" in America since the 1904–08 awakening, there have been localized or more specialized revivals in this century. The late 1940s and the 1950s was a time of unparalleled church growth and evangelism. The Southern Baptist Convention's greatest years of growth came then. J. Edwin Orr, in his final message delivered before his death, noted that "about 1949 there was a wave of revival in colleges throughout the United States."[34] Writing during this period, Orr stated: "The backsliding of Evangelical Christendom began in the theological schools. Its reviving is beginning there too."[35] Orr said the first college revival in the period began in 1949 at Bethel College, Minnesota. He recounts what occurred:

> What happened in Bethel College? I remember one night in Minneapolis, four of us—Billy Graham, at that time President of Northwestern Schools; Bill Dunlap, a Presbyterian; Jack Frank of Forest Home, and I—four of us, young men, praying that God would send a moving of revival to the students of the twin cities. . . . On a Thursday at chapel, at the end of the message, a student got up, ignoring me, spoke directly to the president, Dr. Wingblade, saying, "Dr. Wingblade, can I have a week off to go back to Iowa? I stole a thousand dollars and I can't live with this anymore."[36]

In addition, many other colleges experienced revival. In Minnesota, Northwestern School, St. Paul Bible Institute, and the University of Minnesota were touched. At the Northern Baptist Theological Seminary in Chicago, professor Julius Mantey observed: "Nearly every student that I have asked says he was deeply stirred. . . . We are all on a higher plane."[37] The year 1951 saw a notable spiritual stir on the campus of Baylor University. President W. R. White commented favorably about revival there.

Wheaton College was touched during this time. Fred Hoffman stated, "Perhaps one of the most remarkable and powerful spiritual awakenings was the one experienced at Wheaton College in February 1950."[38] After numerous prayer meetings were inaugurated by student leaders the previous fall, the revival began when a student shared a testimony of his changed life in an evening meeting. Others began testifying, and this continued for over two days without end. Asbury College in Kentucky experienced revival as well. Historian Clifton Olmstead noted further the impact made by Youth for Christ, a parachurch movement that began in 1944.[39]

The Jesus Movement—A Youth Awakening

In the middle of the youth protests surrounding the Vietnam War the Jesus movement served to call youths to a radical commitment to Jesus. The closest thing to spiritual awakening, which particularly affected youth, was the Jesus movement of the late 1960s and early 1970s. This movement generally paralleled the overall unrest among America's youth in the era. Only a brief summary can be offered here.[40]

While many familiar with the Jesus movement tend to emphasize the countercultural Jesus people (or Jesus freaks), the renewal among youth was actually much broader. It included powerful revivals in churches, campus awakenings, as well as the more colorful phenomena such as the underground newspapers, coffeehouses, communes, and new music. It was expressed in youth choir tours, youth evangelism conferences, and music festivals. One observer noted the variety in the movement:

> The label "Jesus Movement" has misled many who associate the term with the Jesus Freaks who have been responsible for the Christian communes and who mostly have come out of the hippie or drug scene. In associating the Jesus Movement with such a narrow group, one misses the national pattern of the religious phenomena, which is touching in one way or another most of the youth of the nation, those still at home, in school and out.[41]

There were different streams to the movement. The best known were the Jesus people, characterized by persons like Ted Wise in the Haight Ashbury district of San Francisco; Lonnie Frisbee of Haight and later at Calvary Chapel, Costa Mesa; and Duane Pederson. *Time* magazine carried the following description:

> Jesus Freaks. Evangelical hippies. Or, as many prefer to be called, street Christians. . . . They are the latest incarnation of that oldest of Christian phenomena: footloose, passionate bearers of the Word.[42]

Pederson, who coined the term "Jesus people," said this group consisted of the thousands of young people who traveled to California in the sixties and seventies whose lives were changed by the gospel.[43] The Jesus people began interesting ministries through coffeehouses, Christian communes, and underground newspapers, and they were fervent in personal evangelism.

A second major stream included the more traditional church and parachurch ministries that exploded in the youth field. While many Southern Baptist churches reacted negatively to the countercultural features of the movement, there was nevertheless a significant impact on the denomination. Most observers concur that the impact could have in fact been even greater.

The Southern Baptist Convention reported records in baptisms in the early 1970s, propelled mainly by a remarkable increase in youth baptisms. For example, the SBC record for baptisms was in 1972, with 445,725. Of that number, 137,667 were of youth, the largest number and the largest percentage of youth baptisms in SBC history. The second highest number of youth baptisms was in 1971 (see table below). It is clear that the record total in baptisms was fueled by substantial youth baptism figures. The Jesus movement reached its peak in 1970–72.

Youth Baptisms in the Southern Baptist Convention 1971–88[44]

Year Baptized	Youth Baptized	Total Youth	Percent U.S. Population	Youth Population	Percent of Youth Baptized
1971	126,127	409,659	30.7	N/A	N/A
1972	137,667	445,725	30.8	24,997,000	0.550
1973	119,844	413,990	28.9	25,287,000	0.473
1974	115,345	410,482	28.1	25,454,000	0.453
1975	116,419	421,809	27.6	25,420,000	0.457
1976	103,981	384,496	27.0	25,305,000	0.410
1977	88,838	345,690	25.6	25,014,000	0.355
1978	97,118	336,050	28.9	24,549,000	0.395
1979	93,142	368,738	25.2	23,919,000	0.389
1980	108,633	429,742	25.2	23,409,575	0.464
1981	101,076	405,608	24.9	22,757,000	0.444
1982	102,259	411,554	24.8	22,358,000	0.457
1983	97,984	394,606	24.8	22,199,000	0.441
1984	91,431	372,028	24.6	21,958,000	0.416
1985	86,499	351,071	24.6	21,632,000	0.399
1986	86,387	363,124	23.8	21,300,000	0.405
1987	79,900	338,495	23.6	21,100,000	0.379
1988	80,506	346,320	23.2	N/A	N/A

In addition, record enrollments and continuous increases characterized all six Southern Baptist seminaries for the decade following the Jesus movement.

Campus Crusade for Christ, a parachurch ministry, held Explo '72 in Dallas. It resulted in what was to that point "the most massive gathering of students and Christian laymen to ever descend on one city."[45] Over 80,000 registered for the event, with some 150,000 attending a Saturday music festival concluding the meeting.[46] Also, Billy Graham, who called Explo a Christian Woodstock, was very favorable toward what he called the "Jesus Revolution." Aside from writing a book about the movement,[47] Graham noted that during the period he had an unusually high number of youth attending and professing faith in Christ at his crusades.[48]

Probably best known among evangelicals from this period was the revival at Asbury College in 1970.[49] The revival began during a chapel service on February 3, 1970. From that service sprang a movement of prayer and confession which lasted for 185 hours. Students from Asbury scattered across the country to share their experience. As a result, many other campuses were touched by revival. Southwestern Baptist Theological Seminary was one of the schools so influenced.[50]

Many other instances could be named. A stirring example in a local church is Houston's First Baptist. John Bisagno came to First Baptist in 1970, when the church was a typical, declining, downtown church. Bisagno kept an eye on the Jesus movement in California. Unlike many in Southern Baptist circles, Bisagno affirmed the youth of the day, arguing that he would rather see youth "yelling for Jesus than sitting barefoot on a park slope taking drugs."[51] Bisagno led the church to involvement in an effort called SPIRENO (SPIritual REvolution NOw), led by evangelist Richard Hogue. As a result the church baptized 1,669 for the church year 1970–71, the vast majority of them young people.[52] One reporter stated, "By taking the initiative, they gave their church and hundreds of others in Houston a chance to jump into the flow of this Jesus movement."[53]

Coffeehouse ministries, ocean baptisms, new music, personal evangelism, and many other phenomena characterized the period. There were controversial elements, including at times a simplistic approach to the gospel and emotional experiences, the charismatic movement, and the appearance of many of the countercultural converts. The benefits certainly outweighed the liabilities, however. Beyond the evangelistic results cited above, the Jesus movement helped many traditional churches to focus again on the work of the Holy Spirit. Also, many leaders today in evangelism were converted during or radically touched by the Jesus movement.[54]

The greatest enduring impact made by the Jesus movement was in the area of music. Contemporary Christian music, now a multimillion-dollar industry, as well as recent developments such as praise choruses and celebrative worship, can be traced to the Jesus movement. An obvious way to gauge the influence of music from the Jesus movement is by examining the 1975 and 1991 editions of the *Baptist Hymnal*. A large number of contemporary songs have made their way into these editions.[55]

Conclusion

God in his sovereignty has chosen to use not only the seasoned in his work. Scriptural examples include Jeremiah, David, and Timothy, among others. Subsequent history has likewise recorded unique individuals used by God from their youth. The preceding is only a summary of notable examples of the role of students in historical spiritual awakenings. The point is this: What God *has* done he *can* do again. Students are perhaps the most fertile field for the Spirit of God to work through in a fresh way. The following is an attempt to examine possible lessons we can learn from history.

First, given the heritage of students in revival, particularly related to college students, evangelical schools have not only an obligation to teach the academic disciplines of the faith once delivered, but an equally vital responsibility to impart a fervent spiritual passion. Far too many schools founded during great revival or on those principles have lost their soul. The model of William Tennent teaching classical subjects while infusing a passion for evangelism in his pupils could be copied with greater regularity in our day. Perhaps the growing current interest in spiritual formation on many college and seminary campuses will temper the past generation's almost incessant devotion to intellectualism.

Second, a subtle trend in local churches needs to be addressed, i.e., the segmentation of youth ministry apart from the church mainstream. For example, over the past two decades the number of vocational youth ministers has grown, while at the same time youth baptisms have declined. This is not an indictment of youth ministers, but demonstrates perhaps that the growth of youth ministry as an entity of its own has helped to take young people out of the mainstream of the church. In many churches with significant youth ministries, the only time young people are noticed is when they return from camp or an occasional youth emphasis during revival services.

Many churches today can place a higher priority on youth. They are not the church of the future; they are the church of today. Churches need both the wisdom of mature believers and the zeal of youth. During the Jesus movement and the years following, youth choirs filled the lofts of hundreds upon hundreds of churches. They were a focal point of the service and a source of great inspiration. While I am not arguing that we should return to that particular method, surely there are ways students can be brought into the heart of church life.

Third, the church and evangelical institutions bear a responsibility to guide students. Certainly some of the zeal they have may be misguided. History is replete with overly enthusiastic, spiritually immature persons who have harmed the church. On the other hand, entire generations have suffered at the hands of anemic, narcoleptic, catatonic believers and churches, whose lives make a mockery of the God they serve!

Rather than focusing on quenching the fire of youthful zeal, mature Christians should help young people to channel their fervency in ways that honor Christ. We can affirm their concern for unsaved friends and their vision for making a mighty impact, and encourage them to maintain convictions. The recent *True Love Waits* campaign is a beautiful illustration of the multitude of godly young men and women who seek to honor God with their bodies. "See You at the Pole" and similar emphases are other examples. The author is grateful to God for a church that affirmed and encouraged him to make a radical commitment to Christ as a teenager.

Finally, and most importantly, those of us who are a little "longer in the tooth" can listen to young people. They too can hear from God, and to hearken back to the words of Edwards, at times they listen more sensitively to the voice of the Spirit than many of us do. May the following sober words remind us all of the importance of zeal, regardless of our age:

> If we look at the ranks of middle-aged men and women we observe that there is all too often no spiritual fire, no urge to achieve things for God. That condition does not suddenly come upon people at that age; you need to be on guard against it now, whatever your age. *It is when one has found his niche that imperceptibly zeal flags and lethargy creeps in.* Oh, to keep burning brightly to the end![56]

Endnotes

1. "Reign of Terror," *Newsweek* (19 June 1989): 14–22.

2. The term student is intended as a generic reference to young people from their teens through their twenties. While primarily the reference relates to college students, the term as used here is more inclusive and will at times be used synonymously with the expressions youth, young people, and young adults.

3. The author would like to acknowledge the influence of Roy Fish on this subject. Fish has always been open to and affirming of the work of God among young people.

4. The notable exception is J. Edwin Orr, *Campus Aflame*, ed. by Richard Owen Roberts (Wheaton Ill.: International Awakening Press, 1994). Two recent books offer a popular examination of students in spiritual awakening: Dan Hayes, *Fireseeds of Spiritual Awakening* (San Bernadino, Calif.: Here's Life, 1983), and David L. McKenna, *The Coming Great Awakening* (Downers Grove, Ill.: InterVarsity Press, 1990). Other works have alluded to the role of students in revival. For example, Leon McBeth, *The Baptist Heritage: Four Centuries of Baptist Witness* (Nashville: Broadman, 1987), 442, noted that in the 1800s "Baptist colleges in the South also became effective agents of revival and evangelism."

5. Fortress Press continues to publish the book, illustrating its status as a classic in Christian spirituality.

6. Earle E. Cairns, *An Endless Line of Splendor: Revivals and Their Leaders from the Great Awakening to the Present* (Wheaton, Ill.: Tyndale House, 1986), 34.

7. See David Howard, "Student Power in World Missions," in *Perspectives on the World Christian Movement* (Pasadena: William Carey, 1981), 211–14.

8. Jonathan Edwards, "A Faithful Narrative of the Surprising Work of God, in the Conversion of Many Hundred Souls, in Northampton, and the Neighbouring Towns and Villages of New Hampshire, in New England; in a Letter to the Rev. Dr. Colman, of Boston," in *The Works of Jonathan Edwards*, ed. by Sereno E. Dwight (London: Banner of Truth Trust, 1834) 1:347.

9. Ibid.

10. Jonathan Edwards, "Some Thoughts Concerning the Present Revival of Religion in New England, and the Way in Which It Ought to Be Acknowledged and Promoted, Humbly Offered to the Public, in a Treatise on That Subject," in *The Works of Jonathan Edwards*, ed. Sereno E. Dwight (London: Banner of Truth Trust, 1834) 1: 423. Emphasis added.

11. W. W. Sweet, *The Story of Religion in America* (New York: Harper, 1930), 140.

12. George Whitefield, *George Whitefield's Journals* (Edinburgh: The Banner of Truth Trust, reprint, 1985), 354.

13. Cairns, *Endless Line of Splendor*, 42.

14. For further information on the life of John Wesley, see Nehemiah Curnock, ed., *The Journal of John Wesley*, 8 vols. (London: Epworth Press, 1938); John W. Drakeford, ed., *John Wesley* (Nashville: Broadman, 1979); Robert G. Tuttle, *John Wesley: His Life and Theology* (Grand Rapids: Zondervan, 1978); Arthur Skevington Wood, *The Burning Heart: John Wesley, Evangelist* (Grand Rapids: Eerdmans, 1967).

15. Daniel Dorchester, *Christianity in the United States* (New York: Hunt and Eaton, 1895), 316.

16. Benjamin Rice Lacy, *Revival in the Midst of the Years* (Hopewell, Va.: Royal Publishers, 1968), 70.

17. Quoted from Hill's biography in Arthur Dicken Thomas, Jr., "Reasonable Revivalism: Presbyterian Evangelization of Educated Virginians, 1787–1837," *Journal of Presbyterian History* 61 (Fall 1983): 322.

18. See Lacy, 68ff; Arthur Dicken Thomas, Jr., "Reasonable Revivalism: Presbyterian Evangelization of Educated Virginians, 1787–1837," 322ff.

19. See Chauncy A. Goodrich, "Narrative of Revivals of Religion in Yale College," *American Quarterly Register* 10 (Feb. 1838): 295–96.

20. Cairns, *Endless Line of Splendor*, 92. See also McKenna, *The Coming Great Awakening*, 18.

21. See Gardiner Spring, *Memoir of Samuel John Mills* (Boston: Perkins and Marvin, 1829); Thomas Richards, *Samuel J. Mills: Missionary Pathfinder, Pioneer, and Promoter* (Boston: Pilgrim Press, 1906); Cairns, 261–262.

22. Bennett Tyler, ed., *New England Revivals, as They Existed at the Close of the Eighteenth Century, and the Beginning of the Nineteenth Centuries* (Wheaton, Ill.: Richard Owen Roberts, 1980).

23. See the chapter by Preston Nix elsewhere in this book.

24. J. Edwin Orr, *Fervent Prayer* (Chicago: Moody Press, 1974), 11-12.

25. John Pollock, *Moody* (Chicago: Moody Press, 1983), 34.

26. Ibid.

27. Howard, "Student Power in World Missions," 216–218.

28. Cairns, *Endless Line of Splendor*, 177, gives the priority to the Pentecostal Movement in characterizing the significance of what he calls a "Global Awakening" beginning in 1900.

29. Klaude Kendrick, *The Promise Fulfilled: A History of the Modern Pentecostal Movement* (Springfield, Mo.: Gospel Publishing, 1961), 36; Cairns, *Endless Line of Splendor*, 179.

30. Ibid., 64–65.

31. W. T. Stead, *The Story of the Welsh Revival* (London: Revell, 1905), 42–43.

32. See J. Edwin Orr, *The Flaming Tongue* (Chicago: Moody Press, 1975), 3–7; Stead, 66, 67; Bob Eklund, *Spiritual Awakening* (Atlanta: Home Mission Board, 1986), 31.

33. Llewellyn Brown, "The Torrey Mission in Cleveland," *Watchman* (14 February 1907): 32.

34. J. Edwin Orr, *Revival Is Like Judgment Day* (Atlanta: Home Mission Board, 1987), 9.

35. J. Edwin Orr, *Good News in Bad Times* (Grand Rapids: Zondervan, 1953), 85.

36. Ibid.

37. Ibid., 63.

38. Fred W. Hoffman, *Revival Time in America* (Boston: Wilde, 1956), 164. See also Cairns, *Endless Line of Splendor*, 213.

39. Clifford E. Olmstead, *The History of Religion in the United States* (Englewood Cliffs, N.J.: Prentice-Hall, 1960), 590.

40. For further study see Alvin L. Reid, "The Impact of the Jesus Movement on Evangelism among Southern Baptists," Ph.D. dissertation, Southwestern Baptist Theological Seminary, 1991.

41. Walker L. Knight, "Faddists or Disciples?" in *Jesus People Come Alive* (Wheaton, Ill.: Tyndale House, 1971).

42. "Street Christians: Jesus as the Ultimate Trip," *Time* (3 August 1970): 31.

43. Duane Pederson, *Jesus People* (Glendale, Calif.: Regal, 1972), 35–36.

44. Billy Beachem, Student Discipleship Ministries, Fort Worth, Texas, to Alvin L. Reed, Indianapolis, Indiana, 8 January 1990, Transcript in the hand of Alvin L. Reed, and *Quarterly Review* July-August-September 1972, 20-21.

45. "Baptists among 80,000 attending Explo '72," *Indiana Baptist,* 5 July 1972, 5.

46. Ibid.

47. Billy Graham, *The Jesus Revolution* (Grand Rapids: Zondervan, 1971).

48. David Kucharsky, "Graham in Gotham," *Christianity Today* (17 July 1970): 30; "Overflow Crowds of Youth Attend Graham Crusade," *Indiana Baptist* (12 May 1971) : 7.

49. Robert Coleman was on the faculty at that time and edited a history of the revival entitled *One Divine Moment* (Old Tappan, N.J.: Revell, 1970).

50. Henry C. James, "Campus Demonstrations," in *One Divine Moment,* 55. See the chapter by Timothy Beougher elsewhere in this book.

51. Dallas Lee, "The Electric Revival," *Home Missions* (June/July 1971): 33.

52. "Tex. Baptist Church Sets New SBC Baptism Record," *Indiana Baptist* (15 December 1971): 5. The highest number the year before was only 395.

53. Lee, "Electric Revival," 34.

54. There are too many to name, but some examples of those who were touched by or provided leadership to the Jesus Movement were evangelist Jay Strack, Ohio Evangelism Director Mike Landry, HMB Evangelism Section staffer Jack Smith, Glenn Sheppard, who became the first to lead the Office of Prayer and Spiritual Awakening at the HMB, and many others. This writer, whose dissertation was on the Jesus Movement, was amazed to discover how many people today testify to the enduring positive impact on their lives.

55. See Reid, "Impact of the Jesus Movement," 98–137, for further elaboration.

56. A. J. Broomhall, *Time for Action* (London: Inter-Varsity Fellowship, 1965), 132. Emphasis added.

16
Cosmic Revival in Our Time

Robert E. Coleman

*Robert Coleman serves as director for the Institute of Evangelism at the
Billy Graham Center at Wheaton College and also as the director of
the School of World Mission and Evangelism at Trinity Evangelical
Divinity School. Coleman formerly taught at Asbury Theological
Seminary in Wilmore, Kentucky. He has written numerous books on
evangelism and spiritual awakening, including the classic* The Master
Plan of Evangelism.

The sons of Korah prayerfully asked, "Wilt thou not revive us again, that
thy people may rejoice in thee?" (Psalm 85:6, KJV). It was a rhetorical
question prompted by the conviction that God wanted his people to come
alive to his grace and glory. That is the biblical meaning of revival—the
restoration of men and women to their true nature and purpose.[1] Inasmuch
as all of us were made to glorify God, revival simply fulfills his desire that we
know him in the fullness of his Spirit and declare his praise across the earth.

Longing for Revival

Few church leaders will question the need for such an awakening today.
For most people life seems to have lost its meaning; there is no thrill in
personal devotion; no sparkle in the eye, or shout in the soul. The joy of
sacrifice is missing. Self-indulgence is the norm.

While the church flounders in mediocrity, the world plunges deeper into
sin. The sacredness of home and family is forgotten. Moral standards in
public and private are debased. Lawlessness pervades the land.

A day of reckoning is sure to come. Degeneration has its limits. Judgment may be delayed, but on our present course it cannot be postponed indefinitely. That point of no return may be nearer than many of us envision.

Yet there is hope. In other days when catastrophe threatened, men and women of prayer, like the sons of Korah, have turned to the Lord and found in him deliverance and strength. It can happen again if we meet God's conditions: "If my people, who are called by my name, will humble themselves and pray and seek my face and turn from their wicked ways, then will I hear from heaven and will forgive their sin and will heal their land" (2 Chron. 7:14).

In the personal sense of obedience to God, of course, a deep spiritual undercurrent of revival in the life of persons walking with God is always present. God is never without a witness. It is this faithful remnant of Spirit-filled servants that really keeps the church alive. Thankfully, there are seasons when this stream of spiritual vitality breaks forth in great power, renewing multitudes of people and sometimes changing the course of nations.

Such movements of corporate revival can be seen all through the Bible[2] and indeed have occurred in varying degrees throughout the history of the church. As to American Christianity, were it not for these seasons of refreshing during several crucial periods in the life of our nation, it is doubtful whether our country could have survived.[3]

An Exciting Prophecy

Considering the convulsive struggles of our generation, it is not strange that growing numbers of Christians are praying for a mighty spiritual awakening, a concern beginning with ourselves, but soon reaching out to others in need of revival. As the burden grows, eventually it can take on a world dimension. Nothing is impossible with God, so why not believe him for a conflagration of love and power that will sweep across the earth, engulfing the whole church in a mighty witness of transforming grace.[4]

Scripture does point to some kind of a climactic spiritual conflagration, though the time and extent of its coming can be variously understood. Most of the references to this possibility are bound up with other historical situations, such as the return of the Jews from captivity and the restoration of their nation. How one understands the Millennium, Tribulation, and Rapture must also be taken into account. Obviously those who see Christ returning to take away his church before his millennial reign will look at the awakening from a different perspective than those who view it as an aspect of the Millennium. Notwithstanding the differences, nothing in the varying positions necessarily precludes a coming world revival.[5]

Let us admit that the complexity of the biblical prophecies makes any conclusion tentative. Yet, recognizing that we now only see through the glass darkly, it is possible to discern an outline of a future movement of revival that will make anything seen thus far pale by comparison.

A Universal Outpouring of the Holy Spirit

The day is envisioned when the church in all parts of the world will know the overflow of God's presence. No one will be excluded, as Joel prophesied: "And it shall come to pass afterward, that I will pour out my Spirit upon all flesh; and your sons and your daughters shall prophesy, your old men shall dream dreams, your young men shall see visions; And, also, upon the servants and upon the handmaids in those days will I pour out my Spirit" (Joel 2:28-29, KJV). The inclusion of the young, the women, and the servants, persons at that time usually least expected to receive divine favor, underscores the totality of the blessing. That priests, prophets, and kings are not mentioned, people usually most associated with leadership, makes the point even more impressive.

Peter associated this promise with the coming of the Holy Spirit at Pentecost (Acts 2:16-17). Yet the universal dimension of the prophecy of Joel was not experienced fully, in that the Spirit did not then come upon God's people from all over the world. Of course, potentially the first Pentecostal visitation reached to "all flesh," even to them that "are afar off" (Acts 2:39). This was typified by the Spirit-filled disciples' witness to the people present that day from "every nation under heaven" (Acts 2:5).[6] But in actual extent that outpouring was confined to the city. As the church gradually moved out in the strength of the Holy Spirit, the flame spread to Judea, to Samaria, and finally to many distant places of the civilized world. The message is still going out. But complete fulfillment of the prophecy awaits a glorious day to come.

Certainly a spiritual awakening around the world would be in keeping with the all-embracing love of God (John 3:16). In a dramatic way, it would give notice of the gospel mandate to reach "the uttermost part of the earth" (Acts 1:8; cf. Mark 16:15; John 20:21; Matt. 28:19), fulfilling at last the promise to Abraham that in him all peoples on the earth shall be blessed (Gen. 12:3; 22:18). The worship of God by all the families of the nations, so long foretold, would then be a reality (see Ps. 22:27; 86:9; Isa. 49:6; Dan. 7:14; Rev. 15:4), and God's name would be great among the Gentiles, "from the rising of the sun even unto the going down of the same" (Mal. 1:11, KJV).[7] According to this reasoning, the church age began and will end in a mighty spiritual baptism. What happened at the first Pentecost may be seen as the "early" display of the refreshing rain from heaven, while the closing epic is the "latter rain" (Joel 2:23; Hos. 6:3; Zech. 10:1; James 5:7). Water or rain, it will be remembered, is often symbolic of the Holy Spirit (John 7:37-39).

Strange Demonstrations of Power

In describing the Spirit's outpouring, Joel foretells "wonders in the heavens and in the earth, blood, and fire, and pillars of smoke. The sun shall be turned into darkness, and the moon into blood, before the great and the terrible day of the Lord" (Joel 2:30-31; cf. Acts 2:19-20). These phenomena, however, are not mentioned as happening in the account of the first Pentecost,[8] so apparently they are yet to occur.

Jesus spoke of days immediately "after the tribulation" in similar terms, adding that "the stars shall fall from heaven, and the powers of the heavens shall be shaken" (Matt. 24:29; cf. Rev. 6:12-13). Apparently God will summon the forces of nature to bear witness to what is happening on the earth.

Adding to the spectacle, it seems that some persons will have the power to perform wondrous deeds, such as turning water to blood (Rev. 11:6; cf. Gal. 3:5). Naturally, Satan will do what he can to counterfeit that which he knows is real. We are warned of "false Christs" and "false prophets" of this time, who will show "great signs and wonders" to deceive the elect (Matt. 24:24; cf. Exod. 7:10-12; Matt. 7:15-20; 2 Thess. 2:9-10). The sensory appeal is always fraught with danger, which is all the more reason why we are exhorted to test the spirits. If they are not Christ-exalting, then they are not of God (1 John 4:1-3).

Unprecedented Trouble

Those fearful conditions of the last days described in Matthew 24 and intermittently in Revelation 6 to 17 also seem to characterize this period. And things will get worse as the end approaches (cf. 2 Tim. 3:12; 2 Thess. 2:1-3).

Famines, pestilence, and earthquakes of staggering proportions will occur. Wars and intrigue will fill the earth. Hate will bind the hearts of men. No one will feel secure. As moral integrity breaks down, apostasy in the church will increase. Those who do not conform to the spirit of the age will be hard pressed, and many will be martyred. Clearly, the cost of discipleship will be high.[9]

Yet amid this terrible adversity, Scripture indicates that revival will sweep across the earth. When God's "judgments are in the earth, the inhabitants of the world will learn righteousness" (Isa. 26:9). Dreadful calamities will mingle with awesome displays of salvation—the terrors will actually create an environment for earnest heart searching. Not everyone will turn to God, of course. Some persons will remain unrepentant and become even more brazen in their sin. But the world will be made to confront as never before the Cross of Jesus Christ.

How it will all end is not clear. Possibly the revival will close and there will be a "falling away" before the Lord returns (2 Thess. 2:3).[10] Some Bible students believe that the worst tribulation will come after the church is caught up. Others think that Christians will be taken out of the world midway through this dreadful period.

However viewed, Scripture gives us no reason to think that the last great revival will avert the coming catastrophe. Rather, in the providence of God, it appears that judgment prepares the way for revival.

Cleansing of the Church

Through this purging, to the praise of God, his people will be brought to the true beauty of holiness. Our Lord expects to present his bride unto himself "a radiant church, without stain or wrinkle or any other blemish, but holy and blameless" (Eph. 5:27; cf. 1 John 3:2-3; 2 Cor. 7; 1 Pet. 1:13-16; 3:4). The trials of the last days will serve as fires to refine the gold of Christian character. Out of them the bride of Christ, "arrayed in fine linen, clean and white," will emerge ready for the marriage supper of the Lamb (Rev. 19:7-9; cf. Dan. 12:10). To this end, the "latter rain" of the Spirit is intended to bring "the precious fruit" of the church to maturity in preparation for the Lord's return (James 5:7; cf. Song of Sol. 2).

The church should not fear affliction, though it may cause anguish and even death. Suffering may be necessary to convince us that we do not live by bread alone. When received as an expression of God's trust, our suffering can be a means of helping us comprehend more of the love of Christ, who "suffered for us, leaving us an example, that we should follow his steps" (1 Pet. 2:21; cf. Heb. 2:10; 5:8). Without hardship, probably few of us would learn much about the deeper life of grace.

A purified church will be able to receive unhindered the power of the outpoured Spirit, and thereby more boldly enter into the mission of Christ. It is also reasonable to believe that this greater concurrence with God's program will multiply the manifestation of ministry gifts in the body (Eph. 3:7-15; cf. Rom. 12:6-8; 1 Cor. 12:4-11; 1 Pet. 4:10-11). This would further call attention to the momentous awakening on earth.

Tremendous Ingathering of Souls

Evangelism of the lost, though different from renewal in the church, flows out of the same Spirit. The blessing of Pentecost inevitably brings people to call upon the name of the Lord for salvation, and it will be nowhere more evident than in this last great outpouring of the Spirit of God (Joel 2:32; Acts 2:21; cf. Romans 10:13).

The same revival will also prepare workers for that great harvest of souls. People who are full of the Holy Spirit are committed to God's work. They want to be where laborers are needed most, and there is no more pressing need than bringing the gospel to hell-bound men and women. This is why Jesus came into the world (Luke 19:10), and he sends his disciples on the same mission (John 17:18; Matt. 28:19-20).

Significantly, Jesus said that the fulfillment of that preaching task would precede his return: "This gospel of the kingdom will be preached in the whole world as a testimony to all nations, and then the end will come" (Matt. 24:14; cf. Luke 12:36-37; 14:15-23). Doubtless the passion to get out the message while there is yet time will increase with the revival, even as the witnesses multiply. That the gospel will eventually penetrate "every nation, tribe, people and language" is clear from the description of the innumerable multitude of the white-robed saints gathered around the throne of God in heaven (Rev. 7:9; cf. 5:9). The great commission will finally be fulfilled.

Many believe that Jews will be among the lost who turn to Christ at that time. At least, there are prophecies that speak of their general repentance and acceptance of the Messiah (see Ezek. 20:43-44; Jer. 31:34; Rom. 11:24), and of God's pardon and blessing (see Jer. 31:27-34; 32:37–33:26; Ezek. 16:60-63; 37:1-28; Hos. 6:1-2; Amos 9:11-15; Rev. 7:1-17). The world revival seems a logical time for this to happen. Pretribulationists might put the Jewish awakening after the rapture of the church, making a great deal of Romans 11:25-26, which speaks of Israel's being saved when the fullness of the Gentiles is come.[11] This passage, however, could serve equally well to support the idea of revival before Christ comes again.

Whatever position one might hold, there can be little question that the greatest day of evangelism is before us. The harvesting may be short in duration, and may require enormous sacrifice, but it will be the most far-reaching acceptance of the gospel this world has ever seen.

Preparing for Christ's Return

The massive turning to Christ by people from the four corners of the earth will prepare the way for the coming of the King. Our Lord's return may be waiting now on this spiritual revolution. Until then we are exhorted to "be patient, then, brothers, until the Lord's coming. See how the farmer waits for the land to yield its valuable crop and how patient he is for the autumn and spring rains. You, too, be patient and stand firm because the Lord's coming is near" (James 5:7-8).

The fact that our Lord has not already returned to establish his kingdom is evidence of his desire to see the church perfected and the gospel presented to every person for whom he died. God is "patient . . . not wanting anyone to perish, but everyone to come to repentance" (2 Pet. 3:9). But we dare not presume upon his patience. None of us can be so sure of our understanding of prophecy as to preclude his return at any moment. Every day we should be ready to meet the Lord, the more so as we see the night approaching![12]

Anticipation of our Lord's return is a summons to action. We must cast off anything that blocks the flow of the Holy Spirit and commit ourselves to being about the Father's business. World evangelization now is the responsibility around which our lives should be centered. Whatever our gifts, we are all needed in the witness of the gospel.

Uniting in Prayer

As we anticipate the coming world revival, prayer is our greatest resource. The prophet reminds us, "Ask of the LORD rain in the time of the latter rain" (Zech. 10:1, KJV). "When the tongue fails for thirst," God says, "I will make rivers flow on barren heights, and springs within the valleys" (Isa. 41:18; cf. 44:3). Surely it is time to "seek the LORD, until he comes and showers righteousness" upon us (Hos. 10:12; cf. Joel 2:17; Acts 1:14). There is no other way to bring life to the church and hope to the barren fields of the world.

As the First Great Awakening was sweeping America in 1748, Jonathan Edwards, responding to a proposal from church leaders in Scotland, published *A Humble Attempt to Promote Explicit Agreement and Visible Union of God's People in Extraordinary Prayer, for the Revival of Religion and the Advancement of Christ's Kingdom on Earth Pursuant to Scripture Promises and Prophecies Concerning the Last Time.* It was an appeal for the church to unite in earnest intercession for world revival, based on the text of Zechariah 8:20-21, KJV:

> *It shall yet come to pass that there shall come peoples, and the inhabitants of many cities; And the inhabitants of one city shall go to another, saying, "Let us go speedily to pray before the LORD, and to seek the LORD of hosts; I will go also." Yea, many peoples and strong nations shall come to seek the LORD of hosts.*

About this passage Edwards said:

> From the representation mode in this prophecy, it appears . . . that it will be fulfilled something after this manner; first, that there shall be given much of a spirit of prayer to God's people in many places, disposing them to come into an express agreement, unitedly to pray to God in an extraordinary manner, that he would appear for the help of his church, and in mercy to mankind, and to pour out his Spirit, revive his work, and advance his spiritual kingdom in the world as he has promised; and that this disposition to such prayer, and union in it, will spread more and more, and increase in greater degrees; with which at length will gradually be introduced a revival of religion, and a disposition to greater eagerness in the worship and service of God, amongst his professing people; that this being observed, will be the means of awakening others, making them sensible of the wants of their souls, and exciting in them a great concern for their spiritual and everlasting good, and putting them upon earnest crying to God for spiritual mercies, and disposing them to join with God's people . . . and that in this manner religion shall be propagated, until the awakening reaches these that are in the highest stations, and until whole nations be awakened, and there be at length an accession of many of the chief nations of the world to the church of God. . . .

And thus that shall be fulfilled "O thou that hearest prayers, unto thee shall all flesh come" (Psalm 65:2).[13]

Edwards' plea for God's people to come together in fervent and constant prayer for revival still speaks with urgency. Not only does it call us to our most essential ministry of intercession, but it also reminds us of the way God has ordained to quicken his church and to disseminate her witness until finally the nations of the earth shall come and worship before the Lord.

Living in Expectancy

Billy Graham, in his last message at the Lausanne Congress in 1974, expressed succinctly both the realism and the hope we have in awaiting "the climactic movement and the total fulfillment of what was done on the Cross." Then, reflecting upon the future, he added:

> I believe there are two strains in prophetic Scripture. One leads us to understand that as we approach the latter days and the Second Coming of Christ, things will become worse and worse. Joel speaks of "multitudes, multitudes in the valley of decision!" The day of the Lord is near in the valley of decision. He is speaking of judgment.
>
> But I believe as we approach the latter days and the coming of the Lord, it could be a time also of great revival. We cannot forget the possibility and the promise of revival, the refreshing of the latter days of the outpouring of the Spirit promised in Joel 2:28 and repeated in Acts 2:17. That will happen right up to the advent of the Lord Jesus Christ.
>
> Evil will grow worse, but God will be mightily at work at the same time. I am praying that we will see in the next months and years the "latter rains," a rain of blessings, showers falling from heaven upon all the continents before the coming of the Lord.[14]

All of us should join in this prayer, even as we look expectantly to what lies ahead. Something great is on the horizon. You can almost feel it in the air. Though forces of evil are becoming more sinister and aggressive, there is a corresponding cry for spiritual awakening. Across the world never has there been more yearning by more people for spiritual reality, nor has the church ever had the means it now has to take the glad tidings of salvation to the lost, unreached peoples of the earth. What a day to be alive!

Does this mean that there will soon be a world revival, and that the coming of the Lord is imminent? We cannot know. But it does appear that this long awaited event is now a breathtaking possibility.

Certainly this is not a time for despair. The King's coming is certain. And in preparation for his return, we may be the very generation that will see the greatest movement of revival since the beginning of time.

Endnotes

1. Altogether the term is used in its various forms more than 250 times in the Old Testament. It comes from a root meaning "to live," which originally conveyed the idea of breathing. Revival, or life, was "breathing in the breath of God." The word may be translated revive, live, preserve, heal, prosper, flourish, or even save. Examples are Ezekiel 37:5, 7; Job 33:4; 1 Kings 17:22; Genesis 7:3; 19:32; Hosea 6:3; 14:7; Habakkuk 3:2, to cite a few. In the New Testament the comparable word means "to live again" (Rev. 20:5; Rom. 14:9; Luke 15:24, 32). Other terms liken revival to rekindling of a slowly dying fire (2 Tim. 1:6) or to a plant which has put forth fresh shoots and "flourished again" (Phil. 4:10).

2. For a popular presentation of major revivals in the Old Testament, see Walter Kaiser, Jr., *Quest for Renewal* (Chicago: Moody Press, 1986); or the older study of C. E. Autrey, *Revivals of the Old Testament* (Grand Rapids: Zondervan, 1960). Revivals of both Testaments are considered in less detail by Ernest Baker in *Great Revivals of the Bible* (London: Kingsgate Press, 1906). There are also many selected studies available, such as Wilbur M. Smith's little book *The Glorious Revival under King Hezekiah* (Grand Rapids: Zondervan, 1945). Of course, commentaries and histories will allude to revivals in the course of their interpretation of Scripture, and sometimes these accounts are rich with insights.

3. The history of American revivals has been variously treated by many historians. A few of the more general works include: F. G. Beardsley, *A History of American Revivals* (New York: American Tract Society, 1904); W. L. Muncy, *A History of Evangelism in the United States* (Kansas City: Central Seminary Press, 1945); Fred Hoffman, *Revival Times in America* (Boston: Welde, 1956); Bernard A. Weisberger, *They Gathered at the River* (Boston: Little, Brown and Company, 1958); and a more biographical approach, Keith J. Hardman, *The Spiritual Awakeners* (Chicago: Moody Press, 1983). For a good bibliography on revival from the Great Awakening to the present, especially focused on the American scene, see Earle E. Cairns, *An Endless Line of Splendor* (Wheaton, Ill.: Tyndale House, 1986), 345–365. Further bibliographic information on revival may be found in Gerald Ina Gingrich, *Protestant Revival Yesterday and Today* (New York: Exposition Press, 1959); Nelson R. Burr, *A Critical Bibliography of Religion in America*, 2 vols. (Princeton: Univ. Press, 1961); and Richard Owen Roberts, *Revival* (Wheaton, Ill.: Tyndale House, 1982).

4. The substance of the remaining portion of this chapter first appeared in *Christianity Today,* July 16, 1971, and is used by permission. A reprint of the article is in *Perspectives in the World Christian Movement,* a reader edited by Ralph D. Winter and Steven C. Hawthorne (Pasadena: William Carey Library, 1981), 355–358. A revised and enlarged statement appears as chapter 8, "The Hope of a Coming World Revival" in *The Spark That Ignites* (Minneapolis: Worldwide, 1989), 125–134.

5. Strangely the idea of a last great world revival is given little specific mention in biblical theology, although it is often implied. Martin Bucer, the mentor of John Calvin, seems to be one of the first advocates, in his development of Augustinian amillennialism, by projecting a widespread conversion of Jews following the reformation of the church. With some modifications, this view became common among Puritans, such as John Owen and William Perkins, and Pietists, like Jakob Spener and J. A. Bengel. For more information, see Peter Toon, *Puritans, the Millennium and the Future of Israel: Puritan Eschatology, 1600 to 1660* (Cambridge: James Clarke, 1970); and Ian Murray, *The Puritan Hope* (London: Banner of Truth Trust, 1971). In the seventeenth century some theologians moved to a premillennial position, adopting the presuppositions characteristic of the early church fathers. Others took a more postmillennial turn, a view which largely dominated the thought of eighteenth and early nineteenth century American revival teachers like Jonathan Edwards, and later, Charles G. Finney. Yet as Richard F. Lovelace points out, in this spectrum of millennial opinion there was unanimity in the teaching of a great world awakening, "since even the premillennialists believed that the outpouring of the Spirit and the conversion of large numbers of Jews and Gentiles would precede the millennium" (*Dynamics of Spiritual Life* [Downers Grove, Ill.: InterVarsity Press, 1979], 408). This thinking among revival-minded premillennialists, positive amillennialists, and postmillennialists continued into the middle of the nineteenth century. As a more liberal social agenda absorbed the thrust for renewal, most evangelicals, following Moody, adopted some form of premillennialism, a trend that has continued into the twentieth century.

6. The fifteen nations mentioned in verses 9-11, while not inclusive of every group in the world, could be said to represent "people from all over the known world." See I. Howard Marshall, *The Acts of the Apostles* (Grand Rapids: Eerdmans, 1980), 71; cf. Richard B. Rockham, *The Acts of the Apostles* (Grand Rapids: Baker, 1964), 22.

7. It is interesting to note that the modern missionary movement was rooted in the optimism inspired by exponents of world revival, like Jonathan Edwards, reflected in his edition of David Brainerd's *Diary;* and Isaac Watts as seen in his hymn "Jesus Shall Reign." It was this longing for the universal reign of Christ that burned in the heart of missionaries like William Carey, Henry Martyn, and Charles Simeon, causing them to recite again and again Habakkuk's prophecy: "For the earth shall be filled with the knowledge of the glory of the Lord, as the waters cover the sea" (Hab. 2:14). In addition to Lovelace, *Dynamics,* 409-410, see J. A. deJong, *As the Waters Cover the Sea: Millennial Expectations in the Rise of Anglo-American Missions, 1640–1810* (Kampen: Kok, 1970).

8. I. Howard Marshall observes that, if we do not accept that the reference is to the cosmic signs which accompanied the crucifixion (Luke 23:44-45) then it looks "forward to the signs which shall herald the end of the world; these are still future, and they belong to the 'end' of the last days, rather than to their 'beginning', which is just taking place." See *The Acts of the Apostles,* 74.

9. Significantly, in recent years, the number of Christians tortured or executed for their faith has been rising. According to research consultant David Barrett, approximately 335,000 persons now are martyred each year, and it is estimated that the annual average will climb to 500,000 by the year 2000. "As a 'sign from God'," he says, "this appalling statistic warns us about the escalating conflict between church and state, and hence our future prospects in global missions." See David Barrett, "Annual Statistical Table—Global Missions: 1987," *International Bulletin of Missionary Research* 2, no. 1, (January 1987): 24; cf. context in *Christianity Today* 32, no. 1, (15 January 1988): 27.

10. During this awful time there are those who are said to "have repented not" (Rev. 9:20-21; 16:9). The fact that their refusal to repent is called to our attention indicates that the opportunity was there to repent. However, the absence of even these negative references toward the close of the period as Armageddon approaches might indicate opportunity for repentance is finally withdrawn by God.

11. Those who believe that the tribulation will follow the rapture of the church may still allow for a Gentile revival before the Lord's return, thus anticipating two distinct revivals in the end time.

12. It is this expectancy of the Lord's personal, visible, and historical return in the clouds of glory that distinguishes evangelical faith—not any one particular view of the millennium or a revival in the end time. Let us always keep this truth in focus—Jesus is coming again—and where this "blessed hope" of the church is unequivocally affirmed, we will agree to disagree on the way events related to his coming are interpreted.

13. Jonathan Edwards, *Humble Attempt . . . ,* in *The works of President Edwards,* Vol. 3 (New York: Leavitt, Trow and Co., 1818), 432–33. The full discourse, encompassing pages 423–58 lifts up the promise of world revival, and the need to pray unitedly for it, more than any other writing in the English language. The appeal for concerts of prayer also comes out in George Whitefield's ministry during this same period, and indeed, continued in revival efforts through the nineteenth century. In recent years it has been picked up again by such international voices as the Lausanne Committee for World Evangelization. For a contemporary exposition of the movement, and practical direction in how you can become involved, see Robert Bakke, *The Concert of Prayer: Back to the Future* (Minneapolis: Evangelical Free Church of America, 1993); also the books of Edwardo Silvoso, *That None Should Perish* (Ventura, Calif.: Regal, 1994); Evelyn Christensen, *A Study Guide for Evangelism Praying* (Colorado Springs: AD 2000, 1994); David Bryant's *With Concerts of Prayer* (Ventura, Calif.: Regal, 1984) or *Operation: Prayer* (Madison: InterVarsity Christian Fellowship, 1987); historical background is given by J. Edwin Orr in *The Eager Feet: Evangelical Awakenings, 1790–1830* (Chicago: Moody Press, 1975).

14. Billy Graham, "The King Is Coming," in *Let the Earth Hear His Voice,* Official Reference Volume for the International Congress on World Evangelization, Lausanne, Switzerland, ed. by J. D. Douglas (Minneapolis: World Wide Publications, 1975), 1466.

PART 4
Roy J. Fish:
Evangelist Extraordinaire

This exceptional collection of essays was conceived of, gathered, and published as a way of bringing honor to someone who has honored Christ in his life. Roy J. Fish has been a model teacher, father, and evangelist. This collection is dedicated to him for the glory of God. In this section Steve Fish profiles his dad's life and ministry. Steve Gaines concludes the essays with Dr. Fish's professional history.

17
A Profile of Roy Fish

Steve Fish

Steve Fish, son of Roy Fish, is pastor of the James Avenue Baptist Church in Fort Worth, Texas. Steve formerly served as the associate pastor of the Trinity Heights Baptist Church in Carrollton, Texas. He graduated from Baylor University and earned an M.Div. from Southwestern Seminary.

Two college students were praying on a hillside on the campus of the University of Arkansas one starry night. Burdened, they prayed for the salvation of a lost student, a junior in engineering named Robert White. Their prayers went along the lines of Matthew 18:19: "Again I say to you that if two of you shall agree on earth as touching anything that they shall ask, it shall be done to them by my father who is in heaven."

One of the praying students was my dad, Roy Fish. He had told his friend of Matthew 18:19 and the importance of agreement in prayer after he had learned it from a godly woman in his church. They took the promise very literally, praying specifically, intrepidly, that Robert White would be saved before tomorrow ended. The next day, a few minutes before midnight, my dad prayed with Robert White, who at that moment received Christ as his own Savior.

That was the first time. Dad had told others the gospel, but this was the first time anyone had ever responded by making a commitment to Jesus. It was the first time of many times, for leading people to do what Robert White had done that night became the driving passion in the life of Roy Fish.

Early Life

Roy Jason Fish was born on February 7, 1930, in Star City, Arkansas, population 816, in a frame house on Drew Street. He was the third child of Effie Grace Vick and Curtis Wayne Fish. His father sold cars; however, he could not afford one himself. The family was, in fact, poor. At one point my dad almost had rickets from calcium deficiency because there was not enough milk.

Poverty did nothing to keep him from enjoying a happy childhood along with his older brother, Dudley, and sisters Betty and Doris. The family's Sunday pilgrimages in Aunt Ruby's car to his grandparents' home in Garnett were a weekly highlight. His grandfather would take them to the country store he owned, and the children would pick out gum and candies. Extended family, in particular, became the cornerstone of his childhood. He learned to read as a four-year-old under Aunt Rhoi's instruction, and his wealthy Uncle Clyde took him riding in the rumble seat of his roadster. He and five or six of his friends were constant companions, who regularly explored the woods, ate plums and possum grapes, smoked grapevine, and made plans to build a submarine that would go to the bottom of the town's sizable lake.

During the summer of 1938 the Fish family moved to Abilene, Texas, where Curtis, my dad's father, discovered he could make a better living by working with his wife's brother-in-law, Oscar Rose, a contractor. After Star City, Abilene (population 25,000) seemed monstrous, and indoor plumbing was a luxury. My dad's father, after he had worked a few months—first as a common laborer and then as a bookkeeper—could afford his first car, a dark blue 1937 Plymouth. In 1940 they were able to buy a house.

My dad blossomed in Abilene, making top grades in elementary school. By the fifth grade, he was among the top three in the class declamation contest—the stirring of his love for language and rhetoric. He was a natural athlete. In 1941 he was named to the all-city football team by the *Abilene Reporter News.*

The Fish children were part of a large circle of friends in Abilene. When the Japanese attacked Pearl Harbor, my dad was playing with other boys in Catclaw Creek on Sunday afternoon. The war brought out the leader in him. He remembered that he had been named after an uncle, Roy Jason Fish, a World War I pilot who had died in an accident, flying above England in 1917. Dad organized all the boys in the class into a platoon of soldiers, all with assigned rank. He was the general. The class responded in grand style:

Almost every boy in the class reported regularly to the creekside for maneuvers for the duration of the sixth-grade year.

The most meaningful relationships of his Abilene childhood were with aunts, uncles, and cousins. During a visit to Star City when he was ten, his Aunt Vergie fulfilled one of his great childhood wishes by taking him fishing on the bayou. When his Uncle Clyde and Aunt Audie moved to Abilene with a fishing boat and a need for a fellow fisherman, going out with them that summer cemented in Roy Fish a great love for fishing. Throughout his childhood in a timely way, uncles and aunts filled the gap left by his father, who spent little time with his son.

My dad's mother, a wonderfully patient person and a devout Christian, made sure her four children attended Sunday school and revival meetings at church. In Star City, the First Baptist Church had most powerfully impressed my dad when the pastor preached a vivid sermon on hell. He awakened in the night crying, remembering the sermon and that he had no hope of escaping that hell. The beginning of spiritual awareness was painful.

In the fall of 1939, Dad walked down the aisle of First Baptist Church, Abilene, and joined the church. He received a card and was instructed to fill it out. The nine-year-old's idea of getting into heaven thus became a vague process of joining the church, being baptized, and living as good a life as possible. After he joined the church, his father began to attend rather regularly, which was a source of satisfaction to him.

He remained sensitive to spiritual things. After his best friend in junior high, Wayne Haynes, lay critically ill for weeks after falling forty feet out of a tree, Dad noted that the people of Abilene credited prayer as the reason God spared Wayne's life.

In 1943 Dad attended vacation Bible school at First Baptist, Abilene. A missionary from Hong Kong, named Jaxie Short, led a discussion on the human condition—which she illustrated by shaking a solution in a jar to change it from clean to dirty and back to clean again: dirty from sin, and back to clean again only by the entrance of Jesus into one's heart. At this point Roy Fish very reluctantly admitted to himself that although he possessed the external credentials of baptism and church membership, he was not really a Christian.

The awareness that he had never been saved troubled him less once he enrolled in Abilene High School. He pledged the high school fraternity that most of the premiere athletes pledged. He was elected vice president of the junior class, lettered in track, served as captain of the track team, and won the 440-yard dash at the regional track meet. His high school annuals abound with references to him as a swell buddy, a fast runner, and a booming voice in the a cappella choir.

My dad continued to have a preponderance of friends, who nicknamed him "Jade." In 1947 he and three of his friends took a six-thousand-mile trip to the west, northwest, and far western parts of the United States. The twenty-day trip was a thrill and the beginning, perhaps, of Roy Fish's energetic and still unforsaken love for travel. He, his brother, Dudley, and a friend took another trip after his high school graduation, this time to St. Louis and Chicago, where they saw their first major-league baseball games.

Dad had always wanted to go back to his native state to attend college at the University of Arkansas. McMurry College in Abilene, however, awarded him a track scholarship. He accepted it, lived at home, and ran track at McMurry. In the fall of 1948, when he matriculated at the University of Arkansas in Fayetteville, he began working out with the track team, and some of the coaches noticed his unusual speed. That next spring, he was offered a partial track scholarship.

He settled on English as a major and began to love Shakespeare in particular. But during his sophomore year, the spring of 1949, God began to prod Roy Fish. He wanted to be saved, and he did not know how. He attended church, mostly because so many of his friends did. One Sunday night he heard a sermon on confessing Christ as his Savior. Not understanding what the preacher meant, he walked down the aisle and expressed the desire to be saved. Rather than explaining to him how he could be saved, the man down front said, "God bless you, young man; we are glad you have come." He left the service unchanged, knowing nothing about faith in Christ as Savior.

He did begin to carry around a Gideon New Testament, mostly as a good luck charm; he had heard stories about soldiers who were shot in the war but who remained unhurt because their New Testament stopped the bullet. His thoughts were often occupied with his unsettled spiritual state, and he promised God that he would do whatever he had to do to be saved.

Christian Beginnings

Returning to Abilene for the summer, Dad found that walking down the aisle in the spring had left him an unchanged person, and he continued to run with the usual crowd of friends, doing the usual things. One Sunday in his backyard he felt God had spoken to him, and he responded by saying he would do whatever he needed to do to be saved that Sunday evening at church. Accordingly, during the invitation that night, he left his seat in the choir loft, approached the pastor, and explained that he wanted to be saved because he didn't think he was a Christian. The pastor's reply: "We will pray for you." He left the service lost. For the third time in his life he had gone forward in a church service, and for the third time been met with well-meaning but entirely unhelpful words. No one opened a New Testament and showed him how to trust Jesus as Savior. His desire in future seminary years to see pastors trained to lead to Christ those who respond in invitations found its roots in these experiences.

That night he left the service so oppressed, so much in the dark, and so deeply convicted of his lost condition that he slept little for the next three nights. If he slept, he might die, and if he died, he would go to hell. On Wednesday of that week in July 1949, he walked outside his home, feeling a mighty weight on his shoulders. As he stood on the front porch at noon, the words of the invitation hymn the church had sung on Sunday came to him: "Only trust him, only trust him, / only trust him now. / He will save you, he will save you, / he will save you now." The "him" in the verse was Jesus; this he knew. For the first time he understood that Jesus was the way to God. He told Jesus at that moment, "I trust you as Savior and will trust you to take me to heaven." The huge burden rolled away from his shoulders, and the nineteen-year-old knew in his spirit that he had come to God. All of his own efforts toward Christianity had come to nothing. He now realized he had neither deserved nor earned salvation but could only accept it as Jesus' free gift. Roy Fish's life was changed.

One of the first things he did was purchase a new Bible, an expensive leather-bound Scofield Bible that he used constantly for about two years. Whereas he had previously gone to church simply because church was the place to go, now, knowing that he had a personal relationship with Jesus, he went eagerly even to prayer meeting on Wednesday nights.

Dad was also to discover the world anew as he learned to tell others about his experience of trusting Jesus. Late that summer of 1949, he gave his testimony at the citywide youth revival sponsored by Baptist churches in Abilene. The next day his cousin Earl Rose, a committed Christian, called him on the phone and said, "Roy, I want you to go visiting some of our high school and college friends with me." Dad had never gone to a home exclusively to talk with people about becoming a Christian. He quickly discovered the difference between the fact of knowing Christ and the willingness to talk with others about him. He tried to talk Earl out of taking him, but Earl was persuasive, so he grabbed the huge family Bible off the coffee table and went with him. The friends and their families who opened doors at their knocking looked at those Bibles as one might a loaded cannon, and it seemed that no one in that particular venture was saved by their witness. However, in a few days he began to go out alone to see some of his old friends in an effort to win them to Christ. That invitation to go visiting was the beginning of Roy Fish's lifelong practice of telling others about Jesus.

In the fall he returned to the University of Arkansas as a committed follower of Jesus. He immediately joined First Baptist Church of Fayetteville, started serving in the Baptist Student Union, and began solid friendships with other Christians. However, he still had an unsettled spirit at times as to whether or not he was really a Christian. It was just too good to be true for him. Questioning led him to doubt. Was Jesus really his Savior? He began to read every book he could get his hands on in the library of the Baptist Student Union. He scoured his Bible for assurances and prayed constantly, asking Jesus to be his Savior and telling him that he trusted in him. Yet he didn't feel saved. He realized his reliance on feeling, or mere inner impressions, was part of the problem when God led him to 1 John 5:13, a verse that became perhaps his favorite of all those in the Bible: "These things I have written unto you who believe in the name of the Son of God that you may know that you have eternal life." This verse spoke to his heart's yearning—to know that he had eternal life. Over time, through such promises of God, he came to the place of full assurance, where he could honestly say that he knew that he had eternal life.

At the end of the spring semester, the Baptist Student Union director, Dan Bates, told Dad that the nominating committee wanted him to be the president of the BSU for the coming year. The young man felt overwhelmed; he had already assumed a position working in the college Sunday school department. The Sunday school position was actually not so overwhelming; in truth, he thought the presidency of the BSU was above his head. He turned it down and tried to talk Dan Bates out of asking him again; later, however, Dan convinced him that he should be the president, and he took the role.

One thing that continued unabated among all these changes was my dad's track career. He lettered in track at the University of Arkansas and ran in track meets in Arkansas, Kansas, Iowa, Oklahoma, Louisiana, Alabama, and Texas. In practice one day, he was one of two quarter-milers who broke the existing school record by a full half-second.

Dad spent the summer after his junior year working on staff at Ridgecrest Baptist Assembly in North Carolina, a summer he would later consider as near heaven on earth as any he had ever experienced. He took giant steps in his new faith, establishing deep friendships and listening to some of the finest preachers in the Southern Baptist Convention. Then God began another process: calling him to the ministry.

He preached his first revival meeting with a friend in the little town of Oteen, North Carolina. Night after night people committed their lives to Christ, and revival spread to the rest of the town. A hardened young man who was walking down the street nearby found himself aware of the presence of God and made his way to the meeting to confess Christ. The church voted to extend the meeting another week, and my dad's revival partner left for Oklahoma to begin school, leaving the fledgling preacher to himself. Having exhausted his own supply of sermons, he needed new ones. Faced with a demanding work schedule, though, he had no time to prepare. He preached the sermons of Moody and Torrey, given him by a wise pastor friend, and finished the revival knowing that he had found his calling. The specifics would come later. At this time he simply went forward, full of emotion, after a service to tell the pastor that he sensed God was calling him.

During his senior year in college he was called as pastor by the First Baptist Church of Winslow, Arkansas. The church was a small building, perched on the side of a hill in a small town about twenty miles south of Fayetteville, in the heart of the Boston mountains. Aside from electricity its modern conveniences were few. The restrooms were outhouses, and heat came from a stove in the center of the auditorium. The young pastor rode a bus and then walked through the elements on foot the last two miles to his church. The church, already grappling with several problems, suffered from the inexperience of a first-time pastor during his year-and-a-half term, but managed to survive and is a thriving church today.

A high point of Dad's senior year in college was preaching in the first youth revival ever sponsored by the Arkansas Baptist Convention. Ralph Smith, now pastor of Hyde Park Baptist Church in Austin, Texas, and he preached in the First Baptist Church of Eudora, Arkansas. The church and a good portion of the town found themselves unmistakably in the presence of God, and more than two hundred people made public commitments.

When he graduated from the University of Arkansas in February, 1952, Dad resigned his pastorate at the church in Winslow. He began preaching revival meetings full time during the spring, summer, and early fall, until he enrolled at Southwestern Baptist Theological Seminary.

A Student at Southwestern

The first year at Southwestern was a happy one, full of the new friendships Dad made in the dorm, the awe he had of his professors, and the exhilaration of absorbing new information while at seminary. He became pastor of Salem Baptist Church near Big Spring, Texas, where he made the five-hundred-mile weekly round trip for four years. The church was small, about forty members, and had not shown many signs of spiritual life in previous years. The turning point in his ministry there occurred during his first summer at an outdoor meeting. The men in the church used a flatbed truck for a platform, strung lights out over the parking lot, borrowed chairs, and moved the pews outside. Dickson Rial, who was just seventeen years old and who would later became one of his best friends, was the preacher. Twenty people were saved. Before the end of the first year, the church had an attendance of more than eighty people.

During his ministry at Big Spring, he lived weekends with his parents. In God's providence, they moved across the alley from the George O'Brian family. Mrs. O'Brian, thirty years his senior, whom Dad called the most godly woman he ever met, taught him much about prayer, Bible study, and witnessing. She was the most influential person in his life in his early years of ministry.

When he resigned this pastorate in 1957, Dad pursued full-time vocational evangelism for a summer. "Full-time" is no overstatement; once he preached fifty consecutive nights.

That same year, 1957, Roy Fish got his first degree, a Bachelor of Divinity, now called a Master of Divinity, at Southwestern Baptist Theological Seminary. He had pursued the degree steadily with the exception of 1954, when he dropped out for the fall semester. That year thousands of men—*"brazeros"*—traveled from Mexico to west Texas to pick cotton. Dad and some of his friends felt that God had laid the burden of these people on their hearts, and so they went every night in search of dim lights in cotton fields on dusty west Texas roads. The men from Mexico stayed in everything from old army barracks to renovated chicken coops, living together in groups of ten to one hundred. Dad and his friends brought these men Spanish record albums, sweets from bakeries that had gone unsold the day before, and the gospel. A generous doctor acquaintance provided Spanish New Testaments and other books. Dad was the only one who could speak Spanish, which he had studied since junior high, and so he preached every night to the men, ending by inviting them to accept Christ as Savior. Between three and four thousand of the *"brazeros"* made professions of faith over a period of two years.

Two more things should be mentioned about my dad's time at Southwestern Seminary. First, his fellow students elected him president of the Theological Fellowship, a position which gave him contact with some of the great preachers and Christian intellectuals of the day. The position also made him a logical choice for preaching in chapel when the student council wanted to spotlight an individual from the School of Theology. This task was daunting but thrilling to the young preacher, who spoke about soul winning, using as a text the account of Andrew bringing his brother Simon to Jesus. Second, he met Jean Holley, an extremely bright and equally beautiful new student. She was the daughter of J. Andrew Holley, dean of education at Oklahoma State University. The two dated for three years while Dad completed residence work for his doctorate at Southwestern. He seems to have had to exert himself to persuade Mom to commit herself seriously to an engagement. However, this area is in general problematic for the historian, since each holds to charming but fully conflicting accounts of their courtship. They were married June 11, 1960, at University Baptist Church in Fort Worth, Texas.

Shortly after Dad began his doctorate, he was called as pastor of Live Oak Baptist Church in Gatesville, Texas. The fellowship of the church was divided when he came, but the division was healed during a prayer meeting that was called during a crisis. Within a year a spirit of revival had broken out, and people flocked to Live Oak. In twelve months, more than one hundred people were baptized into the fellowship of this open country church. The church later called Gayle Bone as minister of music and youth, and he and Dad began a strong and lasting friendship. Of the fourteen years Dad had served as pastor, the three years at Gatesville were the richest.

My mother was teaching in the School of Business at Arlington State College (now the University of Texas at Arlington). When the drive from Gatesville to Arlington began to prove too tiring for her, Dad felt he ought to assume the pastorate of Ash Creek Baptist Church in Azle, Texas. Here he would be close enough to the seminary to work on his dissertation. During this time he almost lost his life when a private plane in which he was a passenger crashed while landing. After this experience, it was several years before he would fly again in a private plane. After a year and a half at Azle, he was called as pastor to First Baptist Church of Fairborn, Ohio.

Fairborn was a joyful and interesting time. The church itself was large for a Southern Baptist church in the Midwest. Nearly four hundred members crowded together for worship in a makeshift auditorium. Shortly after his arrival, the church called Gayle Bone as minister of music, education, and youth. After Gayle arrived, the church extended its education space and built a temporary auditorium.

Within three years the church had baptized nearly three hundred people, and Sunday school attendance reached six hundred. During his third year as pastor, my dad was elected president of the State Convention of Baptists in Ohio. He drove to associational evangelism conferences with Dr. Leonard Stigler, from whom he learned much about evangelism.

Faculty at Southwestern

The three years in Ohio were happy ones, but Dad left the pastorate to pursue a calling that he had received eight years earlier, while he had been pastor in Gatesville, Texas—a calling to equip young men and women who themselves had been called to the ministry. His own words best tell the story of that calling: "I was walking down a country road one Saturday night, thinking about my Sunday morning message. It was dark, and I found myself aware of the Lord's presence. I started thinking about my reasons for working on a doctorate at Southwestern, and I suppose I asked out loud why I was beginning this advanced degree. It was almost as if the Lord himself spoke audibly, saying, 'You are doing this because some day you will be teaching evangelism at Southwestern Seminary.' " He never told this to anyone except to my mom after they had married.

More than eight years later, in 1965, as he pulled his car into the driveway after an afternoon of visitation in Ohio, my mother uncharacteristically ran out the front door to meet him with news of a phone call. Dr. Robert Naylor, president of Southwestern Seminary, had called about a newly opened position in evangelism. Ken Chafin had resigned to go to Southern Seminary in Kentucky. Dad's response was immediate and joyful. He regarded the position as one of the most strategic in the kingdom of God and has maintained this regard for thirty years.

So strong was the calling to come to Southwestern that he has found it impossible to leave, though fine pastorates, state directorships, and college presidencies have been offered to him. For almost thirty years he has taught hundreds of students each semester, over fifteen thousand altogether. He has served as interim pastor in more than forty churches, in states as far west as Arizona and as far east as Florida. His four children grew up most of their lives in Fort Worth. My mother underwent brain surgery to remove a tumor in 1981, from which she recovered with grace and tenacity, covered with prayer. She was able to return to her part-time teaching at a junior college.

In training young men and women to share the gospel, Dad found a calling in which God sustained him and our family with an inner blessing and vigor.

In this way the young boy who wanted to fish grew up to be a fisher of men. It must be added that Dad is also a good fisherman when it comes to the fishing pole. Several Saturdays a year find him at his favorite fishing hole in Cresson, Texas. He fishes with a combination of skill and sheer enjoyment characteristic of everything he does. Our family recently unearthed a tape recording of our 1974 Christmas Day. The tape's most outstanding feature is the conversation between our dad and us kids: alternating discussion and laughter on his part. The twenty years since that recording have seen a household made of much joy. He swung baseball bats, attempted skateboarding, and endured Scout camp. Until recently, he played tennis with his daughters regularly. He played the ukelele, sang, read stories, and recited poetry. He attended soccer, baseball, and softball games and listened to his children's speeches and award ceremonies as well as their piano, guitar, trombone, baritone, trumpet, French horn, and clarinet playing. He took us to the western states that he had come to love, and he walked us off our legs in foreign cities. And, of course, he taught everyone to fish. Mostly by example, he taught all of us about evangelism. As naturally as he cast a fishing line, he engaged people in conversations about eternity and salvation. We have watched him earnestly talk about life in Jesus in pulpits, in taxicabs, in our own home. When we awakened early enough during our growing-up years, we saw him on his knees, praying, in the living room. We knew he was praying for us.

Then there is our mother, Jeanie. He has always been fascinated with her. Knowing them both, we have never found this particularly surprising. Mom used to smile when people asked her about her husband's busy schedule and the revivals and meetings that kept him away so often. The whole family missed him, but when he was home, he was so much a father and husband that his presence filled the whole house, and the absences were overshadowed.

The schedule is still busy and our mother still often misses him, but she is still smiling.

Roy and Jeanie's first two children, my sister Holli and I, were born in Ohio in 1963 and 1964. Our younger brother and sister, Jeffrey and Jennifer, were born in Fort Worth. I am presently pastor of James Avenue Baptist Church in Fort Worth. My wife, Marci, and I are the parents of three children. Holli, an environmental scientist, is the wife of Dan Lancaster, a pastor in Hamilton, Texas; they have two children. Jeff is pursuing a doctorate in classical literature at the University of Texas, and Jennifer is in graduate study in English at Baylor University. These children of his, who have written this synopsis of his life, have since childhood felt lavished with his attention, affection, wisdom, and constant prayer. Roy Fish's life has very much reflected Paul's testimony in 2 Corinthians 4:13: "I believed. Therefore I have spoken." Not only has he spoken the gospel; he has taught others to speak the gospel as well.

18
Professional History

Steve Gaines

Steve Gaines is pastor of the First Baptist Church of Gardendale, Alabama, one of the largest churches in that state. Previously he served as the pastor of West Jackson Baptist Church in Jackson, Tennessee. During his seminary studies, he also served as the pastor of Lake Shore Baptist Church in Lake Dallas, Texas. Steve graduated from Union University and earned both his M.Div. and Ph.D., majoring in preaching, at Southwestern Seminary. Gaines was a grader for Fish while in seminary.

Dr. Roy Fish is a master teacher. Any student who has enjoyed the privilege of sitting in one of his classes understands something of the rare gift Fish possesses in the area of pedagogy. He is a member of the Academy of Evangelism in Theological Education. He has been listed in *Who's Who in Religion, Dictionary of International Biography,* and *Personalities of the South.* It is this writer's opinion that Fish's effectiveness in the classroom is due, in part, to his experience as a pastor, preacher, and writer.

Pastoral/Preaching Ministry

Fish was converted to Christ at the age of nineteen. Within a matter of months he sensed the Lord calling him to full-time Christian ministry. He recalled: "A year after I was saved I began preaching."[1] Since those early days when his first sermons were preached in youth revival meetings in churches near Ridgecrest, North Carolina, Fish has been used by God to preach extensively throughout the United States and abroad.

Pastorates

The vast majority of those who study under Fish at Southwestern Seminary are training to serve as ministers in Southern Baptist churches. Fish relates well with them because he has personally served as a Southern Baptist pastor. While attending the University of Arkansas, Dr. Fish was the pastor of Winslow Baptist Church, Winslow, Arkansas (1950–52). While attending Southwestern Seminary, he served as the pastor of Salem Baptist Church, Big Spring, Texas (1952–57), Live Oak Baptist Church, Gatesville, Texas (1957–60), and Ash Creek Baptist Church, Azle, Texas (1960–62). During the writing of his Ph.D. dissertation, Fish served as the pastor of First Baptist Church, Fairborn, Ohio (1962-65). He continued to serve that church for two years after he graduated from seminary.

Denominational service

During Fish's years in Ohio, he was elected president of the Ohio Baptist Convention for one term (1964–65). He also served on the Executive Board of the Ohio Baptist Convention for three years. He later went on to serve in key denominational leadership positions, such as being a member of the Committee on Committees of the Southern Baptist Convention, a member of the Program Committee of the Baptist General Convention of Texas, a member of the Urban Strategy Committee of the B.G.C.T., and a member of the Strategy Planning Task Force of the Home Mission Board of the Southern Baptist Convention.

Interim pastorates

Dr. Fish has continued to utilize his preaching and pastoral gifts by serving as interim pastor at over forty churches during his years of teaching at Southwestern, including many of the greatest churches in the Southern Baptist Convention. These churches include Casa View Baptist Church, Dallas, Texas; Cottage Hill Baptist Church, Mobile, Alabama; Council Road Baptist Church, Oklahoma City, Oklahoma; Eastside Baptist Church, Marietta, Georgia; First Baptist Church, Bossier City, Louisiana; First Baptist Church, Broken Arrow, Oklahoma; First Baptist Church, Dallas, Texas; First Baptist Church, Lake Jackson, Texas; First Baptist Church, Lawton, Oklahoma; First Baptist Church, Lubbock, Texas; First Baptist Church, Moore, Oklahoma; First Baptist Church, Pasadena, Texas; First Baptist Church, West Palm Beach, Florida; First Baptist Church, Wichita Falls, Texas; Henderson Hills Baptist Church, Edmond, Oklahoma; Hoffmantown Baptist Church, Albuquerque, New Mexico; Richardson Heights

Baptist Church, Richardson, Texas; and Second Baptist Church, Springfield, Missouri.

These interim pastorates have helped keep Fish in touch with local churches within the Southern Baptist Convention, and have added immeasurable depth to his classroom ministry.

Conferences, conventions, and crusades

In addition to his pastorates and interim pastorates, Dr. Fish has preached at over one hundred pastor's conferences, convention meetings, and evangelism conferences for Baptist state conventions. He has preached at both the Southern Baptist Pastor's Conference and the annual meeting of the Southern Baptist Convention. He has preached in over six hundred revival meetings and evangelistic crusades for Baptist associations and local churches.

Southwestern Seminary

Since his arrival at Southwestern Seminary, Fish has been one of the most popular preachers on campus. He has preached in seminary chapel many times. One of the greatest honors bestowed upon Fish was being invited to preach the annual Fall Revival at Southwestern Seminary, September 11–14, 1990. The theme of the revival was "Return to the Lord with All Your Heart," which was taken from Joel 2:12. During those four days of revival services, which were held in Truett Auditorium on Southwestern's campus, students packed the seats and aisles, and even stood along the walls of the room to hear Fish preach. During the final service alone there were over 225 decisions made.

Dr. Bud Fray, professor of missions and chairman of the 1990 Revival Committee, described the four-day meeting by saying, "I feel that we have every evidence that the Lord came and met with us. It is evident in the changed lives and how God invaded the lives of our students, faculty and administration."[2] Fray's summary is not surprising, because without a doubt, Roy Fish has been one of the most effective and popular Southern Baptist preachers in the twentieth century.

A. Webb Robert's Library, on Southwestern's campus, has a number of Fish's sermons available on audio- and videocassette. These include "Bringing the Dead Back to Life" (TC 1384), "Doctrine of Salvation" (TC 12276), "Dynamics of Reaching People" (TC 491), "Following God's Assignment" (TC 5699), "Harvesting" (TC 9303), "Home of Your Heart" (TC 5698), "How to Get More Out of Your Christian Life" (TC 5698), "How to Get Rid of Heart Trouble" (VHS 1678), "Returning to First Love"

(TC 10547), and "River of Blessing" (TC 5697). The sermons Fish preached during the 1990 Fall Revival at Southwestern are also available (TC 12792–95; TC 12814–15). Other seminary chapel sermons include those preached on 9/25/86 (TC 10956); 10/20/87 (TC 11481); 9/23/88 (TC 12016); 1/28/93 (TC 16659); 9/7/93 (TC 17037); and 1/18/94 (TC 17311).

Writing Ministry

Another avenue of ministry for Roy Fish has been that of writing. Aside from his Ph.D. dissertation,[3] he has written four books and contributed chapters to nine others. Fish has also written papers for conferences on evangelism, and many articles for various Southern Baptist journals and magazines. He also helped write *Continuing Witness Training,*[4] which was developed by the Home Mission Board to help equip pastors and lay people to effectively share the gospel with lost people.

Books
The first book Fish wrote was a study guide to Robert Coleman's book *The Master Plan of Evangelism.*[5] Coleman's work is a classic, having been widely read by students of evangelism for the past three decades and having undergone over sixty reprints, with over two million copies in print. Fish's study guide[6] was written nine years after Coleman's book was originally published.

Fish's second book is entitled *Giving a Good Invitation.*[7] In this volume, Fish suggests why all biblical preaching should be concluded by allowing the hearers to respond personally to the message. Attention is also given to the basic ways an invitation can be extended, as well as using positive psychology and exhortation in giving the invitation.

The third book written by Fish is entitled, *Every Member Evangelism for Today.*[8] In this work, which is an update of J. E. Conant's classic published in 1922, Fish analyzes God's program for evangelism through the church by giving special attention to New Testament commissions to evangelize, evangelistic strategy, and satanic opposition to evangelism. He also points out God's purpose for evangelism regarding both the spiritual renewal of the church and the redemption of those outside the church. The book concludes by emphasizing the spiritual power necessary for a church to practice evangelism that involves all of its members.

Dr. Fish's fourth book is entitled *Dare to Share.*[9] This book was written to serve as a youth church study course for the Church Training Department of the Sunday School Board of the Southern Baptist Convention. The book emphasizes the biblical imperative of evangelism for all Christians, including teenagers. Specific attention is given to the content of the message that should be shared in personal evangelism, as well as the help God provides through the indwelling Holy Spirit to empower teenagers to lead their friends to faith in Christ.

Chapters in books

Fish contributed to *The Lord's Free People in a Free Land.*[10] He drew from his background in church history to explain how spiritual awakenings impacted evangelism and church growth. This book was written by various Southern Baptist theologians in honor of Robert A. Baker, professor of church history, Southwestern Baptist Theological Seminary. Fish has also contributed the following chapters to these books:

"The Need for Reaching," *Sunday School Evangelism* (Nashville: Convention Press, 1967).

"The Road to Renewal," *How to Win Them* (Nashville: Broadman, 1970).

"The Man with the Burning Heart," James Ponder, ed., *Evangelism Men* (Nashville: Broadman, 1974).

"The New Evangelism," George Worrell, ed., *Resources for Renewal* (Nashville: Broadman, 1975).

"I Would Give More Time to Personal Soul-Winning," Rick Ingle, ed., *If I Had My Ministry to Live Over* (Nashville: Broadman, 1977).

"Speaking the Gospel," Joel Heck, ed., *The Art of Sharing Your Faith* (Tarrytown, New York: Revell, 1991).

"The Missing Thrust in Today's Evangelism," Charles R. Chaney and Granville Watson, eds., *Evangelism Today and Tomorrow* (Nashville: Broadman, 1993), 41–46.

"Blood on Our Hands," Jack Smith, ed., *Fifty Great Motivational Soul-Winning Sermons* (Atlanta: Home Mission Board, 1994).

Papers and articles

Dr. Fish has participated in major conferences on evangelism, during which he presented papers. For example, in 1994 Fish wrote and presented a paper entitled "The Calling and Gift of the Evangelist," at the North American Conference for Itinerant Evangelists, which was held in Louisville, Kentucky, June 28–July 1.

Fish has contributed extensively by writing articles for Southern Baptist journals and magazines. Articles for the *Southwestern Journal of Theology* include "The Missing Thrust in Southern Baptist Evangelism,"[11] in which he exposed the limitations of "come and hear" evangelistic methodologies, such as revival meetings and Sunday school, and stressed the need to engage in the most effective form of evangelism—*personal* evangelism. He also wrote "Evangelism in the Gospel of John,"[12] in which he describes the personal evangelism of Jesus in the fourth Gospel.

Fish also has written many other articles for various Southern Baptist publications. These are:

"Church, Mind Your Business," *Baptist Men's Journal* 39 (January 1968): 10.

"Tell Others? Why?" *The Sunday School Builder* 50 (January 1969): 6.

"Getting to the Subject," *The Sunday School Builder* 50 (February 1969): 6.

"What Does Witnessing Mean?" *The Sunday School Builder* 50 (March 1969): 10.

"The Gospel According to You," *The Sunday School Builder* 50 (April 1969): 8.

"Is the Good News Meant for Children?" *The Sunday School Builder* 50 (May 1969): 12.

"The Imperative of Prayer," *The Sunday School Builder* 50 (June 1969): 10.

"Is Witnessing Relevant?" *The Sunday School Builder* 50 (July 1969): 12.

"Power for the Job," *The Sunday School Builder* 50 (August 1969): 12.

"Preaching to Change the World: Preaching from the Book of Acts," *Proclaim* 12 (July 1982): 19–24.

"Motivating Sunday School Workers and Members to Make Evangelistic Visits," *Sunday School Leadership* 6 (November 1985): 6–9.

"Evangelism in Southern Baptist History," *Baptist History and Heritage* 22 (January 1987): 2–3.

"What's the Good News?" *The Student* 67 (December 1987): 4–6.

"What the Bible Says about Fasting," *The Commission* 51 (April 1988): 58–60.

"Equipping Youth to Share Their Faith," *Discipleship Training* 2 (September 1991): 36.

"Universalism: The Passive Destroyer," *Evangelism Today* (Summer 1993): 7.

Teaching Ministry

Perhaps no person in human history has taught evangelism to more ministerial students than Roy Fish. Since 1965, Fish has served as professor of evangelism at Southwestern Baptist Theological Seminary in Fort Worth, Texas. During those years, in addition to his duties at Southwestern, Fish has served as a guest lecturer at several other colleges and seminaries, including Golden Gate Baptist Theological Seminary, Mill Valley, California; Midwestern Baptist Theological Seminary, Kansas City, Missouri; Canadian Baptist Seminary, Cochran, Alberta; Columbia Bible College, Columbia, South Carolina; and Free Will Baptist College, Nashville, Tennessee.

At Southwestern Seminary, Dr. Fish has taught courses leading to the degrees of Master of Divinity, Doctor of Ministry, and Doctor of Philosophy. For the Master of Divinity degree, Fish has taught Church Growth Evangelism (331); Personal Evangelism (332); Early Church Evangelism (533); Spiritual Awakenings (534); Jesus and Personal Evangelism (535); Contemporary Evangelism and Church Growth (536); Vocational Evangelism (537); and Discipleship Evangelism and Church Growth (540). He has led the Spring Evangelism Practicum (545), also known as "Pioneer Penetration," in which students participate in a week-long evangelistic outreach emphasis during the seminary's spring break. In advanced studies, Fish has taught "Evangelism and Church Growth in Contemporary Culture" (675) for Doctor of Ministry students, and "History of Spiritual Awakenings" (763–764) and "Effective Church Growth Evangelism in the Contemporary World" (765–766) for Doctor of Philosophy students. Fish and colleagues James Eaves and Malcolm McDow were catalysts in instituting a Ph.D. major in evangelism at Southwestern Seminary.

Both "Church Growth Evangelism" (TC 5519, V. 1–11) and "Personal Evangelism" (TC 5530, V.1–11) are available in synopsis form on audiocassette in the seminary library. Other teaching tapes by Fish available at Southwestern are "How to Give an Evangelistic Invitation" (VHS 1287), "Introducing Children to Christ" (TC 1794), "On to Maturity: A Study in Biblical Follow-Up" (TC 1132), "The Pastor, His Own Evangelist" (TC 7470), "Preach the Unsearchable Riches" (TC 3996), "Revival" (TC 2498), "River of Blessing: Get the Weeds Out of Your Yard" (TC 5697), and "Spiritual Awakening at Southwestern" (TC 4848).

Conclusion

No one has affected evangelism in the history of the Southern Baptist Convention more than Roy Fish. His entire life has been dedicated to training others to fulfill Christ's command to "make disciples of all the nations" (Matt. 28:19). Through his preaching, writing, and teaching ministries, Fish has impacted a host of Christians and has encouraged and inspired them to sow the seed of the gospel that they might reap the conversion of lost souls for Christ's glory. Evangelism is not merely a course to be taught for Fish. It is his life. May his ministry live on through those of us who have sat at his feet in the classroom, and have walked with him in life. May we remember the lessons he has shared, and dedicate ourselves to be fishers of men for Jesus.

Endnotes

1. "Evangelism Professor Fishes for Lost Souls," *Southwestern News* 47 (May 1989): 8.

2. "Annual Revival Offers 'Fresh Glimpse of God' to Seminary," *Southwestern News* 49 (November/December 1990): 9.

3. Roy J. Fish, "The Awakening of 1858 and Its Effects on Baptists in the United States," (Ph.D. diss., Southwestern Baptist Theological Seminary, Fort Worth, Texas, 1963).

4. *Continuing Witness Training* (Atlanta: Home Mission Board of the Southern Baptist Convention, 1982).

5. Robert E. Coleman, *The Master Plan of Evangelism* (Old Tappan, N.J.: Revell, 1963). Revell released a special thirtieth anniversary edition in 1993.

6. Roy J. Fish, *Study Guide to The Master Plan of Evangelism* (Grand Rapids: Revell, 1972). Revell includes Fish's study guide in some editions of Coleman's work.

7. Fish, *Giving a Good Invitation* (Nashville: Broadman, 1974).

8. Fish and J. E. Conant, *Every Member Evangelism for Today* (New York: Harper and Row, 1976 update of Conant's original, *Every Member Evangelism,* 1922).

9. Fish, *Dare to Share* (Nashville: Convention Press, 1982).

10. Fish, "The Effect of Revivals on Baptist Growth in the South, 1740–1845," in *The Lord's Free People in a Free Land,* ed. William R. Estep (Fort Worth: Evans Press, 1976).

11. Fish, "The Missing Thrust in Southern Baptist Evangelism," *Southwestern Journal of Theology* 8 (Spring 1966): 71–78.

12. Fish, "Evangelism in the Gospel of John," *Southwestern Journal of Theology* (Fall 1988): 37–41.